MW01094781

MAKING CAMP

MAKING CAMP

Rhetorics of Transgression in U.S. Popular Culture

HELENE A. SHUGART and CATHERINE EGLEY WAGGONER

The University of Alabama Press   *Tuscaloosa*

Copyright © 2008
The University of Alabama Press
Tuscaloosa, Alabama 35487-0380
All rights reserved
Manufactured in the United States of America

Designer: Michele Myatt Quinn
Typeface: Minion & Impact

∞

The paper on which this book is printed meets the minimum requirements of American National Standard for Information Sciences-Permanence of Paper for Printed Library Materials, ANSI Z39.48-1984.

Library of Congress Cataloging-in-Publication Data

Shugart, Helene A., 1966–
    Making camp : rhetorics of transgression in U.S. popular culture / Helene A. Shugart and Catherine Egley Waggoner.
         p.   cm. — (Rhetoric, culture, and social critique)
    Includes bibliographical references and index.
    ISBN 978-0-8173-1607-5 (cloth : alk. paper) — ISBN 978-0-8173-8011-3 (electronic : alk. paper) 1. Popular culture—United States. 2. Camp (Style) I. Waggoner, Catherine Egley, 1962–
II. Title.
    E169.12.S5154 2008
    306.0973—dc22

                                                                                              2007033572

CONTENTS

ACKNOWLEDGMENTS

This book, like most, is a result not only of our own time and efforts but that of others, as well. We would like to acknowledge the staff of The University of Alabama Press for assistance and guidance throughout the publication process, as well as the two anonymous reviewers of our manuscript, whose thoughtful insights and suggestions were key in strengthening and refining it.

Wittenberg University provided generous assistance in the form of a research leave and a grant, and we also thank our colleagues at Wittenberg University and the University of Utah for their valuable support. Juliann Cortese assisted with research early in this project, and we thank her for her contributions.

An early version of portions of this book originally appeared as the journal article "A Bit Much: Spectacle as Discursive Schism," in *Feminist Media Studies* 5 (2005): 64–80. Permission to use this material is courtesy of the Taylor and Francis Group (www.taylorandfrancis.com).

Finally, we would like to thank our families, notably Edward Bennett, Anni Shugart, Laura Egley Taylor, and Dana Waggoner, for their patience, for their support, and especially for their creative insights throughout this endeavor. As we have learned in the course of writing this book, even the study of a phenomenon as inherently playful, delightful, and dynamic as camp has the potential to be desiccated and fossilized beyond all recognition when subjected to intense scrutiny. If it has escaped that terrible fate here, they, more than we, are to thank for that.

MAKING CAMP

Introduction

Trail Map

In October 2004, U.S. television audiences and critics alike noted with delight the debut of a prime-time drama sporting a distinctive aesthetic. A cross between a somewhat sanitized *American Beauty* and *The Stepford Wives* delivered with a wink, *Desperate Housewives* sends up suburbia in a nicely wrapped, ironic package of bucolic domesticity. The aesthetic that constitutes the key motif of the show is *camp*, a parodic, ironic, over-the-top, and often nostalgic sensibility that is arguably a hallmark of popular U.S. media fare today. Indeed, camp is pervasive in contemporary popular media, apparent, for instance, in the recent spate of films that pay comic tribute to television classics of yore, such as *Charlie's Angels, The Brady Bunch, The Dukes of Hazzard,* and *Starsky and Hutch,* as well as films that hearken back to a particular era and aesthetic, such as the *Austin Powers* trilogy and *Undercover Brother.* In addition to *Desperate Housewives,* contemporary mainstream television delivers camp to its audiences via shows like *Xena: Warrior Princess, Buffy the Vampire Slayer,* and *The Simpsons.* Popular musicians increasingly feature camp in their songs, music videos, or even personas; arguably, Madonna is and long has been quintessentially camp, mining as she does historically popular cultural forms in ironic ways for her renowned reinventions, and Macy Gray similarly embodies and ironizes a bygone aesthetic. Musicians such as Prince, Missy Elliott, Pink, and Christina Aguilera all have periodically, to a greater or lesser extent, drawn on a camp sensibility in their careers. In short, one cannot consume popular culture today without also consuming camp.

Because mediated popular culture—that is, culture as represented and made available via electronic and print technologies—is by definition notoriously dynamic and fluid, camp's relative stability and its steadily increasing presence are intriguing. Clearly, something about this sensibility resonates with contemporary audiences. Furthermore, its versatility affords it not only endurance but mobility across a variety of venues, genres, and forms—from the mediated popular cultural forms mentioned above to mass-marketed commodities, including T-shirts, Hallmark cards, and bumper stickers. For these reasons alone, camp warrants closer examination as a barometer of sorts of contemporary U.S. culture.

Given the wide variety of shapes that camp assumes, many have questioned whether the character and function of camp are consistent across all forms and representations. For instance, is the camp sensibility we observe in *Desperate Housewives* equivalent to that performed by Prince; is the aesthetic that infuses *Charlie's Angels* similar to that available in *The Simpsons?* And if camp does in fact vary across instances, how exactly does it vary and with what implications? More broadly, how does camp "fit" within broader conversations regarding the nature and function of the media, culturally and politically?

Such questions intrigue scholars who are interested in tracing how power is negotiated in the landscape of popular media—that is, with respect to how conventional notions of what is "true" or "real," which benefit certain groups and interests, might be challenged, modified, and even resisted in certain mediated texts. With respect to camp, in particular, many scholars have noted that it is frequently—if not always—anchored in conventional notions or "discourses" of gender and sexuality, and accordingly, their questions circulate around whether and, if so, how camp may function as a key strategy by which those discourses might be renegotiated. As others note, however, perhaps camp's popularity in contemporary culture says more about the ability of dominant media interests, invested in preserving conventional discourses, to appropriate and defuse potentially threatening strategies and sensibilities. In either case—and certainly in the intersection of the two—camp serves as an intriguing site for analysis for those interested in understanding the cultural landscape of contemporary media in general and its implications for gender and sexuality in particular.

Our interest here is in identifying and examining ways in which resistive possibilities might be realized through camp in the broader context of contemporary mediated conventions and practices. Although we concede that camp does indeed assume normative dimensions in mainstream contemporary popular culture fare, we suggest that the elements of play and critique that are inherent to camp in any guise, and perhaps especially those performances that turn on gender and sexuality, are infused with critical promise. We submit, first, that some contemporary and popular camp texts, icons, and performances might realize that promise more than others; and second, that those performances might feature a particular constellation or configuration of elements—a logic, as it were—that distinguishes them from their camp peers in popular culture. To that end, we turn our attention to contemporary camp icons whose performances, we assert, constitute transgressive camp not only by mobilizing conventional camp sensibilities but by configuring contemporary aesthetic practices in a specific, predictable pattern—a pattern that simultaneously aligns these performances with normative conventions and facilitates their resistance of those very conventions. Our project here is to identify and assess the precise elements of this resistive camp logic, as well as the movement of that logic, within the broader context of constraint—the contemporary mainstream mediascape—in which it occurs. Our broader theoretical aims are to address the ways in which these camp performances converge with and diverge from camp as historically theorized; to contribute to contemporary cultural studies work relevant to the negotiation of resistance; and to illuminate the value of a critical rhetorical attitude in animating political critique.

Camp Girls

The camp icons that we assess as a springboard for our discussion are the television character Xena, of the action/fantasy series *Xena: Warrior Princess* (played by actor Lucy Lawless); the character Karen Walker (played by actor Megan Mullally), of the television situation comedy series *Will and Grace*; singer/songwriter Macy Gray; and singer/songwriter Gwen Stefani.[1] Specifically, we examine mediated representations of these contemporary female camp performances, including concert footage, music videos, television interviews, and profiles printed in popular magazines. Via extensive and close analysis of these texts, we identify, analyze, and evaluate particular verbal, visual, acoustic, and performative codes that characterize these camp performances in order to interpret and assess the discursive logics that constitute them as transgressive.[2]

Our rationale for selecting these particular cases for analysis includes the following criteria: first, a "camp" aesthetic—understood at the most basic level as over-the-top, playful, and parodic—clearly marks each of them and is easily apprehended by audiences. The figure of Xena, an action/fantasy heroine set in days of yore and modeled on similar figures, such as Hercules and Wonder Woman, arguably is inherently camp merely by dint of her moorings in that genre. In different ways, Karen Walker also is "campy" insofar as her character is an extreme parody of the spoiled, incredibly wealthy socialite. Although Macy Gray and Gwen Stefani are not characters, their public personae also feature strong camp sensibilities; Gray is known for her almost cartoonish "retro" 1970s *Soul Train* aesthetic, and Stefani is renowned for mining highly recognizable icons and aesthetics from the past and incorporating them, in excessive and ironic ways, into her public persona. Thus, each of these women embodies and reflects the camp sensibility that pervades popular culture in general and popular media fare in particular.

Indeed, this pervasiveness speaks to another of our criteria: that each of these characters is squarely located in "mainstream" popular culture via similarly mainstream media venues. Although *Xena: Warrior Princess* concluded active production in 2001, it was an extremely popular series throughout its six-year run, regularly garnering high ratings; and it is still widely broadcast in syndication, suggesting that it continues to resonate with mass audiences. Similarly, *Will and Grace,* which features the character of Karen Walker, concluded its run in the spring of 2006, but during its eight years in active production, it was a top-rated prime-time series for NBC. Even before it ceased production, it was being syndicated and rebroadcast by a number of stations nationally, and this continues to be the case. Gray and Stefani are both popular musicians, featured regularly (in concert with "new releases" of their music and attendant touring) on billboard charts and receiving heavy radio and music video rotation. Stefani is also distinctive for her status as a fashion icon, both as a trendsetter and, most recently, as a designer. These singers, like the characters of Xena and Karen Walker, have thus figured and continue to figure fluidly and prominently in the landscape of popular culture, embodying and/or reflecting sensibilities that are at least congruent with those of "mainstream" audiences.

We also have elected to assess specifically female camp performances of femininity. As many theorists have noted, and as we will address further in the following chapter, gender and sexuality are key axes on which camp has turned historically, especially as available in gay male and cross-dressing cultures and epitomized in "drag." In large part, this has led a host of scholars to suggest that camp performances that draw on this legacy are inherently subversive, insofar as they challenge conventional sensibilities regarding gender and sexuality. As such, cross-sex performances would likely be relatively less available in mainstream popular culture and media fare. Further, given their volatility in terms of the challenges they pose to conventional discourse, they are typically highly managed in such a way as to defuse or trivialize any critical potential, more often rendered as a quirk of an eccentric if sometimes lovable oddball, as with Nathan Lane's character in *The Birdcage*. If camp—and, more specifically, its critical potential—continues to turn on gender and sexuality, then, we surmised that popular performances of either femininity by women or masculinity by men might be a fruitful location for analysis, given the likelihood that critical sensibilities might be imported into those performances under the cover of gendered and sexual conventions.

Our decision to examine femininity as "camped" by women is informed by two primary considerations: first, although several scholars have decried the eradication of women from the received history and culture of camp as inappropriate, femininity certainly is the playing field of camp within that history and culture; thus, we understand femininity to be an established "home" for camp. Second, aside from camp, conventional discourses of femininity and contemporary sensibilities overlap in interesting ways as relevant to the artifice and excess that are understood to characterize both. This is not the case with masculinity, which, as Halberstam (1998) has argued, is conversely assumed to be "natural," authentic, essential, unadorned, and uncontrived. Accordingly, we surmise that female performances of femininity might be the likeliest contemporary cultural site for camp performances in general and, perhaps, critical camp performances as well. This rationale further illustrates our interest in examining the specific convergence of contemporary aesthetic practices, camp, and femininity in contemporary popular culture at this historical moment. We are particularly interested in discerning how attendant new venues and modalities might give rise to innovative critical opportunities and, more specifically, logics and rhetorics of resistance, specifically as realized through camp and as relevant to gender and sexuality.

As we have noted, however, the mere fact that a camp sensibility is present does not necessarily afford resistive potential. Thus, we also identified our four cases because the camp that characterizes them, as we will demonstrate, is distinguishable from the broader camp sensibility as it is available in contemporary popular culture. In this regard, we take our cue from Robertson (1996), who, in tracing "feminist camp," acknowledges (as have other critics) that since the 1960s, camp has become virtually interchangeable with "pop and . . . postmodernism," manifest as an "ironic sensibility [that] eulogizes a fantasy of the baby boomers' American innocence through nostalgia" (pp. 119–121). She argues, however, that even if this trend could be taken as evidence of camp's demise, not all camp in this context ought to be dismissed. To this end, she considers Madonna as a case in point—someone who certainly embodies a "pop" camp sensibility but who nonetheless "takes that sensibility into the terrains of gender and sexual difference, aligning herself with some of the traditional concerns of camp" (p. 123) and its attendant, critical potential. Specifically, Robertson (1996) argues, Madonna's reliance on gay subcultures (especially drag), gender bending, and female masquerade all distinguish her in important ways from the rather fetishistic and narcissistic nostalgia that characterizes the camp media milieu in which she operates.

Like Madonna, the camp performers that we have chosen for analysis are distinctive in the contemporary popular landscape insofar as they similarly turn on gender and sexual difference. Also like Madonna, they suggest that "camp can still be a political and critical force—perhaps even more so since becoming a more public sensibility" (Robertson, 1996, p. 138). Robertson ends her historical discussion of camp as a feminist practice with Madonna, noting precisely the tensions and constraints posed by a postmodern, "pop" media environment thoroughly saturated with camp sensibilities and its significance for "spectatorship." She calls for close scrutiny of "our camp icons, and our own camp readings and practices, to ensure that we do not naively substitute camp for politics" (p. 138). Our interest in this endeavor is to do precisely that—to identify more clearly, and with a specifically rhetorical eye, the features and forms that might characterize and perhaps typify critical, potentially transgressive camp performances, as distinct from the broader contemporary camp/pop environment in which they occur. That is, we identify a discursive logic that, we argue, characterizes "resistive" contemporary camp performances—a logic distinguished by specific, predictable premises that invite a reading of those performances as subversive, even as the movement of that logic functions in novel ways that reflect the environment in which they occur. In so doing, we hope to contribute to broader cultural studies conversations regarding the media as a dynamic and shifting site of contestation and, more broadly, opportunities for resistance in a context of constraint. We launch our analysis of the critical potential and implications of camp in a contemporary era from a brief but necessary discussion of the ways in which four arenas of scholarship—critical media studies, critical rhetoric, cultural studies, and performance studies—shape our apprehension of camp.

Media, Culture, and Power

The major premise of critical media studies is that the mainstream media collectively occupy a unique position as an institution that serves as both a repository and creator of cultural discourses that reflect and promote dominant interests. A number of scholars across disciplines have noted the ways in which both media content and format are managed to the end of establishing and reinforcing power and privilege (e.g., Fiske, 1987, 1989; Gitlin, 1986; Hall, 1980; Poster, 1990). Such hegemonic goals are accomplished via a number of techniques and strategies ranging from the exclusion of certain images to the inclusion of stereotypical representations. Furthermore, the techniques and strategies by which consent is secured have become increasingly sophisticated, subtle, and even insidious as media technologies and programming have evolved in concert with broader cultural and social changes. Thus, what might appear to be progressive or even transgressive may well be positioned and delivered in such a way as to require the acceptance of quite conventional notions. The contemporary landscape of popular culture is littered with myriad performances of race, sexuality, class, and gender that appear to challenge cultural norms but are nonetheless subsumed and framed by conventions that have expanded to contain them (Schwichtenberg, 1993; Shugart, Waggoner, & Hallstein, 2001).

Some contemporary cultural critics, however, cognizant of these dynamics, hold out optimism for the resistive potential of some, especially new, mediated forms, texts, and messages. Although Hall (1980) and others (e.g.,

J. Collins, 1992; Giroux, 2000) have noted the possibility of negotiated and even oppositional readings of "dominant" mainstream texts, perhaps most notable among these is Fiske (1986, 1987, 1989), who argues that contemporary "postmodern" mediated texts, characterized as they are by chaos, randomness, inconsistency, and irony are inherently polysemous, such that audiences can construct from them, from within those audiences' own social contexts, empowering messages. In this way, he asserts, these texts function as "do-it-yourself meaning kits" with endless and significant resistive potential (1986, p. 74).

Controversial as this claim is among cultural critics, it complicates a critical apprehension of mediated texts. Fiske's assertion that audiences have agency in spite of the ideological dimensions and functions of media content not only affords audiences a potential role other than that of cultural dupe (Hall, 1980); it also reflects a relatively recent shift in cultural studies to consider new forms and technologies of media and their messages. In this vein, Grossberg (1989) has argued that certain postmodern mediated texts, like MTV, empower viewers to control their moods and attitudes; Chen (1986) has argued similarly that the "postmodern semiosis" of such texts "provide[s] a cultural politics of resistance" (p. 68). McRobbie (1994), also championing the postmodern features of contemporary media fare, argues that "far from being overwhelmed by media saturations, there is evidence to suggest that [marginalized] social groups and minorities are putting [contemporary media fare] to work for them" (p. 392), cobbling and crafting distinctive and politically significant—resistive—cultural forms from a pastiche of images and ideas. Although these critics acknowledge the dominant ideological discourses in which these polysemous texts are mired, they nonetheless assert that the very polysemy that characterizes said texts can be appropriated and employed resistively by audiences.

Many critics, including those noted above, have identified striking and substantial changes in communication patterns and practices over the last several decades, especially as apparent in means, aesthetics, and sensibilities. Some have labeled those patterns and practices as "postmodern" or "late capitalist," linking them historically to particular social, cultural, political, and technological conditions. While the context for these changes is indisputably relevant, their identification as postmodern arguably gives rise to an inclination to apprehend them as contained within and defined by (or conflated with) a specific era—a tendency that may constrain understanding of how they function more broadly beyond specific social conditions. As such, identifying these aesthetic practices and sensibilities as "postmodern" may no longer be the most appropriate or efficient way to engage their significance and implications. Like many contemporary critics, we are interested in apprehending these dynamics in ways that resist sedimenting them, belying their fluidity and amorphousness as cultural conditions continue to shift and change. Thus, our interest is in assessing aesthetic practices and sensibilities that have, in some cases, been identified by earlier critics as postmodern but that now might best be understood beyond the confines of their consideration as such—especially as they are mediated and especially as they are relevant to power.

Nonetheless, the aforementioned critics' assertions regarding "postmodern" media practices remain relevant beyond that characterization: while the media may be ideologically driven, the aesthetics and sensibilities that characterize the contemporary media landscape, by definition, disallow the certainty of the attendant assumption that the hegemonic function of the media will be realized (J. Collins, 1989; Fiske, 1989; McRobbie, 1994). That is, given the randomness, variety, chaos, and speed of media fare that is available today, the likelihood that a coherent and consistent ideology or set of ideologies is articulated through media fare, much less gleaned from it, is small. On the contrary, these critics assert, the critical opportunities for resistance afforded by such mediated texts are profound and veritably limitless; in an environment of infinitely various and inherently inchoate ideas and images, audiences are left to their own devices to cobble together interpretations tailored to their own desires, experiences, and worldviews—that is, they are granted far more freedom and creativity in interacting with mediated texts, such that they may "read" those texts as they wish, unfettered by the clearly defined and ideologically driven conventions and constraints of modernist media fare.

Not surprisingly, this assertion has met with considerable criticism in the arena of cultural studies across disciplines. Many theorists argue that contemporary, apparently potentially resistive, media practices might better be understood as *strategies* of dominant ideology—that is, if the aesthetics and sensibilities that render media texts dynamic and unstable are not themselves a fabrication of said ideology designed in such a way as to belie its ideological moorings and hegemonic function, they have at least been appropriated and manipulated in contemporary media fare in such a way as to camouflage said ideology and hegemonic ends (Condit, 1989; Harms & Dickens, 1996; Jameson, 1983, 1991; Shugart, Waggoner, & Hallstein, 2001; Tetzlaff, 1991). Texts that may appear to be random, chaotic, incoherent, and infinitely various may in fact be highly organized—the ostensibly polysemous and infinitely malleable images and ideas presented in contemporary mediated texts, in other words, are still determined and edited by the "dominant interests" controlling media content, such that what appears to be ideologically inconsistent and even pluralistic may in fact be configured in such a way as to support very conventional discourses of privilege (Harms & Dickens, 1996; Shugart, Waggoner, & Hallstein, 2001; Tetzlaff, 1991).

We align ourselves firmly with this latter theoretical stance regarding contemporary media aesthetic practices and sensibilities: that they warrant considerable skepticism and that the apparent "free for all" of contemporary media fare is likely configured in such a way as to privilege particular readings—readings highly consistent with dominant discourses. That is, contemporary sensibilities are configured in such a way in contemporary media fare as to camouflage their ultimately hegemonic function. Mindful, however, of the constructions and assumptions of audience suggested by this position, we urge a reconsideration of the assumptions of contemporary media *texts*, which, with few exceptions (e.g., Cooper, 2001, 2002; Cooper & Pease, 2002; Shugart, 2001), tend to be characterized in the debates thus far as either "authentically" inchoate or random—and thus unstable, malleable, and potentially resistive—or strategically rendered and ultimately hegemonic. Specifically, we contend that even if contemporary media content has appropriated unstable, dynamic, and potentially resistive sensibilities to nefarious ends, the very nature of those sensibilities, which are defined after all by multiplicity, parody, irony, and inconsistency, may in turn permit entrée for certain resistive texts, or at least moments, under that rubric.

We contend that camp occupies just such an ambiguous and arguably liminal space in the contemporary mediascape: that is, camp itself constitutes an appropriation of contemporary media aesthetics, practices, and tactics, even as they might have been and continue to be appropriated in contemporary media fare. Indeed, camp sensibilities are highly compatible with—complementary to—these sensibilities, turning as they both do, in large measure, on parody, irony, an emphasis on aesthetics, and incoherence. A few theorists, directly or indirectly, also have noted the affinity between "postmodern" sensibilities, as they have identified them, and camp, as well as camp's perhaps predictable pervasiveness and prevalence in popular culture. Jameson (1991) equates camp with "postmodern pastiche," or the random, heterogeneous, nostalgic, and dehistoricizing "imitation of dead styles" that so thoroughly infuses popular media fare. For Jameson this practice is tragic; it is devoid of a satiric and thus potentially critical impulse. Although Hutcheon (1991) is more generous in her apprehension of the critical potential of postmodernism, she draws a distinction between "high" postmodern parody and what she calls "ahistorical kitsch" of the variety Jameson describes. Robertson (1996) connects this conversation directly to camp, arguing that "whereas postmodern pastiche may privilege heterogeneity and random difference, camp is productively anachronistic and critically renders specific historical norms obsolete. . . . [Unlike postmodern pastiche,] camp redefines and historicizes . . . cultural products not just nostalgically but with a critical recognition of the temptation to nostalgia" (p. 5). Although the nature and function of camp as available in contemporary popular culture is thus contested, its critical potential—which has been addressed by numerous scholars, as we describe in the following chapter—suggests alternative ways of thinking about and directions for critical media studies.

Rhetoric, Power, and Culture

Our examination of the rhetorical dimensions of mediated camp culture is situated theoretically at the intersection of rhetorical studies and cultural studies. Broadly speaking, our project is rhetorical in that we seek to understand and explicate the frameworks for meaning embodied in public discourse. In so doing, we hope to contribute to an understanding of the political employment of those meanings, and our goal is commensurate with others who call for an overtly critical dimension to the analysis of public discourse (Grossberg, 1996; McKerrow, 1989; Sloop & Olson, 1999). Our assumption of the connection between expressive forms and the maintenance (or subversion) of power relations marks our project as inherently critical, as we seek to illuminate the invisible and anonymous strategies for control that are embodied within public discourse, believing that "structures of representation are also structures of consciousness" (Rosteck, 1999, p. 241). As many critical scholars have noted, cultural texts that are not overtly marked as political ought nonetheless to be apprehended as embodiments of power relations with a significant impact on social order (Brookey, 1996; Brookey & Westerfelhaus, 2001; Cloud, 1992; Cooper, 2000, 2002; Dow, 2001; Sloop, 2000). We hope that theorizing camp as a rhetorical practice, predicated in certain instances on an identifiable rhetorical logic, will contribute to greater understanding of how resistance is rhetorically negotiated more generally, especially in the context of ideological constraint—in this case, as found in contemporary popular culture.

Nelson and Gaonkar (1996) remind us that discourse is "the primary form in which culture survives" (p. 9); elaborating on this point, Nelson (1999) urges the apprehension of discourse as "at once the record of the past and the mode of its present reconstitution" (p. 225). Discursive texts are more than repositories of cultural ideas; they are performed ideologies. Thus, texts are "the best means to disclose the prerogatives of a culture set in specific conditions of reception—conditions that necessarily entangle the critic in cultural, economic, and political intertexts" (Rosteck, 1999, p. 232). Indeed, rhetorical analysis helps to illustrate the textualization of ideology, the very process by which cultural politics are enacted (Sloop & Olson, 1999, p. 250).

We situate our project within cultural studies, as well as rhetorical studies, insofar as we seek to examine cultural texts in which "relations of power and domination are 'encoded'" (Kellner, 2003, p. 12) and through which "social practices are produced, circulated, and enacted . . . and given meaning and significance" (Giroux, 2000, p. 9). Although cultural studies encompasses and can accommodate a vast number of foci given the infinite manifestations of culture, the bulk of cultural studies scholarship has attended to the media as a mobilizing agent—mobilizing to the extent that media "work to secure certain forms of authority and legitimate specific social relations . . . [and constitute] a set of practices that represents and deploys power thereby shaping particular identities, mobilizing a range of passions, and legitimating precise forms of political culture. Culture in this instance becomes productive, inextricably linked to the related issues of power and agency" (Giroux, 2000, p. 9). The focus on media has become ever more warranted in a contemporary era of exploding media technologies; as Hall (1997) notes, "the means of producing, circulating, and exchanging culture have been dramatically expanded through the new media technologies and the information revolution" (p. 209).

Perhaps not surprisingly, many cultural studies scholars have focused on mediated popular culture, in particular, as a barometer of contemporary dominant ideologies and attendant hegemonic practices (Bennett, 1986; Fiske, 1987, 1989; Hall, 2000; Hebdige, 1991; Jhally, 1995; Jhally & Lewis, 1992; McRobbie, 2000; Miller, 1998). As Miller (1998) states, "there *is* power, it *is* productive, and it works through the production and dissemination of truth, disciplining the citizen through a pursuit of the popular" (p. 265). Other cultural critics call for a more nuanced approach to the study of popular culture, citing the need "to identify both those aspects of popular culture which serve to secure consent to existing social arrangements as well as those which, in embodying alternative values, supply a source of opposition to those arrangements" (Bennett, 1986, p. xii).

This integrated approach is, with some exceptions (e.g., Cooper, 2000, 2002; Cooper & Pease, 2002; Shugart, 2001), underrepresented in cultural studies scholarship, as is a consideration of mainstream mediated texts that may contain resistive messages for particular audiences. On its face, this appears entirely incommensurate with the fundamental premise of cultural studies and critical media studies: that the media are ideological, their texts framed in and reproductive of powerful dominant discourses. Yet the advent of novel—apparently dynamic and polysemic, and thus unstable—aesthetic practices in contemporary media texts and, accordingly, media studies specifically directed to that turn, has, for all the debate about implications thereof, marked a significant change in the way those discourses are made available to audiences. If the possibility exists that resistive messages may be inferred from contemporary mediated texts infused with these sensibilities, as several cultural critics contend, might the possibility not also exist that these messages may, on occasion, be strategically embedded in those texts for particular if not general audiences? That is, the polysemous nature of contemporary media texts may make them not only pliable for audiences seeking alternative, resistive messages; it may also make the texts themselves more malleable. We contend that certain camp performances available in contemporary mainstream media fare constitute just such texts—that is, they are configured in such a way as to constitute a peculiar discursive logic that makes available a resistive reading of gender and sexuality even as they conform to established conventions. At this historical moment, then, contemporary sensibilities as practiced specifically in popular mediated texts, camp, and gender—and, more specifically, in femininity, the established playing field of camp—have converged in such a way as to offer new venues and modalities for camp, potentially providing critical opportunities as relevant to gender and sexuality. To better understand how that critical potential might be logically and rhetorically configured, we turn to an assessment of the performative nature of gender.

Gender, Performance, and Camp

We apprehend gender as a discursive site of struggle; in this regard, we situate ourselves with other critical and feminist rhetorical scholars seeking similar goals with respect to the discursive practices constituting gender (Brookey, 1996; Cloud, 1992; Condit, 1989; Cooper, 1999, 2001; Dow, 2001; Flores, 1996; Frentz & Rushing, 2002; Harms & Dickens, 1996; Hasian, 2002; McGee, 1980; McKerrow, 1989; Morris, 1998, 2002; Ono & Sloop, 1995; Sloop, 2000; Wander, 1983). The notion that gender is not simply constructed but performed, consciously or not, in everyday practices, utterances, and rituals, has been advanced by scholars across disciplines (Butler, 1990, 1993; Doane, 1982; Phelan, 1993; Riviere, 1929; Russo, 1986; Tseelon, 2001). Much of this work is conceptually linked to the contention that performance is "the ground zero of the feminine" (Bell, 1993, p. 351)—that, in Spivak's words, from her first deliberate performance of faked orgasm, woman performs (1983, p. 169)—and also to Lacanian theory explaining the complicated structure of female subjectivity in a psycholinguistic world ruled by masculine logic. Theories of gender as performance thus cover a wide spectrum of ideas, ranging from the performative nature of women's everyday experiences as objects of the male gaze to a complicated explanation of theoretical underpinnings of gendered identity and essence gleaned from a wide variety of "texts" (e.g., drag shows, performance art, films, novels, and casual conversations). These theories are united in the assumption that, as Bell notes, body politics have always been women's politics, and there exists a special relationship between femininity and performance.

Some theorize feminine performance as oppressive—as compulsory and enforced to the end of maintaining normative conventions of gender. Doane (1982) argues that femininity is "produced very precisely as a position within a network of power relations" (p. 87), a position characterized as *image,* preventing women from assuming a position of agency in the same way as men and encouraging women to engage in performance. In this vein Wolf (1991) asserts that the real issue is not whether women "make our clothing and faces and bodies into works of art or ignore adornment altogether" (p. 272) but the lack of *choice* in such performances.

Other theorists, however, understand the performance of femininity to be *masquerade,* rife with resistive potential. Riviere (1929) first introduced this concept in her analysis of the behaviors of professional women who used their bodies as disguise in order to resist patriarchal positioning, masking themselves in womanliness, and thus, constructing a "fetish of the castrated woman" in order to deflect masculine anxiety arising from their "wrongful" assumption of subjectivity (Tseelon, 2001, p. 10). Doane (1987) also notes the resistive potential found in the artifice or "double mimesis" of feminine masquerade, when the "despised signs of femininity are 'put on' to the woman's own advantage" (pp. 181–182).

Russo's (1986) analysis of hyperbolic representations of femininity found in carnivals echoes the transgressive potential found by others in feminine masquerade. The carnivalesque suggests "a redeployment or counterproduction of culture, knowledge, and pleasure" so that feminine masquerade within carnival culture may be seen as a "site of insurgency, and not merely withdrawal" (p. 218). Like Doane, Russo recognizes the critical potential that occurs when women "act like women," which differs significantly from the masquerade that occurs in transvestism: "Deliberately assumed and foregrounded, femininity as a mask, for a man, is a take-it-or-leave-it proposition; for a woman, a similar flaunting of the feminine is a take-it-*and*-leave-it *possibility.* To put on femininity with a vengeance suggests the power of taking it off" (Russo, p. 224). Moruzi (1993) also notes the resistive promise in the "reappropriation of the traditional designations of the feminine" (p. 257). In her call for a critical reassessment of feminine performance, she argues that when woman "actively impersonates the style that defines her lack, she may at least begin to evade the necessary determinations of her own subordination" (p. 264).

Sounding something of a cautionary note regarding the critical promise of performance, Butler offers perhaps the most extensive examination of gender and performance, noting that gender is not just an act or performance but is materially *performative.* Butler's distinction describes the manner in which gender is a fictionalized rather than fixed ontology. Gender, she asserts, is "the reiterative and citational practice by which discourse produces the effects it names" (1993, p. 2). Thus, one does not necessarily assume gender at will, but gendered identity is constituted in time through repeated and rehearsed acts; "'culture' and 'discourse' *mire* the subject" (Butler, 1990, p. 143) so that enactments of gender are compulsory and, for the most part, unconscious reiterations of heterosexual premises. As Diamond (1996) explains, "Gender is both a doing—a performance that puts conventional gender attributes into possibly disruptive play—and a thing done—a pre-existing oppressive category" (p. 4). When one "performs," one enters an "act" that has been going on before. The resistive power of feminine performance, thus, may be compromised at best.

A form of gender performance that does offer critical potential for Butler, however, is drag as found in gay male communities. Although she notes that "transgender" in any form "not only mak[es] us question what is real, and what has to be, but . . . show[s] us how contemporary notions of reality can be questioned, and new modes of reality instituted (2004, p. 217), she singles out (gay male) drag as "a way not only to think about how gender is performed, but how it is resignified through collective terms" (p. 216). When men impersonate women, consciously assuming the feminine in exaggerated form, they enact a parody of femininity that reveals its constructed nature and offers the critical distance necessary for resistance. In her analysis of *Paris Is Burning,* a 1991 film about drag balls in Harlem, Butler notes that "if the film establishes the ambivalence of embodying—and failing to embody—that which one sees, then a distance will be opened up between that hegemonic call to normativizing gender and its critical appropriation" (1993, p. 137). Similarly, Halberstam (2005) notes that drag-king shows— which feature women impersonating men—"seem to appeal to spectators' desire for a deconstruction of maleness rather than a reconstruction of masculinity elsewhere" (p. 134). But drag is not to be embraced wholesale; in its mocking of gendered stereotypes, drag may reify those very representations. Indeed, Butler herself notes that one of the dangers of men's parodying of women is the articulation of a "unified picture of 'woman'" (1990, p. 137), and Evans (1998) echoes this concern, arguing that "the aura of transgression" associated with drag films (e.g., *The Crying Game*) is paradoxically combined with the endorsement of extremely conservative ideas about gender and race (p. 210).

Curiously absent from most discussions of gender performances are analyses of subversive performances of femininity by women or of masculinity by men. Those who have examined such performances have reached different conclusions regarding their critical potential. Several express skepticism at the ability of these performances to do anything more than reiterate the power structures inherent in traditional gender norms (Hanke, 1998; Lockford, 1996; Morris, 2002). Others have examined the subversive potential available in the performance of femininity by women and how that potential might be realized (Shields & Coughlin, 2000; Shugart, 2001; Waggoner, 1997; Waggoner & Hallstein, 2001).

Our contention is that certain forms of female camp also constitute subversive feminine performance—that is, they constitute discursive sites of resistance within the context of mainstream, contemporary popular culture. That camp is performative is a fundamental premise of our argument: "Camp thus presupposes a *collective, ritual and performative existence,* in which it is the object itself to be set on a stage, being, in the process of campification, *subjected* . . . and transvested" (Cleto, 1999, p. 25). Similarly, we contend that camp is defined by its distinction and relatively easy discernment as "play" or artifice.

Another premise of our argument is that camp is political; although most theorists concur, this is not a universally held assumption. In her landmark essay "Notes on Camp," Sontag (1964) argues that "to emphasize style is to slight content, or to introduce an attitude which is neutral with respect to content. It goes without saying that the Camp sensibility is disengaged, depoliticized—or at least apolitical" (p. 53). But her argument is itself predicated on an assumption that style precludes content—that that which is aesthetic cannot be political—and although some share those sentiments, others have registered vigorous dissent, implicitly or explicitly (Babuscio, 1977; Bronski, 1984; Dollimore, 1999; Ross, 1999). Ross (1999) contends that "camp was a highly developed way of talking about what nonessentialist feminism has come to call sexual difference . . . [and] has been directly responsible for the most radical changes in the constantly shifting, or hegemonic, definition of masculinity in the last two decades" (p. 325). Reminiscent of Bakhtin's (1968) concept of the carnivalesque, Dollimore (1999) similarly asserts that "the masquerade of camp becomes less a self-concealment than an attack. . . . Camp thereby negotiates some of the lived contradictions of subordination, simultaneously refashioning as a weapon of attack an oppressive identity inherited *as* subordination, and hollowing out dominant formations responsible for that identity in the first instance. So it is misleading to say that camp is the gay sensibility; camp is an invasion and subversion of other sensibilities" (pp. 224–225).

Because camp is so closely aligned with gay male subculture(s), often manifest in those contexts as drag—and several critics, as noted above, assert that its predilection for taking the feminine as its object reflects misogynist attitudes—the relationship between women as *subjects,* camp, and performance has not received extensive scholarly treatment. Although she does not utilize camp as a theoretical device, Silverman (1993) does address drag as relevant to heterosexual women performing femininity, raising the question of whether such performances may be legitimately called "drag" at all. For drag to work—for it to constitute more than heterosexual titillation—there must be a sleight of hand or joke involved. Accordingly, argues Silverman, drag works best for lesbians. Robertson (1996) engages the notion of "feminist camp" explicitly and extensively, however, and she theorizes it rather more broadly than Silverman engages female drag. Noting that "camp's appeal resides in its potential to function as a form of gender parody" (p. 10), she asserts that in this regard, camp is entirely compatible with an apprehension of gender—and more specifically, femininity—as performed: as double mimesis, as masquerade, and as drag. In a highly congruent fashion, camp exposes the artifice of gender; a woman who "camps" "plays at being what she is always already perceived to be" (p. 12). Robertson seeks, then, "to emphasize the crucial role women have played as producers and consumers of both gay and feminist camp" (p. 19) and, more specifically, to consider its critical potential as a feminist practice within a context of domination.

Our own interest is much aligned with Robertson's, and in some ways, this project can be understood as beginning where hers concludes. In tracing camp and its relevance to gender and feminist politics through such cultural icons as Mae West, Joan Crawford, and Madonna, Robertson has not only clearly documented the history of female camp performance in popular, mediated culture but also has theorized its implications for "female spectatorship." As she concludes her project, she calls for increased attention to "whether or how camp can be consciously redeployed as an aesthetic counterpractice from within dominant institutions" (p. 153). It is at this point that we engage this project, which is a close examination of *how* camp sensibilities play out in popular media fare in such a way as to hold critical promise. Like Robertson, we focus on female camp performances, specifically with respect to their resistive potential; where our project diverges is with respect to its rhetorical focus and emphasis on the particular configuration of strategies, which we contend forms an identifiable logic that constitutes "transgressive" camp. Our focus, then, is on tracing how those features engage and intersect with the aesthetic practices and sensibilities that characterize the contemporary mediated context in which camp occurs, as well as identifying and assessing the shape that resistance assumes in those cases.

In the following chapter we trace the history and origins of camp and identify the central features, themes, and tensions that have characterized and continue to characterize its discussion today. In chapter 3 we engage the particular issues surrounding camp as available in contemporary popular culture, especially with regard to its critical implications; we also advance the logic that we identify as common across instances of "resistive" contemporary, mediated camp performances. In chapters 4 through 7 we trace that logic across four cases, assessing the particular shapes that they assume and how "alterity" is made available and distinct in each case: in chapter 4 we examine how that logic is manifest in the televised character of Xena, Warrior Princess, as the earliest of the four camp figures we have selected, and how the logic that we have identified makes available, in her case, a subversive reading of lesbian sexuality. In chapter 5 we assess how the character of Karen Walker, of the television situation comedy *Will and Grace,* is drawn against this logic in both similar and distinctive ways, manifest ultimately in an invitation to read her character as "transgendered" and specifically as a gay man. We turn to popular music in chapter 6 as we examine singer/songwriter Macy Gray and trace the ways in which race, gender, and sexuality intersect in prominent ways to afford a resistive reading of Black female sexuality. And in chapter 7 we examine singer/songwriter Gwen Stefani as our final case, assessing how the logic of resistive camp is configured in her camp persona to signal an unfixed and essentially unstable female sexuality in ways that subvert conventional discourses of femininity. Finally, we present the theoretical implications of our findings in chapter 8, our concluding chapter, as well as argue the utility and significance of critical rhetorical sensibilities, in particular, to the end of animating political critique.

1

Camp Grounds

Histories and Characters of Camp

Defining *camp* is no easy task. From its stylistic display in fashion magazines and drag performances of the early twentieth-century clandestine urban underworld to its fictionalized outing in Isherwood's (1954) *The World in the Evening* to its more scholarly treatment in Sontag's (1964) "Notes on Camp" and Newton's (1972) *Mother Camp,* camp has been hard to pin down. It is a world constituted by a slippery aesthetic sensibility, an evasive phenomenon characterized by the trite statement, "You know it when you see it." Oscar Wilde, Rudolph Valentino, Tiny Tim, Mae West, Tallulah Bankhead, and Judy Garland have been said to embody it, as have particular films and works of art, including *The Rocky Horror Picture Show* and Andy Warhol's *Marilyn* (M. Booth, 1983; Cleto, 1999; Core, 1984; Sontag, 1964). Furnishings have their place of significance in the camp world, as well, particularly those that collapse the distinction between "natural" and "human-made" such as art nouveau lamps in the shape of flowering plants or living rooms transformed into grottos (Sontag, 1964, p. 517). Over-the-top clothing that emphasizes textures and sensuous surfaces (e.g., ostrich feather dresses) belong in the camp world, as do highly stylized performances saturated with irony, parody, and exaggeration, as exemplified by Greta Garbo, Bette Davis, Joan Crawford, and Barbara Stanwyck (Newton, 1972; Sontag, 1964). Theatricality tinged with humor rules as people, artworks, and artifacts are enmeshed in a performance of celebratory fakery—an embracing of the artificial with a tone of "failed seriousness" (Cleto, 1999, p. 24).

Yet camp's elusive definition has not prevented it from being addressed by a number of scholars across a variety of disciplines; indeed, the study of camp has earned legitimacy in numerous fields, including cultural studies, sexuality studies, gender studies, sociology, and media studies, and is no longer featured only in novels or obscure fashion magazines. In fact, while scholarly investigations of camp have clarified the nature and function of camp, they have also attested to its complexity and "slipperiness." In part, camp is difficult to classify because it assumes many different forms: camp that is embedded intimately within gay male culture, a performative practice rich with potential for disruption of heteronormativity (Babuscio, 1999; M. Booth, 1983; Cleto, 1999); camp that is apprehended primarily in terms of its relevance to gender and, more specifically, subversion of gendered conventions (Case, 1999; Robertson, 1996); and "pop camp," a stylistic appropriation of "authentic" camp sensibility, devoid of resistive potential (M. Booth, 1983; Robertson, 1996; Ross, 1999; Sontag, 1964). A complex discursive relationship concerning gender, sexuality, aesthetics, and cultural context has always characterized camp; its evolution and multiple incarnations render it a particularly intriguing rhetorical phenomenon with respect to where and how those discourses are configured and intersect.

Camp as "Gay Male Sensibility"

Without question, the home of camp historically has been gay male culture. Some theorists point out that "troglodytes sometimes confuse camp with [male] homosexuality" (M. Booth, 1999, p. 70), arguing that "gender parody" (Butler, 1999) rather than homosexuality is the cornerstone of camp, thus accommodating "straight" camp (Robertson, 1996), lesbian camp (Case, 1999), and a host of other incarnations (Reich, 1999; Robertson, 1996). Even these theorists concur, however, that camp has been tightly conflated with gay male culture, accordingly infusing the concept with a "gay sensibility" (Babuscio, 1999). Robertson (1996) traces the genealogy of camp "as an adjective" to the early twentieth century (p. 3), and most theorists identify the roughly concomitant trials of Oscar Wilde as the critical point in the popular apprehension of camp as a gay male practice, alleging that "Wilde's downfall [was] *the* epistemic watershed in the constitutive process of the homosexual-as-type, that process which stabilised the queer sign, and that intervened in the erection of the early twentieth-century epistemic 'nave' of homosexual camp" (Cleto, p. 93; see also Bartlett, 1988; Beaver, 1999; M. Booth, 1983; Cleto, 1999; Core, 1984; Robertson, 1996; Sontag, 1964).

Christopher Isherwood's 1954 novel, *The World in the Evening*, more precisely delineated camp as a gay male practice, distinguishing between "Low Camp"—an "utterly debased form" epitomized, for instance, by "a swishy little boy with peroxided hair, dressed in a picture hat and a feather boa, pretending to be Marlene Dietrich"—and "High Camp," differentiated by "an underlying seriousness" and defined as "expressing what's basically serious to you in terms of fun and artifice and elegance" (Isherwood, 1999, p. 51). Albeit rife with class distinctions that especially informed at least European and North American gay male culture at the time, this characterization nonetheless located camp squarely within the broader gay male culture. Susan Sontag's controversial 1964 essay, "Notes on Camp," although perceived by some as "editing gays out of camp" (Cleto, 1999, p. 21), nonetheless acknowledged the significant and primary relationship between gay male culture and camp in the popular consciousness. Although Sontag clarifies that "it's not true that Camp taste is homosexual taste," she firmly asserts that "there is no doubt a peculiar affinity and overlap. . . . Homosexuals, by and large, constitute the vanguard—and the most articulate audience—of Camp" (p. 529). Indeed, although she does not specifically identify gay *male* culture in this characterization, her discussions of Oscar Wilde as a camp icon, of the "dandy," and of the "aristocratic" dimensions of camp, as well as her assertion that "homosexuals [along with Jews] are the outstanding creative minorities in contemporary urban culture" attributable to the "pioneering force [of] homosexual aestheticism and irony" (p. 529), all clearly reference gay male (upper class) society in particular, given the well-established relative social invisibility and poverty of lesbians (Henry & Browning, 1990; Salholz & Glick, 1993).

The location of camp within gay male culture has been assessed by various theorists. Newton explored the issue in her 1972 monograph, *Mother Camp: Female Impersonators in America,* and she posits there and elsewhere that a camp sensibility is inherent to that culture: "it signifies a *relationship between* things, people, and activities or qualities, and homosexuality" (1999, p. 102). This is epitomized, for instance, in the phenomenon of the "drag queen" or female impersonator that constitutes a significant component of gay culture. Although Newton (1999) concedes that "by no means are all [female impersonators] 'camps'" (p. 102), the artifice and contrived performance that drag, in general, entails lays the foundation for camp, which is more precisely characterized by "strong [recurrent] themes . . . [of] *incon-*

gruity, theatricality, and humor" (p. 103)—defining qualities of camp. But this same performative dynamic is manifest more broadly in the gay community than in just drag, argue Newton and others, insofar as many of its members elect to "pass" as straight. Babuscio (1977) suggests, for example, that passing in this context promotes "a heightened awareness and appreciation for disguise, impersonation, the projection of personality, and the distinctions to be made between instinctive and theatrical behavior" (p. 45). In a similar vein, Cleto (1999) avers that "camp emerges . . . as an exercise in passing, oriented to the *mise en scene* of a performative and transient identity, investing mendaciousness not so much through the 'successful lie' of passing for straight, but rather as its very condition, as the constitutive principle of all 'identity' " (p. 30).

Yet linking camp to performances of passing and, more specifically, to impersonation does not obviate marginalized individuals other than gay men. Some theorists point to the *aesthetic* dimensions of camp as the element that secures its place in gay male culture. Dyer (1999) connects this aesthetic specifically with passing; asserting that camp evolved because "gay men have staked out a claim on society at large by mastery of style and artifice," he argues further that this is so because, "We had to hide what we really felt (gayness) for so much of the time, we had to master the façade of whatever social set-up we found ourselves in—we couldn't afford to stand out in any way, for it might give the game away about our gayness. So we have developed an eye and an ear for surfaces, appearances, forms—style. Small wonder then that when we came to develop our own culture, the habit of style should have remained so dominant in it" (p. 114). This dynamic, however, which would by definition clearly characterize much of the lesbian community, as well, did not result in camp becoming the "province" of lesbians as it has of gay men. Robertson (1996)—addressing the larger question regarding the absence of women in general from camp, given that its historicized practice turns so clearly on the aesthetics of femininity—quotes Dyer in arguing that this is so because "women, lesbian and straight, are perceived to 'have had even less access to the image- and culture-making processes of society than even gay men have had' " (p. 5). This rationale would likely be relevant to people of color, as well, in addition to explaining the elitism that by and large characterizes the gay camp sensibility.

Assuming a more utilitarian stance on the issue, Sontag (1964) states that

camp is associated with gay men because it is an expedient means to their inclusion, if not assimilation, into mainstream society: they "have pinned their
integration into society on promoting the aesthetic sense. Camp is a solvent
of morality. It neutralizes moralization, sponsors playfulness" (p. 530). Beaver (1999) sounds a similar note of cynicism with respect to camp's function
as appeasement of mainstream, heteronormative sensibilities: "homosexuality poses a uniquely peculiar challenge to culture stability because it seems
to threaten the genetic cycle itself and the whole elaborate coding of binary
sexuality. So it must be ruthlessly disarmed of its disruptive power. Transformed to childish dreams and neurotic jokes, it ceases to be serious. In this
way its own transformative role is systematically repressed. . . . Homosexuals too (we have seen) are producers of signs" (p. 168). Most theorists, however, posit an "authenticity" to camp as performed in the gay male community that is simply born of the existential condition of being a gay man. Dyer
(1999) argues that "the camp sensibility is very much a product of our oppression" (p. 114), to the extent that it is "a peculiarly 'gay' way to handle the
burden of stigma" (Cleto, 1999, p. 89). Babuscio (1999) develops this concept, noting that "gays have [always] been regarded with fear, suspicion, and,
even, hatred. The knowledge of these attitudes has developed in us what I
have referred to . . . as a unique set of perspectives and understanding about
what the world is like and how best we can deal with it" (p. 133). Camp, he
argues, is just such a "strategy of survival in a hostile world" (p. 132). Similarly, Newton (1999) states that "the camp ideology ministers to the needs
for dealing with an identity that is well defined but loaded with contempt"
(p. 102); or, as Dyer (1999) puts it, camp "is a form of self-defence . . . the
fact that gay men could so sharply and brightly make fun of themselves
meant that the real awfulness of their situation could be kept at bay—they
need not take things too seriously, need not let it get them down. Camp kept,
and keeps, a lot of gay men going" (p. 110).

Many theorists also note, however, that camp is not inherently or simply
melancholic in nature, a poignant response to conditions of oppression; it
is also characterized by a marked pleasure. Noting that camp is inherently
fun and witty, Dyer also attributes a vital social function to camp: it "gives
you a tremendous sense of identification and belonging. It is just about the
only style, language and culture that is distinctively and unambiguously gay
male. . . . Camp is the one thing that expresses and confirms being a gay

man" (p. 110). Bronski (1984) alludes to these same playful and communal dynamics while ascribing to camp a potentially subversive function: camp, he argues, protects members of the gay community via a "first-strike wit. Wit and irony provide the only reasonable modus operandi in the American Literalist Terror of Straight Reality" (p. 46). The history of camp as a gay male sensibility in the popular consciousness, while laden with implicit issues of privilege, is rich, complex, and multifaceted. Although camp in its contemporary incarnations may have broken loose from those moorings, the very richness of that history ensures that this sensibility remains very much inscribed in virtually all camp performances.

Gender: Axis of Camp

In spite of what many argue are camp's distinctly "homosexual" origins, camp has evolved to encompass more than the narrow domain of gay effeminacy, expanding its gay sensibility in many cases to include "the whole apparatus of theatricalized performance of gender signs and gender roles" (Cleto, 1999, p. 203). A primary axis on which camp turns, then, is the performance of gender that is not necessarily restricted to a gay male context. Robertson (1996), for example, details how heterosexual same-sex (female) mimicry constitutes camp and has the potential to serve a critical function for feminism. Whatever their stance on the proper "home" for camp, scholars agree that camp is funded by gender in a number of ways. Signs of ostentatious femininity (e.g., makeup, wigs, feather boas) overtly characterize camp performances, enabling a celebration of that which is excessively feminine, whether performed by men in drag or by women such as Mae West and Madonna, albeit with perhaps different effects.

The feminine is utilized in more nuanced ways in camp, as well, having less to do with artifacts and more with demeanor. The exhibition of emotions coded specifically as feminine (e.g., sentimentality and fragility) pervades camp, facilitating an aesthetic that is distinctly feminine. Sedgwick (1999) points out that sentimentality, "like the very lives of women, is typically located in the private or domestic realm, has only a tacit or indirect connection with the economic facts of industrial marketplace production, is most visibly tied instead to the 'reproductive' preoccupations of birth, socialization, illness and death, and is intensively occupied with relational and emotional labor and expression" (p. 210). Sentimentality, typically manifest as melancholic nostalgia, is a vital part of camp, Sedgwick notes, pointing out that camp's icons are often imbued with tragic loss. Judy Garland is one such example; her performances, viewed in the context of her heartrending personal life, marked by exploitation and drug abuse, evoke a sentimental response from audiences. The sentimental, coded as feminine, constitutes excellent material for camp's inherently gendered performances.

Another gendered hallmark of traditional camp is the dichotomous interplay of masculinity and femininity and their associated binaries: feminine passivity and masculine agency (Bergman, 1993; M. Booth 1983; Newton, 1972; Ross 1999). This interplay is presented sometimes through gender inversion, such as in cross-dressing, when men "put on" the feminine to pass as women and thus "[re]structure meaning in a symbol-performance matrix that crosses through sex and gender" (Reich, 1999, p. 255). Transgender passing reveals the arbitrary nature of gender, as masculine and feminine signifiers are cut loose from their anatomical moorings and reinscribed. Butler (1990, 1993, 1999, 2004) has chronicled extensively the significance of such moves for our understanding of gender, noting that drag performances uproot the claim of heterosexuality's "naturalness." Significantly, the semiotic significance of camp performances turns on the recognition that the performance is, indeed, a forgery. Camp is an ironic viewing/reading practice that is only available to an elite audience. Further, for irony and attendant elitism to inhere, camp depends on the presence of a bifurcated audience: "for there to be a genuinely camp spectator, there must be another hypothetical spectator who views the object 'normally'" (Robertson, 1996, p. 17).

Some theorists have examined the particular dynamics that inhere in female transgendered performances, arguing that they differ from male-to-female gender inversions in important ways. Piggford (1997) assesses the performances of androgyny by women and finds them to be distinctive in the following respects: "These female/androgynous figures do not simply dress as men; rather, they are women who dress, perform, write, appear as gendered identities that might be placed in a range between masculine and feminine. [They] employ a camp sensibility—a code of appearance and behavior that mocks and ironizes gender norms—in order to undermine the gender assumptions of their specific cultures" (p. 39). Piggford's study of female androgyny highlights the importance of recognizing the camp performer's sex "behind the mask" when analyzing the gender interplay of camp. His assessment raises the question that many camp scholars address: Is camp wedded to a heteronormative logic that turns on and reproduces gender binaries? His examples of inversion and even androgyny suggest as much; while they tweak the traditional arrangement of gender norms, they nonetheless operate on the grounds of heteronormative logic and desire.

Some theorists have argued that traditional camp is gendered in precisely this way, for even as it utilizes and embraces the feminine, it reifies heteronormative logics, often to the further detriment of femininity—and, by extension, women. Male-to-female drag, they argue, constitutes an appropriation of the feminine aesthetic and even female celebrities for gay men but does not—cannot—serve the same purpose for women who "camp." That is, women, given their established status as *objects* of camp, cannot serve as camp *subjects*. Although cognizant of these tensions, Robertson (1996) proposes that female same-sex mimicry may nonetheless qualify as camp. She posits that, for example, Mae West, Bette Davis, and Madonna perform excessively heterosexual femininity to the extent that they rupture gendered conventions, thus resulting in *feminist* camp.

Robertson's work draws on the literatures of film criticism and visual culture, especially those literatures that attest to the compromised positioning of women in visual culture. Many theorists in these traditions have postulated that women can negotiate these tensions effectively via feminine masquerade or mimicry (De Lauretis, 1984; Doane, 1982, 1991; Mulvey, 1975; Riviere, 1929). Robertson argues that gender parody self-consciously engages in masquerade to the end of creating distance between the performer's self and her/his performance of gender, thus disrupting the assumptions regarding the "naturalness" of femininity. Robertson's interest, however, is not relevant to the masquerade of transgender cross-dressing; rather, she addresses the phenomenon of women masquerading *as women*. Camp, says Robertson, in addition to the gender parody that constitutes it, also allows for a particular form of feminist spectatorship that differs from those heretofore identified by film theorists, most notably Mulvey (1975)—the promotion of overidentification in female viewers or the assumption of the male gaze: "Camp necessarily entails assuming the mask as a spectator—to read against the grain, to create an ironic distance between oneself and one's image. Camp not only allows for the double nature of the masquerade (the spectator in disguise will always see through two pairs of eyes) but also accounts for the pleasure of the masquerade (typically unacknowledged), its status as amusement and play for both the masquerading viewer and the performer" (Robertson, 1996, p. 14). Here the humorous "tongue-in-cheek" tone that permeates camp is not to be underestimated. Questions about what sorts of viewing pleasures are available to women within the dominant culture have long perplexed film theorists and visual culture scholars. Robertson suggests that camp, in lighthearted, exuberant fashion, constitutes a virtual playground for gender, a world in which fakery—often associated with femininity in general and female sexuality in particular—is enthusiastically endorsed and refashioned as subversive.

What It Means to Be Camp: Qualities and Characteristics

As noted previously, camp is a quintessentially elusive phenomenon, resisting attempts at definition with respect to nature, form, content, context, and significance. Indeed, one of the primary slippages with respect to camp is how it can describe an active, strategic performance, one that "express[es], or [is] created by, a gay sensibility," as well as the mere reception of a particular event or person, such that "camp resides largely in the eye of the beholder" (Babuscio, 1977, pp. 40–41). That is, drag may well constitute an example of camp, but so does Judy Garland. This is a paradox not easily resolved. Although most theorists agree with Babuscio that both scenarios are, indeed, camp, because the latter case is more amorphous, attempts to define *camp* have focused on the former. Although many critics have contributed to our understanding of the nature and function of camp, Babuscio (1999) has provided perhaps the most extensive treatment of the defining features of camp, identifying irony, aestheticism, theatricality, and humor as inherent in the camp sensibility (M. Booth, 1999; Case, 1999; Cleto, 1999; Robertson, 1996; Ross, 1999; Sontag, 1964). We modify and expand his definition slightly here to accommodate other critics' ideas, noting that five qualities consistently emerge across their work: parody, irony, performance, aesthetics, and resistance.

Parody
The centrality of parody to camp has been established in much of the existing camp literature. Flinn (1999) notes that although it may do other things, camp is largely defined by its practices of "send[ing] up or parody[ing] con-

ventions" (p. 440). Some theorists posit that parody is an extreme, sometimes inevitable, manifestation of the act of passing: "The experience of passing is often productive of a gay sensibility. It can, and often does, lead to a heightened awareness and appreciation for disguise, impersonation, the projection of personality, and the distinctions to be made between instinctive and theatrical behavior. . . . The experience of passing would appear to explain the enthusiasm of so many in our community for certain stars whose performances are highly charged with exaggerated (usually sexual) role playing" (Babuscio, 1999, p. 124). The parody or peculiar "theatricality" of such camp performances, argues Babuscio, is "a way of poking fun at the whole cosmology of restrictive sex roles and sexual identifications" (p. 125).

The parodic dimensions of camp are readily apparent in gender parody in particular, especially in gay male culture. M. Booth (1999) notes that camp frequently "parodies [the traditionally feminine] in an exhibition of stylized effeminacy" (p. 69). The drag queen is the most obvious example of gender parody within the gay male community, as Newton (1999) has established; drag, she avows, is role playing, which further implies "distance between the actor and the role." Its parodic dimensions inhere in the fact that camp demands that "the actor should throw himself into it; he should put on a good show" (p. 105). Butler (1999), speaking to the same parodic quality of drag, asserts that it "effectively mocks both the expressive model of gender and the notion of a true gender identity" (p. 363).

But gender parody as a key component of camp is not limited to drag as manifest in gay men impersonating women. Several theorists have noted gender parody and, potentially, the presence of a camp sensibility in women masquerading as men or women. Case (1999) addresses both of these scenarios in her argument that the lesbian "butch-femme aesthetic" essentially parodies gender as heteronormatively defined, insofar as both roles "offer a hypersimulation of woman as she is defined by the Freudian system and the phallocracy that institutes its social role" (p. 197). Similarly, Doane and Russo have assessed feminine masquerade that ultimately functions parodically; Doane (1982) describes the parodic dimensions of masquerade in her description of a woman who would "flaunt her femininity, produce herself as an excess of femininity, in other words, foreground the masquerade (p. 81). Russo (1986) assesses "gender spectacle" in feminine masquerade, constituted by parodic performances of femininity by women. Although neither Doane nor Russo specifically addresses camp in this context, other theorists argue that the performances that they respectively assess are entirely consistent with a camp sensibility (Case, 1999; Flinn, 1999; Robertson, 1996). Robertson (1996) more explicitly addresses the practice of female—or "feminist"—camp, noting that "the concept of the [female] masquerade allows us to see that what gender parody takes as its object is not the image of the woman, but the idea—which, in camp, becomes a joke—that an essential feminine identity exists prior to the image" (p. 12).

Although, as implied in most theoretical apprehensions of camp, parody is most apparent in camp performance qua performance, it also infuses camp as a phenomenon of reception. Sontag (1964) captures the essence of camp parody in this regard in her assessment that "camp sees everything in quotation marks. It's not a lamp, but a 'lamp'; not a woman, but a 'woman'" (p. 517). Similarly, parody is implicit in M. Booth's (1999) example that "china ducks on the wall are a serious matter to 'straights,' but the individual who displays them in a house of otherwise modernist and modish furniture is being camp" (p. 69). Thus, although camp parody is a most accessible strategic camp performance, it also infuses reception of and response to particular texts.

Irony

Although parody and irony often overlap in camp, they are distinct characteristics of the phenomenon; for camp is not always parodic, but it is always ironic (Babuscio, 1999; Newton, 1972). Sontag (1964) recognizes camp's ironic bent when she asserts that "the Camp sensibility is one that is alive to a double sense in which some things can be taken. . . . It is the difference . . . between the thing as meaning something, anything, and the thing as pure artifice" (p. 518). Case (1999) argues that irony infuses camp and, by extension, gay male culture: "Camp both articulates the lives of homosexuals through the obtuse tone of irony and inscribes their oppression with the same device. . . . [It] ironiz[es] and distanc[es] the regime of realist terror mounted by heterosexist forces" (pp. 189–190). Similarly, Babuscio (1999) identifies camp irony with a specifically gay sensibility: "At the core of this perception of incongruity is the idea of gayness as a moral deviation. . . . The inner knowledge of our unique social situation has produced in us a heightened awareness of the discrepancies that lie between appearance and reality, expression and meaning" (p. 120).

In terms of its function, camp, asserts Flinn (1999), turns on the "recontextualization of signs, . . . making them conspicuous and self-consciously ironic" (p. 440). Newton (1999) concurs, noting more precisely that "camp usually depends on the perception or creation of *incongruous juxtapositions.* Either way, the homosexual 'creates' the camp, by pointing out the incongruity or by devising it" (p. 103). Babuscio (1977) makes this claim even more absolutely: "irony is the subject matter of camp, and refers here to any highly incongruous contrast between an individual or thing and its context or association" (p. 41). An ironic sensibility is thus readily apparent in the gender parody that drag constitutes, wherein "the oppositional play is between 'appearance,' which is female, and 'reality' or 'essence,' which is male" (Newton, 1999, p. 99). Similarly, Butler (1999) argues that drag "effectively mocks both the expressive model of gender and the notion of true gender identity" (p. 137). Robertson, although she rejects the contention that camp is exclusively the province of gay men, nonetheless notes that this is true also of women who "camp" femininity, although the ironic effect in this case is subtler and more nuanced: "In opposition to drag, the surprise and incongruity of same-sex female masquerade consists in the identity between she who masquerades and the role she plays—she plays at being what she is always already perceived to be" (1996, p. 12).

But the "incongruous contrasts" that characterize camp irony are not limited to gender, even if that is its most common manifestation. Babuscio (1999) notes that such contrasts also include those of youth and age, sacred and profane, spirit and flesh, and high and low status (p. 119). Interestingly, the examples that Babuscio invokes for these, as well as for ironic masculine/feminine incongruity, are all films and/or celebrities, suggesting that irony is inherent to camp not only as performed but as received, as well. In fact, Britton (1999) takes issue with Babuscio's "multipurpose" application of camp irony, claiming that "irony is badly misdefined: it does not involve incongruity, and it is not, and can never be, 'subject-matter.' Irony is an operation of discourse which sets up a complex of tensions between what is said and various qualifications or contradictions generated by the process of the saying" (p. 141). As suggested by the existing literature on camp, however, most theorists appear to endorse camp as essentially, fundamentally ironic, both as performed and as received, and they likewise would find little or no inconsistency between Britton's definition of irony and the "ironic" sensibility that infuses and characterizes camp. This is apparent, for instance, in Robertson's characterization of camp as "a form of ironic representation and reading" (1996, p. 4). In both capacities, she argues, camp "redefines and historicizes . . . cultural products [via] an ironic, laughing distanciation" (p. 5).

Aesthetics

Camp is perhaps most recognizable as such by virtue of its visual stylistic dimensions. Style of the exaggerated, ostentatious, outrageous sort constitutes camp, rendering it a spectacle. As noted, much of the spectacle that constitutes camp also inheres in irony and incongruence, as apparent especially in plays on gender binaries. Incongruence must be made visible, however, in particular, typically excessive, ways for it to be coded as camp. There is a passionate, exuberant quality to the extravagant aesthetic of camp, as captured in the statement, "It's too much, which means it's just right." Without this passion, notes Sontag (1964), what results instead is *chic*, a pale, aesthetically inferior cousin to camp. Indeed, style is everything to camp, as noted by most if not all scholars of the phenomenon, to the extent that style not only characterizes camp but is its exclusive determinant (Cleto, 1999; Core, 1984; Dollimore, 1991; Sontag 1964). Accordingly, Sontag asserts, substance is antithetical to camp; when characters in a film or novel are developed, their proclivity for camp is mitigated.

Significantly, artificiality plays a vital role in camp's aesthetics. Camp is predicated on artifice, so a double meaning is always advanced. But it is "not the familiar split-level construction of a literal meaning, on the one hand, and a symbolic meaning, on the other. It is the difference, rather, between the thing as meaning something, anything, and the thing as pure artifice" (Sontag, 1964, p. 518). Duplicity inherent to artificiality is embedded in the aesthetics of camp, but it is not a duplicity that is sinister or malicious; rather it is festive, vitalizing, typically affectionately nostalgic, and intensely experiential: "Behind the 'straight' public sense in which something can be taken, one has found a private zany experience of the thing" (Sontag, 1964, p. 518). Indeed, many theorists have identified camp's "failed seriousness," a posture that on the one hand tenderly embraces serious matter (such as opera or fine art) but, in the same moment, just as lovingly parodies that seriousness (Cleto, 1999; Core, 1984; Isherwood, 1954). Camp is a system of humor, as Newton (1972) explains, that facilitates laughter rather than tears at duplicity and incongruity. In camp the conventional distinction between trivial and serious matters is disrupted: "One can be serious about the frivolous, frivolous about the serious" (Sontag, 1964, p. 525). Artifice, as most theorists agree, is the ideal of camp.

While the parody that is so much a part of camp's aesthetic could easily slip into cynicism, it does not. Rather, an important component of camp's style is the presence of self-love rather than contempt, such that camp's performances are presented with an attitude of tenderness within the parody. This, as many have noted, is what distinguishes camp from "kitsch" (Robertson, 1996; Ross, 1999; Sedgwick, 1999; Sontag, 1964). Although they share many similarities, including a preoccupation with the superficial and an unbridled enthusiasm for the style associated with nostalgia and mass-produced objects, kitsch, these theorists argue, entails a smug, implicit disdain for its consumer. Conversely, they claim, camp is predicated on a nostalgic affection for and homage to the subjects of its performances.

Camp articulates alternative aesthetic standards, distinct from conventional apprehensions of aesthetic worth or lack thereof. Camp refuses the distinction between true art and cheap imitations, conferring aesthetic merit to instances of the latter as readily—if not more so—as to the former. Its refusal to value any distinction between the original and the copy—or, in Sontag's (1964) words, its ability to "transcend the nausea of the replica" (p. 528)—affords camp a conspicuously democratic sensibility. This is not to imply that affluence does not have a place in camp; indeed, camp cannot exist outside of the experience or the psychology of wealth, for so much of it is predicated on abundant excess. Robertson (1996) describes camp as "an upper-class sensibility" (p. 18), and Cleto (1999) similarly identifies "aristocratic detachment" (p. 6) as a key element of camp. But camp proposes a different sort of elitism, one characterized by an embracing of and tenderness toward failure and artifice, as appropriately parodied: whereas, Sontag (1964) notes, "the dandy held a perfumed handkerchief to his nostrils and was liable to swoon; the connoisseur of Camp sniffs the stink and prides himself on his strong nerves" (p. 529). Sontag, too, recognizes this aspect of camp, if somewhat less reverently; citing the "relation between boredom and Camp taste," she asserts that "Camp taste is by its nature possible only in affluent societies, in societies or circles capable of experiencing the psychopathology of affluence" (1964, p. 529). Sontag acknowledges the significance of historical milieu, however, in her assessment of the tensions posed for camp by a contemporary context: "Detachment is the prerogative of an elite; and as the dandy is the nineteenth century's surrogate for the aristocrat in matters of culture, so Camp is the modern dandyism. Camp is the answer to the problem: how to be a dandy in the age of mass culture" (1964, p. 528).

Performance

Scholars of camp have noted not only its gendered and aesthetic dimensions but its explicit theatricality, as well. Most, if not all, camp scholars echo Butler's assumptions regarding the performative nature of gender, as presented vibrantly in gay drag performances, with its potential to disrupt gender binaries and sexual boundaries. They concur that camp has a definite performative edge—a "stagey" feel—presenting things in "a way that they are not," epitomizing the metaphors of "life as theatre" and "[b]eing-as-playing-a-role" (Sontag, 1964, p. 517). Camp's performative dimensions are perhaps most apparent in drag queens' hyperfeminine stylings, popularized in gay male culture and documented by camp scholars (Babuscio, 1977; Cleto, 1999; Newton, 1972; Tyler, 1999). Similarly, transgender performances in which women assume masculinity (the "butch" aesthetic) could be considered camp, as Case (1999) argues. Even camp performances that do not turn on inversion, however—for example, androgyny or same-sex mimicry—feature a definite theatrical dimension (Robertson, 1996; Ross, 1988; Piggford, 1997; Reich, 1999).

The highly stylized, visual nature of camp, with its delight in artifice, supports this association with putting on an act or playing a role. Here the incongruity that is so much a part of the camp aesthetic plays a critical function in the camp performance, as the oppositional play between appearance and reality is dramatized. Camp performers, as Newton (1972) explains, maintain a double stance toward role playing, putting on a good show while simultaneously revealing that it is, indeed, a *show*. This performative distance might be revealed in any number of ways—by, for example, a drag queen's flash of a flat, masculine chest, where there should be breasts, or Mae West's over-the-top, stylized hyperfemininity that calls attention to itself rather than to her character. As is the rule with performances in general, an audience, or at least the psychology of one, is necessary for something to be camp. Further, the audience, whether imagined or real, must be bifurcated so that there is always someone for whom the performance is taken seriously and someone who is in on the "joke."

The subject of camp's relationship to performance has inspired much critical reflection. Scholars from a variety of disciplines have pondered the potential for resistance located within camp's performative dimension, assessing how that potential might be realized and for whom. Here Butler's work again provides a theoretical springboard, as critics expound on her postulate that drag, as "secondary" or imitative gender, "stages and erodes . . . the heterosexual construction of coherence . . . [making] heterosexual gendered identities an 'incredible' performative fabrication devoid of ontological priority" (Cleto, 1999, p. 357).

Resistance

Although Sontag infamously averred that "it goes without saying that the Camp sensibility is disengaged, depoliticized—or at least apolitical" (1964, p. 516), most theorists of camp disagree. Camp, as Britton (1999) concedes, at least requires "the *frisson* of transgression, the sense of perversity in relation to bourgeois norms" (p. 138). Others ascribe an even more assertively critical role to camp, claiming that "it works by emphasizing or demystifying the artificiality that passes for natural" (Cleto, 1999, p. 25) and, further, that "camp can be subversive—a means of illustrating those cultural ambiguities and contradictions that oppress us all" (Babuscio, 1999, p. 128). Dollimore (1999) makes this point even more dramatically: "The anarchic and the political, the anger and the boredom, are all active in [camp], and most especially when the survival strategies of subordination—subterfuge, lying, evasion—are aesthetically transvalued into weapons of attack, but ever working obliquely through irony, ambiguity, mimicry, and impersonation" (p. 224).

Given camp's historical location within gay male culture, much theoretical discussion of camp's subversive potential in the existing literature is relevant to heteronormativity. Case (1999) lauds camp's ability to "eradicate the ruling powers of heterosexist realist modes" (p. 189). Many theorists posit that gender, specifically, is the axis on which the critical implications of camp turn in this context; Ross (1999) notes that, "in fact, camp [is] a highly developed way of talking about what nonessentialist feminism has come to call sexual difference" (p. 325). Much of this subversive potential inheres in the gender parody that characterizes camp as it occurs in the context of gay male culture, especially in the practice of drag. Butler (1990) describes the critical component of drag in this way:

> If the anatomy of the performer is already distinct from the gender of the performer, and both of those are distinct from the gender of the performance, then the performance suggests a dissonance not only between sex and performance, but sex and gender, and gender and performance. As much as drag creates a unified picture of "woman" . . . , it also reveals the distinctness of those aspects of gendered experience which are falsely naturalized as a unity through the regulatory fiction of heterosexual coherence. *In imitating gender, drag implicitly reveals the imitative structure of gender itself—as well as its contingency.* (p. 137)

Accordingly, she asserts, by "dramatiz[ing] the signifying gestures through which gender itself is established" (p. viii), "genders can be rendered thoroughly and radically *incredible* through a politics of gender parody" (p. 141). Dollimore (1999) concurs, stating that, even beyond the practice of drag per se, "in a sense [camp] renders gender a question of aesthetics" (p. 225).

In this context, Robertson (1996) perceives distinctly feminist possibilities for camp, which, she argues, "as a performative strategy, as well as a mode of reception, commonly foregrounds the artifice of gender and sexual roles through literal and metaphoric transvestism and masquerade. Since camp has been primarily conceived of as a gay male subcultural practice, its articulation with the concept of female spectatorship will enable us to explore the degree to which the female camp spectator shares her liminal status with another alienated group and also to explore what kind of subcultural resistances are available to women" (p. 14). Piggford is similarly intrigued by the phenomenon of female camp, as well as by its subversive potential, accurately understood only when each performance is viewed in historical context. Those who use female camp androgyny have the potential to "undermine their respective cultures' assumptions about the stable connection between biological sex and gender" (1997, p. 58), but that potential is realized only with the acknowledgment of the historical and social underpinnings of camp's cultural codes.

But some theorists are not ready to embrace camp as categorically subversive. If these critics do not summarily reject a political component to camp, they are more cautious and more cynical than their peers regarding camp's resistive potential. Britton (1999), perhaps camp's harshest critic, is particularly disenchanted with "contemporary" gay camp, citing it as "little more than a kind of anaesthetic, allowing one to remain inside oppressive relations while enjoying the illusory confidence that one is flouting them" (p. 138). Dollimore (1999), in a similar vein, concedes that at least some forms of camp constitute "the quintessence of an alienated, inadequate sensibility" (p. 224). Even Robertson, for all of her optimism regarding camp's feminist potential, is cognizant of its limitations, particularly in the context of contemporary media fare. Although she affirms its utopian qualities, it is, she concedes, "a sensibility more committed to the status quo than to effecting real change" (1996, p. 22).

Notably, the concerns of each of these theorists are contextualized by a broader discussion of the emergence of a camp sensibility into the mainstream of popular culture that is unhinged from its "authentic" (gay male and, thus, presumed subversive) moorings and evacuates it of its attendant critical potential. The consequent repackaging of camp as a repository for and generator of conventional discourses of heteronormativity and gender normativity, cautions Robertson, should prompt us to "scrutinize our [contemporary] camp icons, and our own camp readings and practices, to ensure that we do not naively substitute camp for politics" (1996, p. 138). In the following chapter, we turn our attention to the issues and debates surrounding camp as a contemporary, especially mediated phenomenon, with a particular eye toward its dimensions and potential as a critical device.

2

Breaking Camp

Co-optation and Critical Logics

In the early years of this millennium, Hollywood capitalized on (U.S.) Americans' love for camp with parodic tributes to the late 1970s cult television series *Charlie's Angels* across two sequential films. The first of these, *Charlie's Angels* (2000), featured the action adventures of three female detectives performing impossible crime-fighting feats while clad in stiletto heels and hot pants. One fan reveled in the film's "high-spirited, infectious ridiculousness,"[1] delighting in the tongue-in-cheek antics of the heroic hotties. The film's sequel, *Charlie's Angels: Full Throttle* (2003), was similarly received; fans could not seem to get enough of the "gleefully airheaded and slick" (Rea, 2003) rendition of the bygone TV series, replete with self-referential in-jokes and outmoded, outrageous representations of femininity.

But some critics were markedly less enthusiastic, noting that the films exemplified a trend in which, under the cover of the modish, "hip" ironic and nostalgic sensibility that pervades contemporary media fare, problematic and even downright offensive representations might be "innocently" circulated and thus accepted unquestioningly by contemporary audiences. In the language and literature of camp, which is the very sensibility to which these critics refer, this trend has been identified disdainfully as "camp lite" or "pop camp" (M. Booth, 1999; Case, 1999; Cleto, 1999; Dyer, 1999; Finch, 1999; Robertson, 1996; Ross, 1999; Sontag, 1964). Although the phenomenon has generally been engaged in terms of how it is manifest in and coincides with contemporary media fare, its roots can be traced back to Isherwood's (1954) distinction between "high camp" and "low camp." Isherwood was specifically concerned with distinguishing between clever parody and kitschy imitation, but the elitism that characterized that distinction is also apparent in attempts to distinguish "authentic" camp from "pop" camp. While that issue warrants attention on its own terms, at the core of this distinction is a political question, and it is this question that dominates the debate regarding camp lite: wherein lies the resistive potential of camp? And to what extent might the phenomenon be strategic?

Many theorists assert that contemporary versions of camp so prevalent in current popular culture constitute more than a benign use of the camp sensibility, arguing that this is *appropriation* of authentic camp. Cleto (1999), for instance, describes this shift bluntly as "a brutal appropriation to popular, mass use, of a subordinate strategy" (p. 17), and Dyer (1999) similarly asserts that "something happens to camp when taken over by straights—it loses its cutting edge" (p. 115). Butler, too, notwithstanding her implicit endorsement of camp's subversive potential as it inheres in drag, acknowledges the specter of its appropriation, thus "domesticated and recirculated as [an] instrument of cultural hegemony" (1990, p. 139). Although Robertson does not share in the implicit assumption of these and other theorists that camp is the province of gay men, she agrees that "camp lite" represents a "watering down of camp's critical and political edge" (1996, p. 122).

Initial assessment of the relationship between camp and popular culture originated in a consideration of 1960s "pop art," as epitomized in the work of Andy Warhol, although neither the presence of camp in popular culture nor discussions of it have dissipated since. "Pop camp," most theorists assert, is governed by a metaphor of recycling; it typically "occurs at the moment when cultural products (for instance, stars, fashions, genres, and stereotypes) of an earlier moment of production have lost their power to dominate cultural meanings and become available 'in the present, for redefinition according to contemporary codes of taste'" (Robertson, 1996, pp. 4–5). Accordingly, argues Robertson, "instances of Camp Lite fail to redefine cultural objects critically, because they are steeped in nostalgia rather than a historical sense of camp" (p. 144). Ross (1999) similarly asserts that pop camp is a "parasitical practice" characterized by "a rediscovery of history's waste. Camp . . . is more than just a remembrance of things past, it is the *re-creation of surplus value from forgotten forms of labor*" (p. 320). Furthermore, the sensibilities of irony and pastiche that distinguish contemporary popular culture have a natural affinity with and constitute a natural environment for an appropriately depoliticized and restylized camp aesthetic (Cleto, 1999; Robertson, 1996; Ross, 1999). In this context, camp is repackaged as merely another postmodern sensibility, informed especially by pastiche, characterized by "blank parody" that is dehistoricized and reduced to a mere "discourse of style" (Robertson, 1996, p. 138).

Some theorists, in fact, extend this logic to explain a "cultural economy" (Ross, 1999) of pop camp. Ross argues that "the immediacy and self-sufficiency of the consumption of the Pop experience *already contains the knowledge that it will soon be outdated*—spent, obsolescent, or out of fashion" (p. 319). Because camp is predicated on the retrieval and recycling of "history's waste," camp, Ross avers, was "an antidote to Pop's contagion of obsolescence" (p. 321); he notes further that the consequence of pop camp under these conditions is its influence on the "historical production of the material and cultural conditions of taste" (p. 320). Robertson (1996) explains that pop, given its theoretical premise that

> everyday cultural currency had value . . . , problematized the question of taste itself, rejecting an elitist past based on cultural acts of judgment and the notion that objects had intrinsic aesthetic value. Pop, in this sense, created a context for the mainstreaming camp taste—justifying the democratic spirit of camp, its collapsing of high-low boundaries, while opening the sensibility up to a majority audience. In a curious twist, camp taste became the dominant code. Rather than a covert, cult sensibility, camp becomes a commercialized taste—and a taste for commercialism. (p. 120)

Ross (1999) allows that the infusion of camp into popular culture, especially in the 1960s, "challenged and, in some cases, overturned legitimate definitions of taste and sexuality." He cautions, however, that "we must also remember to what extent this cultural economy was tied to the capitalist logic of development that governed the mass culture industries" (p. 326). Pop camp, he suggests, is entirely defined by the conditions of its production and consumption.

For all of the intuitive sense that the distinction between "authentic" camp and "pop" camp makes, however, and despite the attempts of critics to fix that distinction, it remains rather vague. This is especially true at the level of audience, or spectatorship, to use Robertson's language—if a text is read as critical, irrespective of its designation or location, is this not the best or most appropriate measure of precisely *how* it is camp? Discussion regarding the content of "camp lite" as compared to "authentic" camp is similarly unsatisfactory or incomplete, seemingly drawing rather arbitrary or ultrafine distinctions. It seems that the recontextualization of camp within mass culture and via contemporary media venues is the singular concrete defining feature of pop camp, justifiably prompting the suspicion and skepticism of critics. But the mere fact that camp has been commodified as a sensibility does not *necessarily* entail a qualification of its critical rhetorical potential; indeed, the very features that make up camp may make it more resilient than other critical devices and sensibilities that have gone before it—hence, the possibility that one might indeed read a "pop camp" text as subversive. We are not convinced of the mutual exclusivity of authentic camp and pop camp, and we do not seek to reify it in this project; instead, we venture a closer inspection of the variations of camp available in popular mediated culture with a specifically critical eye.

To this end, it is also important to consider the aesthetics and sensibilities that characterize popular culture, particularly the contemporary mediascape. That is, if contemporary popular culture and the media fare generated within and for it can be understood as characterized by pastiche, artifice, and the endless recycling and recombination of images, perhaps what we understand to be camp is simply a manifestation or variation of that; as we have noted, the two are highly commensurate on several levels, so perhaps they are, for all intents and purposes, interchangeable. And if they are not interchangeable, perhaps camp might best be understood as a logical and even inevitable culmination of those sensibilities; that is, the packaging and commodification of those abstract sensibilities must inhabit the form of camp, an ideal template, such that recycling and recombination take shape as parody, irony, and nostalgia, and texts are aesthetically rendered in such a way—theatrically and excessively—to point up those qualities. As such, the prevalence of "pop camp" that so many critics have decried may be less evidence of conscious or opportunistic appropriation, as they imply, than of evolution and synthesis, a merging of compatible aesthetics at a particular historical moment.

We are inclined to take this latter position (although we would suggest that it nonetheless describes appropriation, simply more broadly defined). If we understand camp to have been absorbed into contemporary sensibilities and practices rather than seized and strategically reconfigured, and if we assume that the qualities of play and critique are inherent to camp—

and, indeed, the very features that call forth contemporary sensibilities and vice versa—then we might apprehend camp as a particularly dynamic and volatile practice. In other words, the convergence of camp and contemporary sensibilities in our current mediascape may well be critically fortuitous, given that camp is largely defined by the "play" of gender and sexuality; the very same camp features that provide fodder for popular mediated texts by dint of their superficial congruence with contemporary sensibilities may have a critical traction that could conceivably be utilized in alternative—and, importantly, largely ungovernable—ways. In other words, camp is not a cipher, an empty form that assumes the dimensions of that which chooses to inhabit it. While its rendering as a contemporary, and for that matter fairly proliferative, practice might eclipse its proclivities for critique, let alone its critical promise, we submit that in certain popular camp texts, that promise is more available than in others. Again, our intent is to distinguish between those texts. Thus, while the role of the reader, audience, or spectator is not irrelevant, we are particularly interested in discerning the *textual* features that do not merely permit but configure a subversive reading, even if that reading is rejected by or is obscure to some audiences.

Contemporary Female Camp Performances

The cases that we have selected as a collective springboard for this discussion of the resistive potential of camp in the context of the contemporary mainstream mediascape—Xena, Karen Walker, Macy Gray, and Gwen Stefani—all embody the characteristics of camp as defined in the literature on camp to date. Robertson (1996) characterizes camp as "both a mode of excess and a method of containment. Camp depends on our simultaneously recognizing stereotypes as stereotypes to distance ourselves from them and at the same time recognizing, and loving, the hold and power those stereotypes have over us" (p. 142). She thus attributes a critical edge if not drive to camp. Accordingly, she draws a fine distinction between camp as such and the conscious production of a "camp aesthetic" that "fails to define cultural objects critically, because [such productions] are steeped in nostalgia rather than a historical sense of camp" (p. 144). Noting that, as a camp icon, "Madonna and her reception provide a caution about too easily conflating camp with progressive politics" (p. 138)—given that Madonna, at least to some extent, may appropriate camp as a "conscious artistic practice"—Robertson concludes that "we need, therefore, to consider whether or how camp can be consciously redeployed as an aesthetic counterpractice from within dominant institutions and not simply from the margins" (p. 153). This is precisely the challenge that we take up with this project.

In part, what separates the performances that we will analyze from the "camp lite" that Robertson finds pervasive in contemporary popular culture but wanting in terms of critical potential inheres in the fact that they also embody other defining features of the camp sensibility as established in the existing literature: irony, aestheticism, performance or theatricality, parodic humor, and resistance. Irony is a prominent feature of each of the performances that we will examine, primarily by virtue of the "incongruous contrast [that] can be drawn between an individual/thing and its context/ association" (Babuscio, 1999, p. 119), for instance. The juxtaposition inherent in the performance of bygone stereotypes in a contemporary context accounts for some of this irony; however, other ironic markers characterize these performances, as well. Stefani's physical performances, for instance, are often coupled with sarcastic lyrics that belie her actions; Gray's "retro funk" look and performance are represented as cutting edge; Karen Walker's socialite, although consistent with the stereotype in terms of appearance and elitist behavior, is also coarse and often socially inappropriate; and Xena exemplifies what Babuscio identifies as the most common manifestation of this incongruity, that of masculine/feminine, insofar as she is a fearless, fearsome warrior who is also conventionally beautiful and "sexy."

Similarly, each of these performances is characterized by aestheticism that often manifests as excess and always is defined by "its opposition to puritan morality. . . . [It] is subversive of commonly received standards." As such, irony is the basis of a camp aesthetic in that "irony, to be effective, must be shaped" (Babuscio, 1999, p. 120). Stefani's performances are extremely excessive aesthetically, sometimes apparent in an over-the-top "baby-doll" look, sometimes the retro "hippie chick" look. Central to these performances is sexuality; Stefani utilizes her sexuality in all of her performances in ways that flaunt conventional discourses of appropriate—controlled—female sexuality. The fact that Stefani pairs stereotypes of passive sexual availability with often aggressive, even quasi-masculine sexual performance suggests the ways in which irony and aesthetics interrelate in camp performances.

Gray's aesthetic is extreme, as well, characterized by a large "Afro" hair-style, enormous sunglasses, precariously high platform shoes, tight pant-suits, and large, faux-fur boas. Her persona, too, is very sexual, as apparent in her physical performances and her lyrics. In addition, her employment of a clearly Afrocentric aesthetic poses a further challenge to specifically raced moral discourses. Karen Walker's excess is most apparent in signifiers associ-ated with class—her wealth is established via frequent reference to her limit-less funds, her jewels, her prestigious East Side address, her limo, her ser-vants, and her casual, wasteful attitude toward all of it. The challenge that she poses to moral conventions is predicated on class, as well—that is, to the degree that she exhibits incongruously crass, crude behavior, most of which, notably, also turns on her sexuality. Xena's excess is apparent in her mascu-line actions—she is featured regularly in physical battle. She is also dressed accordingly in armor, albeit armor that has been tailored for a female form—a skirt, bustier, and thigh-high boots, a veritable caricature of the Wonder Woman or Amazon cultural icon. Again, Xena's camp aesthetic is driven by the incongruity that inheres in a masculine/feminine duality.

Babuscio (1999) argues that performance or theatricality is core to camp, especially as relevant to "the gay situation" (p. 123), which he equates in that context with "passing." Although we believe that the particular camp perfor-mances we analyze are both informed by and have implications for the "gay sensibility" that has historically been associated with camp, we argue that they do so distinctively; thus, theatricality in the sense that Babuscio invokes the concept may not be strictly relevant in these cases. Understood more broadly, however, as conspicuous "role playing" (Babuscio, 1999, p. 123) and the problematizing of gender and sexuality, the camp performances of Ste-fani, Gray, Karen Walker, and Xena arguably qualify at least to the extent that the irony and excess that constitute the bedrock of their performances denaturalize the tropes invoked. As with historic camp icons that Babuscio (1999) references, "their roles provide the means whereby they can project their hyperbolic personae. The more hackneyed the material, the easier it is for them to find spaces with the framework of scene, situation, and direction where they can be themselves" (p. 125). Although our goal in this project is not to determine authentic identity or authorial intent as the measure of these camp performances—rather, our goal is to understand their peculiar rhetorical dimensions and functions—certainly, the excessive, almost parodic incongruity that characterizes those performances renders them conspicuous.

Infused within these parodic performances is a brand of humor that renders camp affectionately playful as opposed to cynical. Babuscio asserts that "humor constitutes the strategy of camp" (1999, p. 126). To some extent, as he notes, "the comic element is inherent in the formal properties of irony" (p. 126); however, he argues further that "the 'serious' is, in fact, critical to camp. Though camp mocks the solemnities of our culture, it never totally discards the seriousness of a thing or individual. As a character in a Christopher Isherwood novel [1954] says: 'You can't camp about something you don't take seriously; you're not making fun *of* it; you're making fun *out* of it. You're expressing what's basically serious to you in terms of fun and artifice and elegance'" (Babuscio, 1999, p. 128). Again, our purpose is not to measure intent as the hallmark of camp; however, we find that the camp performances with which we are concerned are playful on their own terms, even as they retain the element of gravity that Babuscio and Isherwood describe. Stefani's performances, for instance, are often rife with ultrafeminine features—red heart outlines, pink bubblegum, chiffon, and excessive makeup. Although these elements are juxtaposed with features and behaviors that point up their frivolity, they are never rejected—to the contrary, they remain key signifiers positively associated with Stefani's camp persona. In a somewhat different way, even as Gray playfully parodies "hip" 1970s Black funk, her performance also functions as a cultural tribute in conjunction with the "classic" soul and rhythm-and-blues qualities of her music. Furthermore, that aesthetic is semiotically steeped in Afrocentrism, which imbues it with a political sensibility that, while it can be recontextualized, cannot be erased. Similarly, Karen Walker's crass elitism and attendant racism simultaneously ridicule class even as they ultimately salvage the rich, white "fag hag" as the reliable social sponsor of the gay male, the warrant for his urbanity and sophistication. Finally, the incredible success that Xena experiences as a warrior and the attendant dismal failure of those men who would try to defeat her is comic in terms of the sheer unlikelihood of most of those scenarios; at the same time, however, the larger discourse that frames this performance—of women resisting and overcoming male oppression—is poignant and grave.

Gwen Stefani, Macy Gray, Karen Walker, and Xena thus all reflect qualities historically associated with "authentic" camp, yet they are also quintessential examples of contemporary "pop" camp. Our contention is that their performances feature a critical edge and thus embody a variation of camp characterized by the configuration of particular elements that distinguish them from the majority of camp performances, texts, and icons available in contemporary popular media fare. Our project is to identify and examine those features and their configuration in each case, and, accordingly, contribute to an understanding of the evolution of camp, as well as its political and cultural implications. We also hope to make innovative contributions regarding female performances of camp, thus engaging Robertson's (1996) contention that female camp may constitute a feminist practice. Much writing to date on camp has defined the concept as a uniquely gay male sensibility; indeed, the relationship between camp and gay male culture, historically especially but also today, is strong and clear (Babuscio, 1999; Britton, 1999; Cleto, 1999; Dyer, 1999; Ross, 1999; Sontag, 1964). Because of this relationship, most writings on camp have addressed gay male camp in particular—in terms of camp performances, as well as in terms of audiences of and for camp. Our focus on female camp represents a departure from much of the existing literature in this respect, although we find that a gay sensibility remains a highly relevant feature, not least insofar as camp performances of femininity, in particular, if by women in these cases, may be key to the retention of a critical edge to camp in a contemporary popular cultural context. Accordingly, we examine how and to what degree sexual and gender alterity intersect rhetorically in these instances of contemporary female "resistive" camp. We submit that these camp performances are liminal in this respect, discursively conflating and simultaneously challenging conventions of gender and sexuality. While many have identified the ways in which gay male camp accomplishes this, we contend that it inheres distinctively in female camp performances of femininity, specifically in a contemporary, mediated context; our interest is in discerning exactly how it is rhetorically configured.

Critically Configuring Camp

Subversive readings from camp texts are not guaranteed; the parodic nature of camp, after all, transgressive or otherwise, requires the invocation of

often blatant stereotypes. There is a substantive pattern, however—a logic—
to certain performances that belies the contemporary random and pastiche
aesthetic that also characterizes them. These performances do more than
merely permit resistive audience reading *of* or projection of meaning *onto*
the text, insofar as audiences must read "against the grain." Rather, if the appropriate cues are attended to by the audience, resistive readings can emerge
from the text, wholly intact and logically sound. Our contention is that transgressive camp performances are better understood as "double texts," wherein
a distinct and coherent message seemingly at odds with a superficial reading
can be identified in and emerge from the text contingent on the cues foregrounded and attended to by the audience. In this sense, they function as
something of a figure-ground or perhaps "magic eye" perceptual illusion,
where a distinctive and wholly coherent image emerges out of a large, seemingly random and abstract pattern on attending to particular visual cues.
That is, we argue that in these cases, resistive readings coexist with their
own appropriations. In these texts, both dominant and resistive messages
can be identified, contingent on the cues to which the audience attends; accordingly, these texts may be better considered conjoined rather than conflated.

Sender (2004) addresses this dynamic in a specific context in her discussion of advertising to gay consumers in a mainstream context, specifically chronicling how "marketers . . . walk a narrow line between making
gayness visible and making it too visible" (p. 123), in the latter case risk-
ing offending certain of their audiences. To this end, asserts Sender, ads
of this ilk typically invoke "gay subcultural knowledge" or "gay signifiers"
that specifically cue and, accordingly, interpellate gay audiences but that
would not register with "mainstream"—that is, heteronormative and possibly antigay—audiences. Thus, marketers strive for and achieve a "contained
visibility" (p. 129). Although the context that Sender engages—the world of
marketing—significantly shapes the politics of ambiguous messages in the
texts that she considers (for example, how resistance might be characterized,
if at all; the specific targeting of certain audiences; and the necessary presence of overt strategy), we suggest that the dynamic that she identifies has
relevance to our project as well. That is, she implies that the invocation, arrangement, and foregrounding of certain signifiers constitute a logic of sorts

that invites a particular reading, even as those same signifiers might be arrayed or privileged differently to render a different interpretation. Our contention is that certain camp performances available in the contemporary mediascape also feature this dynamic, and our interest is in making explicit the rhetorical logic that drives it in these texts.

Our analysis of Macy Gray, Gwen Stefani, Karen Walker, and Xena reveals that, in addition to the "classic" qualities of camp identified by various critics, their performances feature the elements of trope, spectacle, and anchor and foils; furthermore, these elements serve as premises that configure and make available a subversive reading of gender, especially as it intersects with sexuality. Although some or all of these elements may appear to be mirror images of some of said "classic" camp characteristics, we have identified them as distinctive precisely insofar as they engage compatible contemporary sensibilities, which serve as both context and, arguably, vehicle for these camp performances. These premises distinguish them from the plethora of camp texts and performances that proliferate in contemporary popular culture and media fare. While contemporary and camp sensibilities are conflated in most of that fare, the performances that we assess reflect a peculiar engagement and configuration of those sensibilities.

Trope

Each of these camp performances is patterned after highly recognizable tropes, or stereotypes, of women whose familiarity is established precisely by virtue of their availability in mainstream mediated texts—these tropes function as the "first premise" of (resistive) camp's discursive logic. The allusions to these tropes in the camp performances we examine are very clear; at the same time, the performances are distinctive from and extend beyond those tropes in important ways that secure their camp sensibility and set the stage for the alterity that they ultimately represent.

Traditionally in the fields of literary studies and rhetoric and composition, *trope* has been categorized under "style," referring to a figure of speech involving a turn of phrase or "the use of a word in a sense other than the literal" (Holman & Harmon, 1992, p. 485). Metaphor, synecdoche, and metonymy are commonly recognized as tropes, literary conventions that exploit in significant ways the symbolic function of language and occur with enough frequency in a culture to constitute standard use. Metaphors, for example, are familiar rhetorical forms that function to encourage implicit comparisons between whole objects and ideas (e.g., "the Web," "the war on drugs"), and synecdoche and metonymy to encourage an association between parts and wholes (e.g., "head of a corporation," "heart of the matter"). The familiarity with which they are used and which becomes part of their semiotic constitution causes tropes often to be considered interchangeably with *cliché* or *stereotype*, "standard phrases for a concept, term, or description that is fixed and unchanging" (Morner & Rausch, 1991, p. 329).

Reliant on the human proclivity for symbol use, tropes as wordplay function beyond the ornamental, making use of the associative appeal of patterning for the making of meaning. Words formed in patterns of "comparison, balance, repetition, disclosure, reversal, contraction, expansion, magnification, and series" (Gregg, 1978, p. 4), for example, encourage a mode of reception that transcends literal comprehension. Comparing them to Aristotle's concept of *topoi* or commonplaces, Frye (1957) refers to such recurring word patterns as "associative clusters" or "communicable units" precisely because of their distinctive capacity for communicating emotions, experiences, and feelings. Burke (1962, 1969) also notes that "master tropes" such as metaphor, metonymy, synecdoche, and irony are symbols that extend beyond their figurative use by playing an important role in humans' relationship with their external reality. They are "not merely reflections of the things symbolized, or signs for them; they are to a degree a transcending of the things symbolized" (Burke, 1962, p. 716), fostering new epistemological frameworks. Tropes, then, are heuristic uses of language's inherently symbolic nature traditionally associated with poetic language, but extending into everyday lexicon, as well.

Since its original classification as stylistic word choice, the concept of trope has expanded to suit contemporary needs, its essence often appearing under different labels. Across disciplines, studies of rhetorical forms feature terms such as *archetypal metaphor, imagery, genre, analogy, synecdoche,* and *icon* to refer to recurrent patterns—discursive as well as nondiscursive—turning on implicit comparisons. Osborn's (1967, 1977) renowned analyses of archetypal metaphors demonstrate the figurative value found in age-old symbols such as light and dark, the sea, and the cycle of the seasons;

and Hauser (2002) notes the rhetorical power of imagery created through an amalgamation of symbols. Campbell and Jamieson's *Form and Genre* (1978) represents a decisive collection of essays examining the role of form in rhetoric, in particular the significance of *genre*, "a complex, an amalgamation, a constellation of substantive, situational and stylistical elements" (p. 18), and its relationship to rhetorical action.

Others have stretched the concept of trope to include nondiscursive rhetorical forms or icons, responding to the need for revamped analytical tools in understanding the pervasive visual communication in our media-saturated culture. Messaris (1997), for example, argues that all modes of communication may be described in terms of two properties: the semantic, in which elements of a communication mode (e.g., images, musical tones) are considered in terms of their meaning, and the syntactic, in which the arrangement of those elements are considered as they form larger units of meaning in a type of grammar. The semantic properties of communication, notes Messaris, have long been considered by scholars across disciplines under the category of "semiotics." Inspired by Charles Sanders Peirce's definitive work in the early twentieth century, communication scholars in the area of visual communication have continued the interest in the study of "signs," or "any mark, bodily movement, symbol, token, etc., used to indicate and to convey thoughts, information, commands, etc." (Danesi, 1994, p. xi). The interest in nondiscursive rhetorical forms, then, has evolved from an earlier conception of trope as stylistic wordplay and certainly has relevance for the variation of trope found in female camp.

Although the basic understanding of trope has evolved across time and disciplines, what has remained rather constant is the recognition of the semiotic significance of this rhetorical form. Tropes have semiotic force, in large part, not only because of their symbolic nature but because of their recurrent nature, a fact understood clearly by critics with interest in genres and their rhetorical power. The proliferation, for example, of the "wicked stepmother" trope in children's fairy tales lends that convention power beyond its literal use. Similarly, the reiteration of the "peacekeeping" trope in reference to U.S. military actions in the Persian Gulf furnishes that form with rhetorical force. Such recurrent and repetitive discursive patterns are "given rhetorical force by their habitual use and codifiability" (Gronbeck,

1978, p. 140), allowing them to function as mnemonic sites for those who consume them. As Birdsell (1993) notes, "Tropes can condense arguments, which are then subject to recall in much the same manner as an enthymeme" (p. 179). The result is a particular framing effect for interpretation, one imbued with an aspect of cultural logic and, because of its reliance on established conventions and commonplaces, with hegemonic proclivities.

Although the bulk of scholarship addressing the rhetorical significance of tropes is relevant to their function as linguistic devices of formal argument, tropes are particularly noteworthy—and arguably, hold distinctive rhetorical implications—in contemporary mediated texts, where they are far more likely to assume nonlinguistic—especially visual or aural—forms. A number of cultural critics have noted that a hallmark of contemporary media fare is its self-reflexivity or self-referentiality—that is, it is "constantly recycling images that were previously constituted and communicated by the media" (Harms & Dickens, 1996, p. 215; see also Grossberg, 1983; Kaplan, 1987). Examples of this include, for instance, Madonna's invocation of Marilyn Monroe's performance of the song "Diamond's Are a Girl's Best Friend" in the film *Gentlemen Prefer Blondes* in Madonna's music video for the song "Material Girl"; 50 Cent and G Unit's allusions to characters, scenes, and dialogue from *The Godfather* in their music video "Poppin' Them Things"; and countless advertisements that feature old film clips (e.g., featuring Fred Astaire) and songs (e.g., Edith Piaf) to sell anything from brooms to luxury cars. Of course, not all historical mediated images qualify as tropes; however, some images—and those most frequently referenced in the context of a camp sensibility—are indeed evocative of an era, an ambience, or a set of assumptions and practices that assume the status of trope. Also, although critics concede that the reproduction of cultural texts is not novel or inherently problematic, contemporary media technologies allow those texts to be reproduced and "recombined" in various contexts and in infinite configurations, thus allowing those texts to be endowed with meanings that may serve strategic, even ideological, purposes. That is, whereas the recycling and recombination of images may appear random and reflective of the pastiche that so heavily characterizes a contemporary sensibility, this practice in fact is strategic—particular tropes are invoked in order to secure audience acquiescence to a given message or representation. Accordingly, the media practice of drawing on established cultural (media) tropes ultimately is hegemonic, reproducing discourses commensurate with the dominant interests that drive contemporary media. Thus, although cultural critics do not use the language of "trope" that rhetorical theorists do, they arrive at the same conclusion regarding their tyrannizing force.

Although we concur with the stance that many scholars take regarding the default hegemonic function of trope, we are not yet ready to dismiss the practice as irredeemable, especially in a contemporary mediated context whose hallmark aesthetic is apparently infinite and random pastiche. That is, if tropes invoked in specific contexts and configurations render alternative meanings, might it not be possible to "recombine" them in such a way as to render a resistive or at least critical reading? Just as the manipulation of these familiar and often beloved forms are utilized to secure adherence to ideological conventions, they might well be manipulated to challenge them. If the "wicked stepmother" trope is tweaked in a new version of the children's fairy tale, for example, the repetitive process by which that image might otherwise become encoded as "truth" is effectively disrupted via a type of defamiliarization nonetheless predicated on initial recognition of the trope's cultural legitimacy. Conventional cultural tropes arguably provide fodder for what is understood as camp, given the latter's ironic and nostalgic sensibilities, wherein beloved cultural icons are paid homage and deconstructed simultaneously. Thus, a contemporary media environment, characterized by self-reflexivity and saturated with pastiche and irony, presents an ideal scenario in which established cultural tropes might be reconfigured in very "camp" ways. Of course, "camping" a given cultural trope is not necessarily resistive—as Robertson (1996) notes, the popular mediascape is rife with nostalgic fare, such as the film versions of the television shows *The Dukes of Hazzard* and *Charlie's Angels,* that "eulogize a fantasy of . . . American innocence through nostalgia" (p. 121) for bygone cultural icons. Nonetheless, the potential certainly exists for resistive camp in this contemporary media playground, afforded by those very—highly pervasive—sensibilities. We suggest that contemporary female camp performances—including those of Xena, Karen Walker, Macy Gray, and Gwen Stefani—move beyond simply resurrecting and gently ironizing cultural tropes of gender and sexuality to reconfiguring them, sometimes radically, in a way that realizes the critical and transgressive potential of camp. Notably, nostalgia is not incommensurate with a critical sensibility, however, as Robertson reminds us. Our goal is to elucidate the complicated rhetorical logic found in camp's use of tropes and whether and how they may function subversively.

Spectacle

If "trope" functions as the necessary first premise for the discursive logic that constitutes contemporary, resistive camp, then spectacle is its warrant, assuming "the form of rules, principles, or conventions particular to certain fields" (Inch & Warnick, 2002, p. 318). Undeniably, this is where the substance of camp is contained—the aesthetic dimension characterized by over-the-top, sensational, and particularly image-driven displays or events—that defines camp (Babuscio, 1999; M. Booth, 1999; Case, 1999; Cleto, 1999; Core, 1984; Robertson, 1996; Ross, 1999; Sontag, 1964). Spectacle certainly reflects the hallmark camp quality of aesthetic excess, but it assumes distinctive and significant (and camouflaging) forms within the contemporary media environment. Spectacle alone, however, does not constitute camp, whether of the resistive or pop variety; to the contrary, it is arguably a hallmark feature of contemporary mediated popular culture on its own terms. From Beyoncé's "bootyliciousness" to Janet Jackson's highly public "wardrobe malfunction" to Pamela Anderson's Barbie-doll visage, the landscape of contemporary popular culture is littered with mediated spectacles in the form of outrageous performances of femininity. Contemporary popular music stars like Christina Aguilera and Jennifer Lopez provide additional proof of the ready availability of female spectacle for popular consumption, available in myriad mediated images and texts. Clearly, although the popular music industry is particularly fraught with them, spectacular performances are staples of mediated popular culture.

Cultural critics and theorists from a variety of disciplines and perspectives have noted this pervasiveness of spectacle in contemporary media fare (Baudrillard, 1983a, 1983b; Debord, 1976; Harms & Dickens, 1996; Erickson, 1998; Farrell, 1989; Lyotard, 1984; Procter, 1990). Most of them, in fact, are wary of this trend, arguing that such sensational images may have a stultifying and depoliticizing effect on the audiences that consume them. Best and Kellner (1999) warn of the dangers inherent in living within a "society of the spectacle," wherein audiences are entirely occupied with that which is commodified and their everyday lives are organized around the consumption of images. Critical thinking is compromised, they argue, and audiences become compliant consumers of a world invented by others rather than actively constructing one of their own.

Our notion that spectacle may be used as a tool of domination is rooted in the work of French theorist Guy Debord (1976). His interest in the consumer culture of the 1950s and 1960s and his commitment to the extension of Marxist principles to contemporary social conditions cultivated arguments concerning the hegemonic power of images to lull viewers into social conformity. In Debord's mind, images in contemporary society are not only omnipresent but are increasingly abstract, separated from social reality, and commodified, assuming the form of spectacles with a progressively more sophisticated power of domination. Such spectacles are precarious in that they discourage creative production, fostering instead critical disengagement and manipulating desire into consumption and other modes of social conformity. In a similar vein, some contemporary media critics have assessed the connection between spectacle and social conformity, noting that some mediated spectacles, such as those found on *The Jerry Springer Show,* may function to inscribe dominant moral codes via the appropriation and "spectacularization" of alterity and/or resistance (e.g., Grabe, 2002; Tavener, 2000).

Baudrillard (1983a, 1983b) offers what some consider an extension of Debord's work moving from a focus on *spectacle* to one on *simulation* (Best & Kellner, 1997). Rejecting the modernist assumptions undergirding Debord's notion of the society of the spectacle—in which one might track the source of oppression, for example, or observe a difference between appearance and reality—Baudrillard argues that we have entered into a "postmodern" world marked by implosion, simulation, and hyperreality such that it makes little sense to think of the spectacle in terms of a subject/object distinction. Best and Kellner (1997) explain this move by Baudrillard as a continuation of Debord's work rather than a rejection of said work, as both theorists struggle to explain the role of the commodity object as spectacular image in cycles of semiotic exchange.

Not surprisingly, spectacle has captured the attention of feminist media critics in particular, many of whom have noted the consistent and troubling manifestation of spectacle on women's bodies in contemporary popular culture in such a way as to reinforce conventional discourses of gender, even as they appear to flaunt convention by dint of sheer excess (Battles & Hilton-Morrow, 2002; Brookey, 1996; Brookey & Westerfelhaus, 2001; Cloud, 1996;

Dow, 2001). Harms and Dickens (1996) have attended to the "postmodern media practices" that cultivate this dynamic. Here potentially diverse, resistive representations, including especially the highly spectacularized, are strategically rendered for hegemonic effect. Some critics afford a resistive potential to spectacle, however, citing its proclivity for disrupting normative gender assumptions via the denaturalization of gender. In their view, women who render themselves as spectacles may well be engaging in bold acts of transgression that appropriate the very dominant discourses that would constrain them (Butler, 1990, 1993; Doane, 1987; Russo, 1986, 1995; Silverman, 1993).

Many feminist film theorists have noted the particular implications that spectacle has for gender and have assessed spectacle in precisely those terms. Most of them, in fact, share the reservations of other cultural critics who have engaged spectacle theoretically, identifying the ways in which specifically gendered discourses are inscribed on the female body (De Lauretis, 1984; Doane, 1982, 1987; Mulvey, 1975; Russo, 1986). Mulvey (1975), for instance, assesses woman as cinematic spectacle designed for a male gaze. Positioned in film so as not to threaten men, Mulvey argues, women are denied subjectivity and stripped of their agency via either sadistic voyeurism or fetishism. Indeed, the fetishization of the female body has particular significance for spectacle; Singer (1988) defines *fetish* as a "material object that functions as a penis-substitute, a surrogate for the mother's missing penis.... The fetish assuages castration fear and restores the female body as good rather than as a threat" by recasting the female body as phallic (p. 5). In their study of cinematic male drag performances, Robbins and Myrick (2000) focus on the obsession of fetish as played out on desiring male bodies, noting the ultimately problematic effect for women as men in drag denaturalize gender while simultaneously reifying the power of male authority.

The intriguing correlation between spectacle and gender has been the focus of scholars in other arenas, as well, who assess spectacle as located in the over-the-top displays of femininity found in gay male culture, epitomized in female impersonation, or "drag." While Debord portends the mesmerizing and oppressive power of the mediated spectacle as something to be resisted, others who address spectacle as it occurs in drag performances embrace it as liberatory and even resistive, inviting a consideration of the critical potential of spectacle (Butler, 1990, 1993; Newton, 1999; Ross, 1999;

Sedgwick, 1999). Featuring as it does the display of femininity in the extreme by individuals who are known to be men, hence affording it irony by virtue of incongruity, spectacle in this context functions to challenge and undermine gendered conventions and expectations; as Butler (1990) argues, drag discloses the imitative structure of gender.

Perhaps foreshadowed by the noted relationship between spectacle and drag, scholars of camp likewise have been intrigued by the distinctly aesthetic nature of camp, although few use the term *spectacle* in reference to it. They note that camp "is all about style," particularly an upper-class, white aesthetics typically associated with a gay male sensibility. Not to be confused with *kitsch*, which refers to a voyeuristic disparagement of the "aesthetically shallow or vulgar," camp implies an "affectionate involvement" with spectacle (Babuscio, 1999, pp. 122–123). Camp scholars embrace the superficial—the highly ornate and dazzling artifice—as the very essence of camp. Situated at "the point of emergence of the artificial from the real, culture from nature" (Dollimore, 1999, p. 225), camp promises something other than the stultifying effects described by Debord. Key to this critical potential is the performative dimension also found in the spectacle of camp (Newton, 1999; Ross, 1999; Sedgwick, 1999). Displaying femininity in the extreme, camp avows "Being-as-Playing-a-Role ... life as theatre" (Sontag, 1964, p. 520), suggesting a critical distance between self and the image portrayed (Babuscio, 1999; Britton, 1999; Cleto, 1999; Dyer, 1999; Ross, 1999; Sontag, 1964).

The excessively performative nature of camp not only provides critical distance for the performer, but it also enables viewers' realization of camp's aesthetics, which are only recognizable as a deviation from a norm; without the norm, camp would cease to exist, given the need for hypothetical spectators who do not "get" the joke of camp's parody (Britton, 1999, p. 138). This relationship to a norm is particularly relevant for gender; the spectacle of camp serves to mock or parody and thus denaturalize gender. That promise is realized at least in part in the popular camp representations of Xena, Karen Walker, Gwen Stefani, and Macy Gray. Each of these women clearly trades in spectacle in terms of her mediated representations. As noted, this is not unique to these women in contemporary popular culture. In the increasingly pastiche-laden and image-driven context that characterizes contemporary popular culture, spectacle arguably is a vital feature of any performer who seeks to secure a place in the popular consciousness. But the spectacle available in the performances of these women, we argue, is distinctive, best understood as a convergence and (re)configuration of camp and contemporary sensibilities. That is, rather than spectacle for its own sake, the performances of these women are distinguished by a particular configuration of qualities—namely, parodic excess and juxtaposition—that utilizes and deploys the context of the contemporary mediascape in which they occur to foment a distinctively ironic and, in tandem with the other "premises" of camp that we identify, a potentially critical performance.

Anchors and Foils

Whereas tropes establish important historical and nostalgic referents for the camp performances, and spectacle secures the distinguishing aesthetic dimension necessary for camp, equally germane to contemporary camp performances are the contexts or grounds for these premises, which are crucial in configuring a discursive logic that positions the camp performances for a critical reading. Given the random, pastiche nature of contemporary popular media content, an establishment of context is vital in charting camp parameters. We contend that contemporary benchmarks—anchors and foils— for these camp performances serve as contextual cues for alternative perspectives, helping to define the performances as critical and potentially subversive. In particular, foils are those characters that serve as the contemporaneous backdrop against which camp emerges as such; fairly ubiquitous and conventional in their representations, they provide the contrast that throws into relief the "campiness" of those performances. Anchors are contemporary characters that also serve to define the camp performances, albeit via ironic congruence rather than contrast and furnishing additional critical fodder and dimension.

To say that contextual cues are key to the form and content of logic is not novel; Toulmin (1958), in his work on "practical" or informal logic, is perhaps most noted for his consideration of context in everyday argument. In his efforts to demonstrate the limits of formal logic for practical situations, Toulmin identifies elements of practical argument—backing, modal qualifiers, and rebuttals—that serve to locate the argument in the specifics of the situation rather than rely on universal, abstract principles. Such elements serve to modify the basic, syllogistic structure of formal logic, providing concrete components and accounting for contingencies to help ensure the desired reading of the argument. Although Toulmin's work is focused on linguistic arguments, his revision and modification of the elements of logical argument are also useful for nonlinguistic "arguments," including those broadly defined and diffuse, such as the discursive practices, conventions, and sensibilities available in contemporary media fare.

In fact, the relevance of context in the contemporary mediascape has been the subject of considerable discussion and debate among contemporary media critics. One of the hallmarks of contemporary media fare, all critics agree, is the random, pastiche, chaotic, and apparently incoherent aesthetic that characterizes it—an aesthetic some have identified as "postmodern" but all note as pervasive in contemporary culture. Where critics dissent is with respect to the ideological significance of that aesthetic. Most cultural critics see that aesthetic as hegemonic, contributing to the cultivation of dominant interests and ideology insofar as consumers of the these texts are overwhelmed by the sheer quantity and dissonance of images, alienated by their randomness, cynical regarding their technological manipulation, reconstituted as exclusively sensual and desiring (rather than sentient and reasoning), and effectively paralyzed by the apparent superficiality or constant shifting of signs with which they are inundated (Baudrillard, 1983a, 1983b; Best & Kellner, 1991; Goldman & Papson, 1994; Jameson, 1991). The audience thus is rendered a "black hole" or a "spongy referent" (Baudrillard, 1983b) that "unreflectively absorbs the meaningless messages spewn from the mass media" (Harms & Dickens, 1996, p. 217). As such, immobility and presumption converge to reify and reproduce conventional ideologies and sensibilities; audiences are rendered passive, veritably captive to the onslaught of media fare designed specifically to that end. Others, however, have argued that the very randomness and chaos that these critics cite as politically stultifying are in fact liberatory, offering a vast range of ideas and images from which audiences, acting as *bricoleurs* (McRobbie, 1994), may draw to cobble together and infer an infinite number of meanings, including empowering and even subversive ones. Rather than constraining consumers, contemporary media fare offers incredible opportunities for creative resistance (see, e.g., J. Collins, 1989, 1992; Fiske, 1989; McRobbie, 1994).

Some critics, however, have argued that images are not as random as they might appear, even if that appearance is actively cultivated—that is, what seems inchoate may in fact be strategically rendered in order to actively articulate conventional ideologies. As Harms and Dickens (1996) assert, "What is grossly undertheorized [in the work of theorists lauding the emancipatory potential of postmodern media] are the . . . conditions and foundations for creating meaning and communication" (p. 221). Accordingly, signs are arranged and sequenced in patterned ways that belie themselves to promote particular perceptions or even behaviors—such as, for instance, when a car commercial promoting the safety of the product featured follows on the heels of a news report on a rise in traffic fatalities; including the coverage of a film in a news broadcast of a network that owns the film studio; or following certain, potentially "serious" issues in media programming with a punch line or bizarre cartoon image. These critics imply that the pastiche that characterizes contemporary mediated content might best be understood as a discursive context for conventional ideologies, sensibilities, or, broadly speaking, "arguments" for those conventions (Harms & Dickens, 1996; Shugart, Waggoner, & Hallstein, 2001; Tetzlaff, 1991).

We concur with those critics who are skeptical of the apparent randomness and chaos pervading contemporary mediated texts; we, too, subscribe to the notion that mediated texts, in general, are ideological vehicles, invested in the promotion and dissemination of dominant interests and ideologies. We also subscribe, however, to the idea that, despite the nonlinear nature of contemporary aesthetics and sensibilities, individuals are compelled and even encouraged, under the very guise of those sensibilities, to make narrative sense of that with which they are presented, including dissonant, apparently inconsistent or even unrelated, information. That is, especially in highly uncertain situations, people will rely on all available contextual cues to resolve that uncertainty to the end of establishing narrative coherence. In the case of contemporary mediated texts, this impulse, as critics noted above have averred, generally works hegemonically, in favor of ideological conventions, reflecting the political economy that drives and controls media content.

We posit, however, that *re*positioning contextual cues in relation to certain texts may well utilize the same impulse to foster an alternative reading, one that contrasts with or perhaps even resists conventional sensibilities. That is, resistive messages may be extrapolated from given texts by virtue of their contextualization, via their being drawn with and/or against contemporaneous signs in such a way as to cultivate a negotiated or resistive reading (e.g., Hall, 1980). This is distinct from the argument that the resistive potential of contemporary aesthetics available in contemporary media fare is realized in the highly idiosyncratic and personal interpretations of individual audience members alone. The strategic positioning of text against context is what occurs, we contend, in the camp performances of Xena, Karen Walker, Macy Gray, and Gwen Stefani, and this positioning endows them—in tandem with attendant discursive premises of trope and spectacle—with critical potential. In the case of these performances, that potential is realized in large part via the use of benchmarks—anchors and foils, as we have designated them—within or alongside the performances that serve as contextual cues for their peculiar and potentially resistive discursive logic. Burke's work on perspective is helpful in this endeavor, as he explains this process of using new configurations to create alternative meanings in "planned incongruity" (Burke, 1954). Here, new insights are achieved via planned or deliberate misfits. Categories previously thought to be incompatible are conjoined so that one order of classification is violated, while another one is emphasized (p. 112). Thus, there is critical potential in such juxtapositions, as what is considered to be "rational" order is made anew with an apparently contrary logic (p. 73). Our contention is that the contemporary female camp performances found in Xena, Karen Walker, Macy Gray, and Gwen Stefani feature the use of anchors and foils as juxtaposition, rather than sheer randomness or inconsistency, to enable a critical reading of these women.

We argue that all of these premises—trope, spectacle, and anchors and foils—are present in each of these "resistive" camp performances, if they assume distinctive dimensions in each case. These premises, in fact, represent a convergence of camp sensibilities and the sensibilities that characterize the broader contemporary mediascape. Thus, they are neither precisely "authentic" camp nor "pop" camp, as both of those practices have been characterized by critics, but something of a hybrid or liminal version. In each case, particular manifestations notwithstanding, these premises constitute a logic that makes available a critical reading of gender and sexual alterity, even as that logic occurs within a broader aesthetic that might obscure it. The clearly discernible common pattern that emerges in these performances suggests that a unique discursive logic is at work, one that features significant implications for the articulation and negotiation of resistance in a contemporary context of constraint. These performances further illuminate the political dimensions of the intersection between camp and contemporary sensibilities in popular culture at this particular historical moment; the new venues and modalities for camp, furnished by mainstream, mediated popular culture, invite us to consider alternative ways of thinking about critical acts. In the following chapters, we will address each of the performances in turn to discuss precisely how the logic that we have identified is configured, distinctively yet consistently across various performances, and how resistive possibilities might be realized through camp in the broader context of contemporary, mediated popular culture.

3

Xena

Camped Crusader

The May 30, 2004, issue of *TV Guide* ranked *Xena: Warrior Princess* number 9 in the "25 Top Cult Shows Ever." This came as no surprise to the scores of Xena fans who are committed to watching actor Lucy Lawless play fantasy-action adventure star, Xena, in a camped-up TV version of a "morality play set in a mythical ancient realm" (Martindale, 1999, p. 90). Originally featured as a villain in the syndicated television program *Hercules*, the character of Xena was so popularly received that *Hercules* producers created a spin-off series based on her, running from 1995 to 2001. The eponymous Xena renounced her evil ways and embarked on her quest to aid the innocent, only intermittently plagued by her darker side. To this day, fans cannot seem to get enough of the "bad girl turned good." Although no longer in active production, the syndicated series continues to be rebroadcast in various national and international markets, retaining its cult status. It has been recognized as one of the highest-rated dramas in syndication, second only to a handful of game shows and other television series (Frankel, 2000; Hontz, 1997).

The character of Xena is distinctive for a number of reasons, not least because of her prowess as a warrior; a whirling embodiment of incongruous contrasts, she is known for her anomalous presentation of ambiguity and contradiction. She is simultaneously masculine and feminine—stereotypically masculine in her deportment and athletic prowess, conventionally feminine in her appearance and concern for the welfare of others. Her acute physical strength, typically seen only in male superheroes, is paired with glimpses of her poignant vulnerability—her compassion, for example, for the marginalized or disenfranchised. Her willingness to engage in battle of the most dangerous kind—situations in which she is grossly outnumbered by skilled, bloodthirsty warriors—is mitigated by her vigilant commitment to peace, even if it means that she must spare the lives of the very warriors who attack her or defend her enemies from the others' assault.

This incongruous representation is a rarity in mainstream popular culture, although it is not unheard of; the high-octane heroines Red Sonja and Sheena, Queen of the Jungle, are two such examples. Like these women, in fact, Xena also bears many hallmarks of femininity, primarily evident in her appearance; conventionally beautiful, she wears armor that is designed to flatter and accentuate her voluptuous body, and her warrior repertoire includes seducing men, when necessary. But unlike other historical "warrior queens" (Fraser, 1988) who have preceded her, Xena is not connected with a central, defining male figure that serves to affirm her femininity and thus redeem her (Morreale, 1998, p. 80). Rather, the definition of Xena's character is afforded via her relationship with Gabrielle, her female sidekick and trusted confidante. Indeed, their intense friendship has been interpreted by many viewers and critics of the show as "purposely vague" (O'Neill, 1997, p. 78) and thus implicitly romantic, creating a lesbian subtext for the show and resulting in a large lesbian following (Martindale, 1999; O'Neill, 1997; Stockwell, 1996). Perhaps it is Xena's many incongruities that cause her to have such wide appeal to seemingly disparate audiences. But, more important for our interests, perhaps her very campiness provides her character with its critical edge, resulting in a performance of gendered sexuality that is more than playful retro homage and sexual titillation. A close examination of the logic of Xena's camp performances exposes that promise.

Wonder Queen

At least part of Xena's wide appeal may be attributed to the bygone cultural tropes on which she draws, tropes that resonate nostalgically for audiences. Lawless's action-packed performance as Xena is not an entirely new construction of femininity; in fact, it resurrects an older form. Fans no doubt respond to Xena's invocation of a trope familiar to 1970s television audiences and comic book fans since the 1940s—the gendered archetypal female superhero, quintessentially embodied in Wonder Woman and a number of "jungle queens," of whom Sheena, Queen of the Jungle, is the most renowned.

Debuting in *All Star Comics* in 1941, Wonder Woman was created by psychologist Dr. William Moulton Marston, who was inspired by Greek mythology and female psychology to endow her "with a hundred times the agility and strength of our best male athletes and strongest wrestlers . . . [a]s lovely as Aphrodite, as wise as Athena, with the speed of Mercury and the strength of Hercules" (Gifford, 1984, p. 124). Thus, Diana, daughter of Hippolyte, Queen of the Amazons on Paradise Island, emerged in the United States as Wonder Woman, the voluptuous, star-spangled superhero who avenges evil at the drop of a hat and then retreats to assume the identity of her alter ego, Diana Prince, bespectacled nurse. Similarly committed to protecting the downtrodden from evil, jungle queens appeared as popular superheroes in 1940s comic books. Inspired by Edgar Rice Burroughs's *Tarzan of the Apes,* the first comic book queen of the jungle was Sheena, Queen of the Jungle, appearing in America's *Jumbo Comics* in 1938 (Gifford, 1984, p. 102). Orphaned as an infant in Africa and raised by natives to have telepathic powers with nonhuman animals, Sheena donned skimpy animal skins and wielded a knife in her pursuit for justice in the jungle. She was depicted most often rescuing her male companion, Bob Reynolds, from villains ranging from slave traders to Nazis. Both Wonder Woman and Sheena had enough popular appeal to move from comic books to electronic media. Cathy Lee Crosby starred as Wonder Woman in a 1974 made-for-TV-film of the same name, which spawned a television series, *Wonder Woman,* in 1976, starring Lynda Carter (Daniels, 2000, p. 136). The latter, in particular, made Wonder Woman a popular cultural icon. Although short-lived, *Sheena, Queen of the Jungle,* appeared as a television series in 1955 featuring Irish McCalla, and again 29 years later as a feature film, *Sheena,* with Tanya Roberts (of television series *Charlie's Angels* fame) in the lead role. The move to electronic media venues and formats broadened the appeal of the female superhero as a trope of acceptable feminine strength.

Like her prototypes, Xena's superhuman persona is hypermasculine in several respects: she is physically powerful, apparently invincible, as evidenced by the battles in which she consistently triumphs over any number of men. She has physical strength that surpasses that of normal human beings. Her manner of engaging in physical battle particularly showcases this strength, most obvious when she is dramatically outnumbered by enemies armed with swords, clubs, and knives. Just when it seems that Xena is doomed by these seemingly overwhelming odds, she welcomes the challenge with a puckish glint in her eye, a wry smile, and a patronizing, "Hi, boys." She then uses her statuesque body as her primary weapon, spinning into a dizzying series of back handsprings; leaping 30 feet from a standing position into the air in order to evade attackers or position herself in a brutal kick; and whirling around a pole, knocking out with her feet those who approach her. Her physical prowess also gives her the capability to extract information from her enemy, similar to Wonder Woman's ability to extract the truth from evildoers with her golden lasso. At the end of a physical altercation, for instance, Xena single-handedly grabs her enemy's throat in "the pinch," forcing him to reveal significant details about who was behind the attacks and the details for future evil schemes.

Especially reminiscent of the jungle queen trope, Xena's physical power is characterized by a primal, even inhuman, quality. Like her jungle queen predecessors, this Amazon princess possesses the ability to leap great distances and heights in pantherlike fashion, dodging her assailants and positioning herself for surprise counterattacks. She is animalistic in areas of her life other than battle, as well. As she and her sidekick, Gabrielle, roam the countryside seeking injustice to avenge, they make their homes in the outdoors, sleeping in barns or by a fire in the open air. Their behavior is sharply contrasted with the domesticity of the villagers, particularly the women, who populate the series. Xena also is able to relate to animals in a manner reminiscent of earlier jungle queens' telepathic abilities; she communicates with Argo, her horse, for example, in ways that other characters on the show are not able to emulate with their own animals, sensing his needs and responding to his apparent death with profound grief. Finally, Xena is especially known for her distinctive battle cry. As she springs about in violent battle, she lets forth her piercing signature howl, "yi, yi, yi, yi!" suggestive of the primal nature of her power.

Of course, Xena's magnificent physical strength is accentuated by her appearance, which also conforms to the female superhero prototype. As Xena, Lawless resembles not only the comic book renditions of Wonder Woman but also Lynda Carter, who gave Wonder Woman life on the small screen. Both are "Amazon princesses," tall, statuesque women manifesting a feminine ideal with large breasts, small waists, long legs, flowing brunette hair, and conventionally attractive facial features. Like both Sheena and Wonder Woman, Xena is costumed to emphasize her large breasts and long legs. She wears a bustier, short skirt, and over-the-knee boots as her armor, curious apparel for one who engages in rigorous hand-to-hand combat on a daily basis. While not heavily applied, her makeup skillfully accentuates her eyes and lips—also curious for someone who lives in the elements of the outdoors. Like her prototypes, Xena cuts an impressive figure whose appearance is every bit as important as the action in which she engages, a significance constantly reinforced visually as the camera slowly pans Xena's sensual curves from top to bottom, allowing the viewer to register every detail.

This is not to say that the action in which Xena engages is to be taken lightly. Like the female superheroes before her, Xena fights for justice on behalf of the disenfranchised, usually women and children or those who are poor and sickly. In messianic form, she appears from nowhere to avenge an injustice or right a wrong. Her battles result in significant outcomes: saving villages from total destruction, preventing catastrophic deaths of women and children, or thwarting devastating wars between the gods. The setting in an ancient mythical realm of gods and warlords provides the backdrop that enables such large-scale consequences. Here, for example, winning one battle against Ares, the god of war, can alter the lives of many, and Xena takes her charge as defender of the innocent quite seriously.

It is precisely this nostalgic conjuring of the trope of earlier feminine superheroes that helps to qualify Xena's performance as camp. The trope is more than just lovingly acknowledged; it is showcased, embraced, even adored, rather than ridiculed—indeed, at times in "minimusicals" in which characters break out enthusiastically in song and dance. As Robertson (1996) has warned, however, the mere resurrection of stereotypes in and of itself is not sufficient for camp to be anything other than "camp lite"—easy, cheap nostalgia devoid of critical potential and reconstituted as a vehicle for highly conventional representations of gender, as in the cases of films such as *Red Sonja* and even *Sheena*. Xena's performances, on the other hand, differ subtly but significantly, constituting a recouping and redressing of the female superhero trope to provide the representation with a critical edge in at least three ways. First, the attitude with which Xena approaches her superhero "duties" is significantly different from the way in which her prototypes approached their work. Wonder Woman, in particular, was depicted as being very comfortable, even natural, in her role as superhero dressed in an outrageous outfit. Lynda Carter's comments reflect the earnestness with which she played the role: "what I didn't want to do was play it too tongue-in-cheek" (Daniels, 2000, p. 141). Unlike her more staid predecessor, Xena, while taking her superhero status seriously, is nonetheless often depicted as being very uncomfortable, annoyed, or even frustrated in having to perform her duties. Her nonverbal communication, namely her facial expressions, reflect this attitude of "failed seriousness" so vital to camp and key to its critical edge in providing performative distance; before engaging in a battle, for example, she often sighs deeply in apparent exasperation or at the least, resignation, before launching a swift kick at a charging enemy. Clearly, she would rather be doing something else.

A second way in which Xena alters the female superhero trope is more obvious. Whereas her predecessors are prominent leading characters who are female, a point quite conspicuous in their time of original creation, they nonetheless are connected closely to a leading man. Morreale (1998) refers to this as the "appendage syndrome," whereby historical Warrior Queens typically are connected to a masculine figure, mitigating or softening their power and affirming their heterosexual femininity. Wonder Woman's character, for example, is made possible by Captain Steve Trevor, the American airman who is stranded on Paradise Island and nursed back to health by the beautiful Amazon princess, Diana. Indeed, both Wonder Woman and her alter ego, Diana Prince, are hopelessly in love with Trevor, and much of the *Wonder Woman* story revolves around this plotline. Likewise, Sheena, Queen of the Jungle, is in love with Bob Reynolds, a white outsider to the jungle who must constantly be rescued by his beloved Sheena (Gifford, 1984); thus, he significantly defines her character.

Xena, conversely, is not closely aligned with any man. She has no father or husband, and although references are made to her son, the boy rarely appears onscreen (Morreale, 1998)—and in any case, her status as the boy's mother, the parental authority figure, defies and arguably subverts the conventional pattern. While it is often revealed in various episodes that Xena has had past relationships with men, those relationships have not lasted into her present superhero days; indeed, they often do not last from one episode to the next. Likewise, while she is often the object of affection of both men and gods who ogle her body, flirt shamelessly with her, and attempt to seduce her, she ultimately resists such attention, maintaining her primary relationship instead with another woman, Gabrielle. Further, as noted earlier, her relationship with Gabrielle, if not overtly sexual, is extremely intimate, as they are constant companions who protect each other in battle, sleep next to one another beside the fire, seek comfort in each other's arms in times of grief, and disclose very personal vulnerabilities to one another. Other characters take note of this "odd" relationship and constantly question its purpose. In one episode, for example, Xena is chided by another warlord for traipsing around the world while dragging along a "half-starved child, *pretending* she's a friend" (Sears & Jacobson, 1997).

The resulting lesbian subtext changes the nature of the power manifested in the female superhero trope, namely because it destabilizes the discourse of gendered heterosexuality that typically undergirds it, ultimately qualifying and containing female power. Xena's superhero status is not so mitigated, and the result is a striking tweaking of the Amazon/Warrior Queen trope. Having a lesbian subtext in and of itself, however, does not assure alterity. As others have noted, apparently progressive representations of sexual alterity do not always live up to their promise, as those representations are often couched in discursive practices that function to qualify whatever challenges their presence could potentially pose (Battles & Hilton-Morrow, 2002; Brookey, 1996; Brookey & Westerfelhaus, 2001; Capsuto, 2000; Dow, 2001; Gross, 2001; Shugart, 2003; Walters, 2001). For example, the use of a lesbian subtext, even thinly veiled, often serves the purpose of heterosexual titillation, hardly a progressive representation.

This is ostensibly the case with Xena, whose performance of the Wonder Woman trope within a lesbian subtext evokes a second trope against which her character is drawn—the sexual dominatrix. In her thigh-high boots, armored bustier, and whetted sword, Xena evokes the heterosexual fantasy of the powerful, masochistic female dominatrix, eager to "hurt" men with her take-charge sexual antics that transgress the boundaries of conventional sexual escapades. The appeal of the dominatrix is the ardent display of power and sexuality, a marked deviation from the Wonder Woman trope, which is couched, albeit complexly, in psychological undertones of female submission manifest in the superheroine's affinity for being bound (Daniels, 2000). To be sure, Wonder Woman's creators were criticized for themes of bondage found in her stories, manifest most often in comic book covers that featured a tied and shackled Wonder Woman. In response to such criticism, creator and psychologist Dr. Marston defended his use of female bondage as a psychological undertone in the comic strip: "This [use of 'painless' bond-age] is the one truly great moral contribution of my Wonder Woman strip to moral education of the young. The only hope for peace is to teach people who are full of pep and unbound force to *enjoy* being bound. . . . It is the se-cret of women's allure—women *enjoy* submission, being bound" (Daniels, 2000, p. 63). Certainly, Xena seems to have inverted the philosophy under-girding the Wonder Woman series, as she signifies the dominatrix who con-trols men rather than the woman being controlled. As many theorists have noted, however, inversion in and of itself is not necessarily revolutionary, such that an inverted display of sexual power is not necessarily one possess-ing critical potential. In its fetishization of the female body and its reifica-tion of the conventional sexual power structure of domination/submission, the dominatrix may offer a female sexuality defined in terms of and for het-erosexual male pleasure and desire, serving as merely a performance for het-erosexual titillation, and thus, be severely limited in its critical semiotic sig-nificance.

In the case of Xena and Gabrielle, however, the lesbian subtext redefines the dominatrix dynamic, providing progressive potential. In short, Gabri-elle defines Xena's character in terms other than sexuality. By Xena's own ad-mission, Gabrielle's relatively "pure," altruistic nature enables Xena to resist her own "dark side" and keeps her (Xena) on the "straight and narrow path" of good deeds for the betterment of all humanity rather than submitting to impulses characterized by greed, self-interest, and domination. In one epi-sode, in which Gabrielle was questioning what kind of person she might be if not for Xena's mentoring, Xena turns to Gabrielle, looks her squarely in the eyes, pauses dramatically, and replies, "No, Gabrielle, the question is who would I be without *you*" (Sears & Jacobson, 1997). Gabrielle serves as a re-demptive force in Xena's life, saving her from a life of self-destruction found in the patriarchal, and one may argue, heterosexual world. In this sense, the trope of the female superhero is reconfigured for a new rhetorical effect.

Super Spectacular

It has been argued that stylistic elements such as clothes, adornment, and home décor have the capacity to serve not only as an expression of one's identity but also as a form of "justification in a society which denies one's essential validity" (Babuscio, 1999, p. 122). Style and/or aesthetics, rather than being "merely" superficial, may serve a critical function as well. This is the case with Xena, the Warrior Princess, who is arguably determined by the superficial; what she looks like determines in large measure what she is, and how she does things overrides what is done, as is common in camp. It is not, however, the aesthetics of wealth and glamour that are often associated with camp that characterize Xena. Instead, Xena is defined by a particular visual aesthetic marked by the juxtaposition of opposites, which are rendered in excessive ways, resulting in spectacle that features a distinct camp sensibility.

Physically, Xena is an unusually statuesque woman; standing approximately six feet tall, she cuts a striking and potentially masculine figure. Aesthetically, however, she is coded as excessively, even caricaturishly feminine, in both her appearance and behavior. Like her superhero predecessors, she is a spectacle of fetishized feminine sexuality. Her "uniform"—leather and brass bustier with miniskirt and thigh-high boots—marks her as a superhero that is decidedly female, calling attention to and even fetishizing her large breasts, long legs, and supple skin. Her hair is never pulled back or clipped up, as one might expect for battle; instead, it cascades down her bare back, serving as yet another site of visual fixation. Camera angles and movements also serve a fetishizing function, lingering on Xena's legs as she straps on her boots or focusing on her exposed cleavage as she threatens evil warlords. Her feminine aesthetics are made more apparent via her distinctiveness from other women on the show. Village women are not sexualized in the same manner via costuming, and other Amazon warriors, while often appearing in costumes similar to Xena's, are also presented alternately in everyday dress so that they are not so closely associated with a particular visual aesthetic. Xena's aesthetics, then, are unquestionably and excessively feminine.

In her behaviors, Xena is also coded discursively as feminine in that she models, oddly enough for a warrior, an amalgamation of a commitment to peace and a maternal instinct. Redeemed from her life of evil through her charitable act of saving an infant from being killed by her soldiers, Xena infuses her fight for peace and justice with a compassion for others—even her enemies—that is maternal. She recognizes the good in her enemies, much as a mother is assumed to identify the good in children who have gone astray.

Her compassion for Goliath even as he seeks to kill her, for example, is evident in her rationalization of his "bad behavior" as the result of his losing his family (Winter & Jones, 1996). She is saddened for him rather than enraged by him. And her compassion for childless King Gregor, even as he calls for the death of an orphaned infant, leads her to help Gregor see the value in adopting the infant (Winter & Levine, 1995). Xena carries out her superhero duties, then, in a way that is maternal and thus coded as feminine.

At the same time that Xena is a model of fetishized femininity, she paradoxically embodies masculinity; her feminine aesthetics are juxtaposed with a warrior aesthetic that is discursively coded as hypermasculine, semiotically sharpened via the concurrence of opposites. Her uniform, intended—however incredulously—to serve as armor in life-threatening battle, is constructed of hard metals and leather, the antithesis of soft, compliant femininity. She wields a phallic sword (indeed, often several at once). Her other weapon of choice, the circular chakram, while not phallic, is nonetheless razor-sharp with the capability of killing many men simultaneously in its dazzling whir, and thus is coded as part of the violent masculine war aesthetic. Xena's actions are also a critical dimension of her hypermasculine aesthetic. Her physical dexterity incites wonder on the part of her enemies, who watch awestruck as she leaps thirty feet from a standing position or spins in tornado-like fashion through a crowd of oncoming soldiers, leaving none standing in her wake.

Indeed, Xena's fighting skills—traditionally a hallmark of masculinity—surpass those of any men on the show in both competence and aesthetics. She single-handedly conquers armies of men with ease, demonstrating a myriad of combat strategies and techniques. A certain rhythm characterizes her fighting style, as well, also distinguished by juxtaposition of opposites. It is marked by first a stillness characteristic of objectification and often attributed to women, and second by sudden bursts of extreme, dizzying action, suggestive of unfettered agency and attributed primarily to men. There is no cinematic buildup as a precursor to Xena's action; rather, she erupts from a pose of tranquility to raging, shrieking warrior in a manner of seconds. Finally, Xena's performance of discipline also supports the masculine warrior aesthetic in its employment of oppositions; she is stoic in deportment, coldly barking orders to her fellow warriors and not flinching when she stabs her enemies to death. Such cold-heartedness is held in tension with her maternal compassion, substantiating Xena's status as spectacle. In aesthetics and behavior, then, Xena embodies hypermasculinity while simultaneously being coded as feminine, resulting in spectacle.

Certainly, Xena's performance is redolent of the conventional camp sensibility pertaining to gender, namely the characteristic of theatricality noted by Babuscio (1999) and others that sanctions the performance of the opposite sex (e.g., homosexual drag), and thus has promise for destabilizing gender norms. Xena's performance, however, is not sufficiently explained in terms of theatricality. Her embodiment of oppositions—masculinity/femininity, hard/soft, violence/peace, action/stillness—and specifically extreme characterizations of those oppositions, is without resolution of those tensions, different from the seamless performances of drag in which the "joke" is revealed only in the end with the removal of the drag queen's wig or the revelation of his penis. In contrast, Xena maintains those tensions, signifying indistinct gender, neither androgynous nor characteristic of transvestism yet exceedingly sexual in its potency. She is neither a man in drag nor a woman masquerading as a man. Rather, she is an interplay of oppositions, extreme on their own terms, constituting a spectacle rife with critical potential for the unsettling of normative gender codes in a manner that is spectacular rather than chiefly performative.

The Yin and the Yang

The camp sensibility found in *Xena: Warrior Princess* is established, in part, via Xena's relationships with other characters in the series. Gabrielle, Xena's female sidekick, serves as an anchor for Xena's character, redeeming her in crucial ways. Others, namely two men—Salmoneus and Joxer—serve as foils for Xena, throwing Xena's character and camp sensibility into sharp relief and thus serving as critical reference points for viewers' understanding of Xena's motivations. Gabrielle, Salmoneus, and Joxer are markedly different from Xena; their discursive relationship to her serves a critical purpose, both in establishing Xena and the show as camp and in providing Xena with a critical edge necessary to be more than merely "camp lite."

The power of Xena's display of the embodiment of simultaneous hyperbolic femininity and masculinity is made more apparent by her interactions with supporting characters Salmoneus and Joxer. These two men, who appear recurrently in the series, although not together, serve as the butt of many jokes and provide comic relief to what might otherwise be a dramatic, dark, and very violent mythical world. Both are feminized men, standing in stark contrast to other, hypermasculine men around them. Salmoneus, a parasitic, middle-aged man with the gift of gab, represents a certain stereotypical version of gay masculinity—the eunuch—in both his actions and attitudes. He is characterized by physical weakness; an interest in "feminine activities" such as food preparation, interior decoration, and beauty pageants; and an elite sophistication that manifests itself in materialism. Fearful of virtually everything and unable to defend himself physically, he relies on his quick wit for survival in a world that demands aggression and combat skills in men. When faced with advancing enemies, for example, Salmoneus masquerades as a woman or cowers behind women and children, leaving others—typically Xena and Gabrielle—to fight. Or he will try to manipulate his way into the good graces of the enemy, even if that means switching loyalties. His preferred method of ingratiating himself to others is profuse flattery but always for a self-interested end. He constantly showers Xena with gushing compliments on her appearance and celebrity status ("I'd know those gorgeous gams anywhere" and "What a hero!") so that she will protect him. He does the same with warlords if he fears for his safety, desperately seeking their approval through sweet talk in order to save his own neck. He has no conscience, switching convictions to suit his cause—an attribute that contrasts sharply with Xena, a warrior of unshakeable principles and irreproachable moral fiber. Additionally, his constant pursuit for economic wealth leads him to view every situation as a moneymaking opportunity. After one of Xena's victorious battles, for instance, he scampers along beside her, urging her to let him write her biography, which would "make millions" (Schulian, Green, & Perez, 1995). His schemes, full of references to modern-day capitalism, are out-of-place in this mythical world, serving as a primary springboard for the tongue-in-cheek humor that permeates the show and lends it a camp sensibility.

Another male character that seems comically out of place in Xena's world is Joxer, considerably younger than Salmoneus, with an endearing grin, goofy hat, and childlike, naive spirit, who accompanies Xena and Gabrielle on many of their adventures, providing slapstick comedy along the way. Physically awkward and vaguely burlesque, Joxer bumbles through episodes,

getting hit on the head by rocks, falling down stairs, and walking unsuspect-
ingly into a warrior's punch. He loves adventures and begs to be included if
Xena and Gabrielle threaten to exclude him. But his adventuresome spirit is
more than a bit naive; like Salmoneus, he is cowardly, fleeing scenes when adventures become dangerous. Unlike the more sophisticated Salmoneus, however, Joxer has not developed smooth ways of removing himself from such
situations. Instead, he relies entirely on Xena and Gabrielle to rescue him
from his predicaments, and they always do. Indeed, Xena and Gabrielle treat
Joxer as if he were a beloved but annoying child or pet. His unconditional
love for the two women, unlike Salmoneus's fickle allegiances, renders Joxer
endearing.

The Both Salmoneus's and Joxer's characters are gendered in significant ways.
Like Xena, they serve as amalgams of masculinity and femininity, Salmoneus as eunuch and Joxer as boy-child. Unlike Xena, however, their gendered
representations are devoid of potency, especially sexual power. They serve as
foils for Xena's character, causing her sexual power to be more apparent via
their lack. Their presence serves, as well, to equivocate the binary relationship between genders that positions masculinity as powerful and femininity
as submissive. This potentially threatening subtext is made more palatable
via comedy, an essential component of the camp sensibility. The comedic
element that pervades the characters of Salmoneus and Joxer serves a rather
serious function, enabling a critique of conventional gender polarities.

The primary character against whom Xena is defined is, of course, Gabrielle, who serves to anchor or endow Xena's character with substance. Sweet-
spirited, altruistic, and unabashedly in awe of Xena, youthful Gabrielle represents a contrast to Xena's mature character. Desiring a more exciting life
than what typically was available to young women in her village, starstruck
Gabrielle pesters Xena to allow her (Gabrielle) to join in her journeys. Xena
reluctantly agrees, and Gabrielle becomes Xena's partner in fighting evil.
The contrasts between the two women are many. While Xena is a mature
woman in every sense of the word, Gabrielle represents a young, innocent
girl, not yet skilled in the nuances of performing femininity—particularly
the femininity/masculinity required in Xena's superhero role. She ridicu-
lously attempts to adopt the postures and attitudes of Xena but never quite
pulls it off. When Gabrielle is anointed as an Amazon princess, for example,
she must choose a weapon and learn combat techniques. Her physical inept-

ness is apparent as she awkwardly wields a staff, knocking herself repeatedly in the head (Sears & Alexander, 1995). Her petite stature renders her an unlikely Amazon princess in the first place, and her gentle spirit is anything but aggressive. As she struggles with these incongruities in her effort to become like her idol, Xena, the effect is comic. A vital component of camp is the presence of the "wink" that suggests the presence of an inside joke and hints that what is being presented should not be taken at face value. Gabrielle fulfills this function, as she reveals the performative nature of Xena's gender via her own awkward attempts to mimic it. As in the case of Joxer and Salmoneus, humor serves a serious and critical function as it reveals the constructed and performative nature of Xena's gender.

As the other principal female character in the series, Gabrielle functions as an anchor for Xena's character in at least two additional ways. Xena's "do-good" nature is presented as always situated at the very edge of a dark side, as noted by Lawless, who observed that Xena's inner turmoil causes her to be "very conflicted" and that "it's the dark side of her that makes her so very interesting" (Martindale, 1999, p. 93). Gabrielle serves as her moral compass, keeping Xena on the path toward goodness when she may be tempted to use her power for ill. A primary way in which Gabrielle does this is through the use of words rather than actions; a proficient bard, Gabrielle spins lyrical morality tales as she and Xena travel the countryside in their adventures. In this sense, Gabrielle keeps Xena on the "straight and narrow" and thus is redemptive. Gabrielle's character anchors Xena also in that her presentation of pure, unspoiled femininity recompenses Xena's more masculine femininity. With Gabrielle—and only Gabrielle—Xena, the Warrior Princess, is able to reveal her own vulnerabilities, fears, and unfilled dreams, depicted in many intimate moments, a sharp contrast to the images of mighty Xena tearing up the battlefield. In these moments, Gabrielle assumes the roles of counselor and protector. When Xena fears that she is going insane, for example, she turns to Gabrielle for help; Gabrielle assumes a protective role, assuming responsibility for her friend's well-being. Without Gabrielle's redemptive presence, the masculine dimension of Xena's character overwhelms the feminine, resulting in a character that is less likely to be received positively by viewers. While Salmoneus and Joxer serve as foils for Xena's character, throwing her (especially sexual) power into sharp relief, Gabrielle's character anchors Xena, grounding while not obviating her otherwise masculine sexual potency in the feminine.

The "L" Warrior

The invocation of the familiar tropes of jungle queen and dominatrix, the occurrence of the spectacle of extreme oppositions, and the employment of anchors and foils all result in a presentation of sexual alterity in *Xena: Warrior Princess*, specifically a particular configuration of lesbian sexuality. Indeed, *Xena* has been touted as a media staple in lesbian culture by many mainstream critics, who point to the show's lesbian fans and its cultlike status among lesbians (Martindale, 1999; O'Neill, 1997; Stockwell, 1996). Readily available to the average fan of the show is a subtext of lesbian sexuality, one that at first blush appears quite conventional in its conformity to popularized framings of heterosexist romance. The settings in which Xena and Gabrielle find themselves, the manner in which they hold intimate conversations, and the topics of their conversations all connote a romantic relationship between the two women. They engage in close, face-to-face discussions before a glowing fireplace, and they lie next to one another, sharing their fears and life dreams. They frequently reassure one another of their commitment, promising to be there always for each other and speculating about their future crusades for social justice. Their conversations are peppered with long pauses, knowing smiles, and lingering gazes. They have one another constantly in mind, even in chaotic battle scenes as they look around to ensure that the other is safe. In many cases, Xena spins around just in time to rescue Gabrielle from death via a flying spear aimed right at her. Finally, they console each other in times of grief with lingering, loving embraces.

Such portrayals of intimacy are not that uncommon in the camp world of mediated action heroes and their sidekicks, as found for instance, in the "camp lite" (measured against contemporary sensibilities) dynamic duo of Batman and Robin, whose sexual orientation, however unrealized by the two, has been the subject of much speculation. But Batman and Robin, while demonstrating a notably close bond, shy away from any sexual references at all. Indeed, their seeming unawareness of their own sexual orientation is fodder for many snickers. Conversely, sexuality—and a particular brand of female sexuality—is performed overtly in *Xena: Warrior Princess*. In her "spectacular" embodiment as a big-breasted woman, in bustier and boots, sporting weapons, there is a possible reading of Xena as a female dominatrix, indeed, as noted earlier, a vision for many male fantasies that present female sexuality in heterosexist terms, defining women in terms of their sexual availability and ability to control/be controlled, and positioning them as objects of an implied male gaze. Within the logic of the dominatrix, one would expect to see trappings of this heterosexist framing even in a woman-to-woman relationship; certainly, that allusion ensures sexuality as a frame by which Xena's character—and her relationships with others—is read. But a different attitude toward female sexuality is depicted in the relationship between Xena and Gabrielle, secured in the irony and parody that are inherent in camp and made available via the premises of trope, spectacle, and anchors and foils.

Hints often are provided as to the complicated nature of Gabrielle and Xena's relationship in scenes containing double meanings. When Joxer flings open a barn door, finding a disheveled Xena and Gabrielle in an embrace, he hesitates awkwardly for a minute. A sexy musical score fills the air, suggesting that romance is in the works. In the next second, however, Joxer's face erupts in sheer delight and he pounces on the women, yelling "group hug!" (Bader & Merrifield, 1997). His juvenile response to the otherwise very sexy scene facilitates the double meaning that not only allows the lesbian relationship to remain underground but also codes it as naively natural. Later, when he observes a mark on Xena's neck and blurts out in amazement, "Is that a *hickey?!*" Gabrielle and Xena exchange a brief but meaningful side glance that could be interpreted as either embarrassment for the sexual act or for Joxer's immaturity (Bader & Merrifield, 1997). Here the double meaning not only facilitates the possible reading that "something is not as it appears," but it also challenges ever so slightly the conventional meanings we attribute to sexual acts. Conventionally romantic scenes and situations are deliberately "sent up" for parody, destabilizing conventional norms. The challenge to sexual norms is presented even more overtly in scenes relying on campy, slapstick comedy for their double meaning. As Xena leans over Gabrielle holding two turnips right at the position of Gabrielle's breasts, for instance, she enthusiastically exclaims in a wide grin, "We must seize the day!" (Bader & Merrifield, 1997). This camped up salute to breast fetishization in our heterosexist society offers a critique of that practice even as it affectionately acknowledges it.

Thus, it is not the playful tease of a lesbian female sexuality in and of itself that renders Xena's camp performance critical in terms of sexual alterity. Certainly, lesbian portrayals in mediated texts are often both constrained by and redolent of heteronormative sensibilities and conventional heterosexual sensibilities. As argued earlier, Xena herself dances with these constraints in her dominatrix dress, leading many to claim that *Xena: Warrior Princess* should perhaps be a staple for heterosexual titillation rather than one for lesbian culture. But the critical potential of sexual alterity offered in *Xena: Warrior Princess* exists in the attitude toward female sexuality made available via the interplay of trope, spectacular contrasts, and anchors and foils. Xena's performance of a hypersexual trope—the female dominatrix—is played within a camp context of ironic, spectacular contrasts (masculinity/femininity, aggression/vulnerability, ruthlessness/compassion, frenetic action/reflective repose) that permits, if not encourages, an alternative reading of that age-old sexualized trope. Similarly, Xena's performance of potent female sexuality is couched within a context of parodic humor primarily via the use of buffoonish foils such as Joxer and Salmoneus, providing performative distance from the authority of sexual norms that typically accompany readings of the dominatrix. And, finally, the relationship with Gabrielle serves to complicate further Xena's portrayal of female sexuality, imbuing it with a naiveté and artlessness that ironically renders it more "natural" than the heterosexist models of female sexuality otherwise performed in the show. Thus, *Xena: Warrior Princess* utilizes premises of trope, spectacle, and anchors and foils, permitting an alternative reading of female sexuality that embraces lesbianism while simultaneously critiquing the limited way it has been constructed conventionally. A lesbian subtext is not only given traction via these premises (for one may see the subtext without them), but it is legitimized by them, even as they squarely delineate the performance as camp.

4

Karen Walker

Drag Hag

Like *Xena: Warrior Princess,* the highly popular television situation comedy *Will and Grace* (Kohan & Mutchnick, 1998), which ran in active production from 1998 to 2006 and continues to be broadcast in syndication, is "gay themed," although, unlike *Xena,* that content is explicit. Also, whereas *Xena* is characterized by a specifically lesbian aesthetic, *Will and Grace* is centered on a gay male aesthetic and content. For this reason, given its historic moorings, the presence and prevalence of a camp sensibility on the show arguably is not surprising, and, indeed, it is prominent in the central character of Jack McFarland, a flamboyantly and stereotypically gay man. In light of our interests, however, we focus here not on Jack but on Karen Walker (played by actor Megan Mullally), whose "campiness," while not at all camouflaged, may well be easily overlooked or dismissed in relation to Jack's more classic and familiar camp performance. We suggest, however, that Karen is quintessentially camp, indeed the embodiment of a camp sensibility, and ironically (and we would suggest, more effectively) to precisely the same end as Jack: articulating sexuality in ways that resist or erode conventional discourses of gender and sexuality. Indeed, the sexuality that she advances via her camp performance is a *gay male* sexuality, suggesting that the ways in which the logical premises of contemporary, resistive camp that we have identified—trope, spectacle, and anchors and foils—can be configured in distinctive ways in each case to engage and negotiate the intersections of gender and sexuality.

Described as a "sharp-tongued socialite," Karen is the "rich-bitch assistant" of Grace Adler, one of the leads of the show, which chronicles primarily the lives and times of two best friends, a gay man and a straight woman (Cagle, 1998, p. 48; *OKT* profile, 2001, p. 19;). Although Grace and Will are the best friends in question, their relationship is echoed in many respects—including respective sexual orientations, more or less—in that of Karen and Jack. As part of the "ensemble cast" genre of situation comedies, Karen and Jack are, in fact, the prominently featured secondary leads on the show. Karen is extremely wealthy, married to a multimillionaire who never appears on the show—and who has been, in fact, variously dead and alive on the show, in no particular order. She is materialistic, inappropriate, selfish, crude, superficial, insensitive, obnoxious, alcoholic, bored, and sexually sophisticated. Notoriously politically incorrect, she often directs homophobic, racist, sexist, and classist comments to all those about her; these comments invariably function as humorous punch lines or one-liners for the show.

Rich Bitch Revisited

As with Xena, the trope invoked in the camp character of Karen Walker is an amalgam of a generic female character familiar to media audiences: the malignant rich-bitch socialite. This collective trope is relevant to class (as well as race, for that matter) and is gendered specifically as female. Perhaps most reminiscent of notorious film and television characters played by Bette Davis (e.g., in *All About Eve*), Joan Crawford (e.g., in *Mildred Pierce* and *Possessed*), and, more recently, Joan Collins (e.g., in *Dynasty*), Karen manifests all of their material trappings as well as their qualities. Like her predecessors, she is an extremely wealthy white woman, a feature established by various references to and depictions of her lavish, Upper East Side apartment; her troop of servants to tend to her every whim; her personal, chauffeur-driven limousine; her outrageously expensive jewelry; and her references to her haute couture outfits, shoes, and shopping sprees. Her casual attitude to all of this opulence is further evidence of the magnitude of her wealth; in one episode, she spends thousands of dollars on a pair of Manolo Blahnik boots that she subsequently decides are not quite the right shade, so she gives them to a blind beggar in lieu of change (Kohan, Mutchnick, & Burrows, 1999a).

Karen, like her prototypes, is sophisticated in equal measure to her wealth. Unfazed by others' wealth and fame, she will casually let slip personal tidbits about famous celebrities or royalty that indicate her intimate familiarity with them, as well as, notably, her superiority over them. In one episode, she is on the telephone and says impatiently, "No, Blackie, stop it. I'm not going to tell you which designers I'm buying this year! For god's sake, get your own taste!" She hangs up, muttering, "Best Dressed List, my ass," establishing that her conversation was with eminent fashion critic Tony Blackwell (Lotterstein & Burrows, 2000). Her sophistication also is made comically apparent in her cynicism; perpetually suspicious of others and their motives, she often will accost strangers who, for instance, are crossing in front of her limousine at a crosswalk: "Hey, hey, keep moving, buddy! I know your type: waiting for Driver to fall asleep and hit the gas pedal so you can hit the jackpot! Go on! Move it!" (Lotterstein & Burrows, 1999). Her frequently referenced sexually risqué past and her overtly sexual innuendos and behavior also signify her sophistication; on various occasions, she alludes to numerous lovers, male and female, who have populated her past, establishing both the casual nature of those relationships and her absolute control of them. In one flashback scene, she recounts her torrid, brief affair with a Saudi prince ("or was it a princess? Huh. I can't remember. Anyway, let's just go with a boy") who attempts to win her with jewels, yachts, and palaces; she dismisses him and his offerings because "the dust [in Saudi Arabia] was murder on my suede shoes. Besides, no one there can fix a decent martini" (Janetti & Burrows, 2003). This example captures her wealthy, sophisticated persona, establishing her cavalier attitude toward incredible wealth, her sexual openness, and her relentless urbanity, to the extent that a nationwide ban on alcohol is clearly unfathomable for her.

Like her prototypes, Karen has a distinctly malevolent edge. As they did, she came into money by virtue of relentless gold digging and exploitation of rich men. Her money actually belongs to Stan, her never-seen (later ex-; for a time presumed deceased; and then resurrected and reinstated, yet always invisible) husband, whom she finds physically repulsive; she frequently alludes to his grotesque obesity, and she regularly establishes that she married him for his money. For instance, when she wants to buy a big-ticket item—one that costs beyond a mere several hundred thousand dollars, that is—she sighs ponderously and states, "I guess I'll have to let Stan touch my boobies tonight" (Spitz & Burrows, 2000). Indeed, it has been established in the series that Karen was a con artist with a criminal past; she and her mother, from whom she apparently learned her gold-digging skills, had taken advantage of many men when Karen was young, a practice that she perfected and that culminated in her marriage to Stan (Wrubel, Barr, & Burrows, 2001).

Karen also is extremely superficial, self-centered, and grossly insensitive to others, an insensitivity that is conflated with her upper-class, elite status on the show. Her attitude is of someone privileged and entitled; she presumes the inferiority and servility of all others, and she assumes that her desires far outweigh the needs of others—accordingly, she expects others to recognize this and has no patience with them if they do not. As Grace's receptionist—she has taken the job out of sheer boredom—she refuses to answer the telephone if she is reading a magazine or if she hasn't yet had her quota of prescription drugs and alcohol. She refers to her servants impersonally as "Gardener" and "Driver" and "Maid," with the exception of her personal maid, Rosario, whom she frequently insults and demeans, especially in racist ways; she will tell Rosario to "get on your knees and do what you were born to do" in order to clean the floor "properly" rather than with a mop (Barr & Burrows, 2000). In fact, her controversial reference to Rosario as a "tamale" (Barr & Burrows, 1999) led to that episode's being pulled from broadcast in its originally intended run. Similarly, she frequently makes homophobic references to Will and Jack, calling Will "Wilma" or "you big homo," for instance, or saying sentimentally of Jack, "my little girl is growing up!" As such, Karen's thoughtlessness and selfishness are established as integral personal traits, very much in accordance with the rich-bitch trope; like her predecessors—Davis, Crawford, and Collins—Karen is conniving, materialistic, superficial, cruel, and self-centered, trading on her sexuality for wealth and financial security.

But Karen also differs in important ways from this generic character on which she is modeled, and the camp nature of her performance inheres in these differences. Unlike her more earnest prototypes, Karen has not adopted the refined, cultured attitude and elegant behavior that signal their status as wealthy and upper class. To the contrary, Karen is loud, crassly elitist, rude, and vulgar. She is wont to scream insults across Bloomingdale's at a stranger who is committing a fashion faux pas; indeed, Grace is often the recipient of many of those insults. Karen constantly derides Grace's dress by, for instance, standing in front of Grace, pinching the bridge of her nose as if in pain and saying such things as, "What's going on here, honey? There's a tablecloth missing in New Jersey." Politeness, however superficial, is simply not part of Karen's repertoire, thus lending a comic edge to the character that contributes to its camp sensibility. In a similar vein—and further evidence of her insensitivity—Karen may tell Jack, "Aw, those homeless kids are so cute, so *Les Mis*—let's buy one, put it in the corner for the party" (Kightlinger & Burrows, 2005). Or she may declare passionately, "I want to help people more unfortunate than I am, that's all I've ever wanted!"—at which point she and Jack look at each other for a moment and then dissolve in helpless laughter (Lerner & Burrows, 2000). Karen also behaves physically in ways that give the lie to the conventional upper-class socialite character, especially as regards sex; that is, she will flaunt her body sexually in ways that would be considered crass in those circles. For example, we learn early in the series that she has starred in a porn video (Palmer & Burrows, 1999), and even if this is described as a past indiscretion, her sexual lewdness and crudeness are constants. For instance, mistaking a birdwatcher in the park below her prestigious penthouse apartment for a peeping tom, she tears open her blouse, lifts up her brassiere, and grinds herself against the window, screaming, "Is this what you want, you pervert?! Oh, my god, he's relentless!! Here, Jackie [she says to Jack], help me out of my skirt" (Gabriel & Burrows, 2005). Much of this is a result of her enormous ego—that is, when she wants something and someone resists, she is convinced that if she uses her sexuality, she can attain it. For instance, when Will—a gay man—refuses to allow Karen to stay at his apartment for a few days, she heaves a sigh of resignation, undoes her blouse, and shimmies her breasts at him vigorously, licking her lips and moaning, "Come on, big boy! Oh, yeah" (Bradford & Burrows, 2002b). In this way, the gold-digging aspect of the "rich bitch" is parodied, reflective of the irony and humor that are essential to camp.

Perhaps Karen's most significant departure from the prototype of the gold-digging socialite is that she is not defined by or beholden to the wealthy man who finances her lifestyle. Stan is invoked only through her colorful references to him, and her control over him is absolute; as suggested above, she need only hint at promised sexual favors and he cannot help but do as she commands. His literal absence on the show, in tandem with her control over him, thus substantially qualifies her dependence on him—as does the fact that, by the final episode of the series, she has divorced him. Her brief second marriage, as well, ends on her wedding day, immediately following her new husband's toast to her, in which he thanks her for her sacrifices for (and implied dependence on) him—summarily negating all that he has just acknowledged (Warfield, Lizer, Greenstein, Marchinko, & Burrows, 2004). The show's final episode, in fact, confirms Karen's resolute independence from men as measured against the trope of the wealthy socialite and the conventions of heterosexual marriage: single and unattached save for her enduring relationship with Jack, with whom she now lives, her lavish lifestyle is financed by the wealth that Jack inherited from his partner (Karen's longtime nemesis on the show, in fact)—a partner with whom he took up unwillingly but precisely in order to return Karen's favor in this regard from years prior, for she was left destitute after her second divorce from first husband Stan (Mutchnick, Kohan, & Burrows, 2006). This symmetry further fuses Karen and Jack's characters in significant ways.

But Karen *is* defined, notably, by another man (with whom she ultimately spends the rest of her life, in fact): Jack, the flamboyantly gay man on the show who is her best friend, kindred spirit, and soul mate. Jack is her "little poodle," and he can get her to do things for him that she would not do for anyone else—especially not Stan. Although she is also rude and insensitive to him—and he reciprocates, this is the foundation of their simpatico—she also exhibits compassion for him when she anticipates that he may be truly hurt. For instance, when Jack is told that his off-off-off-Broadway one-man show is nominated for an award, she attempts to shield him from the information—left on his answering machine, which she accesses before he hears it—that it was a mistake, his play was confused with one with a similar title (Bradford & Burrows, 2000). In terms of its significance for camp, this "twist" in Karen's representation serves two important functions: first, by redeeming her, it furnishes the camp object—the rich bitch trope, in this case—with the nostalgic affection that Robertson (1996) and others argue legitimizes camp; and second, through the character of Jack, it establishes gay male sexuality as key to her moral redemption, thus enhancing the critical dimensions of the performance—which are already established by virtue of a less-than-flattering portrayal of the elite upper class—as well as endowing it with a distinctly gay sensibility, a feature historically associated with camp.

Socialite Extraordinaire

If, like Xena, the trope that the character of Karen Walker invokes is marked by "campy" improvisation, the conventionally camp features of Karen Walker's performance largely inhere in dynamics that render it a spectacle, or a caricature of itself, in ways that work very fluently with and build on the rich-bitch trope. Although they play out differently in this case, as with Xena, spectacle is manifest via the aesthetics of excess and juxtaposition that serve simultaneously to confirm and camouflage critical plays on gender and sexuality.

Excess thoroughly infuses the character of Karen Walker. This is perhaps most apparent in Karen's wealth, which assumes fantastic proportions, as established by her extravagant spending sprees and the fact that she has several servants available to cater to her every whim. Perhaps not surprising but notable is the fact that her wealth is conflated with her upper-class status, such that descriptions of her wealth are concomitant indicators of her elite social status. This conflation is especially evident in her appearance, which is redolent of the best taste: her hair, makeup, and fingernails are always salon perfect, and her clothes, shoes, fashion accessories, and jewelry are always haute couture, as indicated by her and others' references to them. Her elite social position is ascertained further by her clearly superior and unchallenged fashion sense, which is a fundamental component of her interactions with Grace; Karen will often make snide comments about Grace's clothing and hair ("Grace, honey, why don't you run along home and change? I think we'll both feel better"). Karen's self-presentation also features these qualities of excess: her clothes are quite fitted, her "designer skirts so butt-huggingly tight she can only just negotiate a staircase" (Bardin, 1999, p. 30), exaggerating her body and especially her breasts, which are typically presented with considerable cleavage and severe décolletage. She wears extremely high heels, which cause her to walk in an exaggerated version of the classic feminine mincing walk. Her voice is perhaps the most apparent element of her excess; she speaks in a comically high, shrill voice—"Betty Boop goes boom," as Bardin (1999, p. 30) describes it—such that the cartoonish qualities of Karen's aesthetic of excess are unmistakable.

Excess is also evident in Karen's behavior. In the first place, her addiction to alcohol and prescription drugs is a staple feature of her character. She is very frequently depicted with a drink in her hand or taking pills, and rarely does she appear in a scene where her addiction to these substances isn't referenced: for instance, Will may ask her if she's "drunk her breakfast yet," or she may attempt to find Grace an aspirin in her handbag, which she empties on a desk to reveal a stockpile of various, unidentified pills. In one episode,

Karen's snack contribution for a "girls' night in" is a large bowlful of assorted prescription drugs (Lizer & Burrows, 2003). She also is notorious for indulging in her substance abuse in inappropriate contexts, such as "guzzl[ing] martinis at her work desk" (Bardin, 1999, p. 30), swilling a drink at her stepson's swim meet, or gobbling a handful of pills during a church service. The quantities of these substances that she consumes also are excessive; in one episode, she lambastes "Driver" for only getting her one case of scotch (Lotterstein & Burrows, 1999) to see her through a weekend by herself. In another episode, she is frantic to secure several drug prescriptions through shady means just prior to a long holiday weekend (Kightlinger & Burrows, 2004). Her behavior on this count similarly functions to delineate her performance as excessive, not only comic but cartoonish in its proportions.

Karen's excessively crude, conventionally unrefined behavior—especially with regard to sexual innuendo and display—contributes to the caricaturish nature of the performance, not least by virtue of incongruence and juxtaposition with her elite, upper-class persona. She engages in much of this sexual play with Jack; they will often "touch stomachs" or "touch boobies" in celebration of some minor feat, and she will always let Jack fondle her breasts or "French kiss" her when he asks, which he frequently does. In one episode, as a prelude to Karen giving Jack cash, they enact a performance of an ATM transaction whereby he slides a makeshift card through her cleavage twice and then, upon her turning around, the cleft of her buttocks: "Denied, denied, accepted," they chant delightedly (Kohan, Mutchnick, & Burrows, 1999a). In another such scene, Karen serves as Jack's assistant for a magic show he has devised; in this role, Karen presents herself physically in a manner reminiscent of a burlesque stripper, straddling her chair, licking her lips provocatively, and fondling her breasts and thighs, and she also makes crude comments: when Jack asks her to "get inside the box," she says, "I haven't done that since college, just a little youthful experimentation" (Bradford & Burrows, 2002a). Karen's crude, crass behavior, which is quite at odds with her refined, upper-class persona, thus takes the shape of excess predicated on irony to establish the performance as caricature.

Karen's unmitigated insensitivity, largely related to her elitism and egocentrism, also contributes to the excess of her performance and the ironic juxtaposition that secures its camp sensibility. Rather than exhibit the sensitivity of the noblesse oblige, even of the patronizing variety, Karen is blunt and offensive, unmoved by the plight of others, acknowledging them only insofar as they affect her. This is manifest, for instance, in her interactions with the less privileged in general: she chastises the homeless for committing serious fashion errors and thus marring her visual landscape; she threatens to deport her servants (they are usually illegal aliens, like her maid Rosario, whom she is exploiting) if they do not perform particularly demeaning tasks, which she demands purely for her own amusement; and she uses her friends—in one episode, she places an urgent call to Will, who is also her lawyer, in the middle of the night, imploring him to come to her home and telling him that she needs his legal expertise immediately. Upon his flustered arrival, she hands him a jar of olives and tells him to open it so that she can properly garnish her martini (Barr & Burrows, 2001a). Karen's insensitivity knows no bounds, a quality that stands in sharp contrast to the world of refinement and gentility of which she is clearly a part. Her unabashed elitism and even cruelty assume excessive proportions, and while they are extreme on their own merits, the dissonance sharpens that excess.

Karen has a curious relationship with her maid, Rosario, in particular, that also is excessive and constitutes spectacle, albeit in novel ways. In fact, Rosario gives as good as she gets in terms of demeaning, humiliating, and hurtful comments and behaviors—she is Karen's match in terms of cruel sarcasm, and Karen is the object of those barbs. Karen enjoys this repartee, however, although in a very patronizing way, as if Rosario is her own special entertainment; in other words, the class dynamic is not only retained but heightened in these interchanges. For instance, in one episode revolving about the specter of Rosario's deportation, Karen hurls some shockingly racist insults at Rosario—about how she was an illegal "tamale" whom Karen bought from her parents and whom she'll send back in a heartbeat to wear a loincloth in the bush if she doesn't watch her step. Rosario bristles and responds, in heavily accented English, "Listen, lady, one more word out of you and I'll mop this floor with your skinny ass!" Karen sniffles, smiles tearily, clasps Rosario's hand, and turns to Will (her lawyer) and says, "See, honey, I can't live without my Rosie; you have to do something to keep her with me" (Barr & Burrows, 1999). Certainly, this relationship constitutes spectacle, both in terms of the juxtaposition between shocking cruelty and deep affection and in terms of excess as relevant to the degree of degradation that characterizes it and the extreme class differential on which it is configured.

The conventional camp sensibility that infuses Karen Walker's performance is ultimately attributable to the aesthetics of excess and juxtaposition that characterize it. In particular, excess is the point at which the irony, humor, and stylistic features that Babuscio (1999) delineates as characteristic of camp converge, established in Karen's case primarily by dissonance and the cartoonish dimensions of her performance. These qualities converge to give rise to Babuscio's fourth criterion, theatricality, in such a way that may well be relevant to the location of the performance in the contemporary popular mediascape. That is, the excessive nature of the performance functions as a shield that practically bifurcates that performance and, thus, the audience. Excess and parody—in this case, of the comic variety—can be appreciated at a very superficial level, such that Karen can be read as a quirky, outrageous character. The audience that accesses this performance may well be unaware of the satire that is available at another level, much like the mainstream—especially heterosexist—audience of conventional camp that reads it as an earnest if somewhat playful nostalgic homage. Conversely, the excess available in Karen Walker's performance may very well be read against the trope on which she is based, a lens that ensures an apprehension of the performance as satirical and even critical, turning as it does on harshly exposing the classism, elitism, and racism that undergird that trope. For this audience, the comic, cartoonish dimensions of the performance are not lost, but they also suggest that hypocrisy and selfishness are attendant to economic privilege. Furthermore, the fact that a considerable degree of the spectacle that inheres in Karen's performance turns on sexuality and, by extension, gender locates a reading of the character in that context; accordingly, "spectacular" gender and sexual play, if not alterity per se, serve as the backdrop against which critique might emerge. As such, along with trope, spectacle constitutes a premise in the logic of transgressive camp performance.

Orientations

The camp sensibility that characterizes Karen Walker's performance also is largely attributable to her relationships with others. In particular, Karen is drawn primarily against the characters of Grace and Jack, such that Grace constitutes the foil and Jack the anchor for her camp character, and these relationships function to further secure a resistive reading.[1] As the female lead on the show and, thus, the only other consistently present female character other than Karen, Grace serves as an obvious reference point for Karen's character. The contrasts between the two women are marked. Grace is younger than Karen, a fact that is not only made explicit but also is apparent in dress and behavior. Unlike the brittle and hard-edged Karen, Grace has a "softer" and more girlish persona—more vulnerable, impressionable, and impulsive—and is more "naturally" feminine in her appearance: her hair is long and usually untamed, in sharp contrast to Karen's flawlessly coiffed hair. She wears less and softer makeup than Karen does, and her clothes tend to be "funkier," more bargain-basement chic than haute couture—this is, in fact, the basis of Karen's formidable criticism of Grace's fashion sense.

Grace also is constructed as naive on the show, at a far remove from Karen's jaded worldliness. This is evidenced, for instance, in Karen's insightful if cutting opinions on Grace's love life, real or potential, which are always on the mark. Karen frequently dismisses Grace's lover at the time as "not gay enough," in reference to what she sees as Grace's unhealthy level of attachment to Will, her gay best friend. In one episode, Karen actively discourages Grace's pursuit of Karen's husband's nephew, who is similarly interested in Grace: "He's a user, honey," she tells Grace. "He's not good enough for you." Lest she be mistaken for caring, she adds, "And besides, he's not gay" (Barr & Burrows, 2001b). Grace is portrayed as sexually naive, as well, unlike Karen, whose ribald and varied sexual experiences are referenced frequently on the show. In one episode, Grace is invited to participate in a "threesome" with an ex-boyfriend and his current girlfriend (Rosenstock & Burrows, 2000). Attempting to fulfill an image of herself as sophisticated and worldly, she agrees, but she is unable to go through with it—she shows up dressed in several layers of bulky and unflattering clothing, and before they are all peeled away, despite her resistance, she calls a vehement halt to the proceedings, insisting that she is a "nice Jewish girl" who simply cannot be what she is not. Her initial determination to participate is fueled by a desire to demonstrate to Karen, Jack, and Will that she can be worldly; all three of them, it is revealed, have engaged in threesomes, and, it is implied, that is the least of their sexual adventures. They are convinced that Grace could never be so adventurous. Thus, in comparing Karen and Grace specifically, Grace embodies conventionally acceptable female (hetero)sexuality, whereas Karen clearly operates far beyond that realm.

Karen and Grace also differ substantively in terms of their personalities. Unlike Karen, Grace is kind, thoughtful, open, and friendly. Although she is also often selfish, hers is a childlike and even endearing selfishness—for instance, she may lie to Will about the fact that the bakery was sold out of chocolate chip muffins and hoard the last one for herself (Lizer & Burrows, 2001). But with respect to "important" matters, like friends' needs and feelings, Grace will invariably—ultimately, at least—put their needs before her own. This is consistently apparent in Grace's and Karen's relationship; whereas Karen always puts Grace down about her appearance and her relationships, Grace will go out of her way to be kind to Karen. For example, when Stan, Karen's husband, is imprisoned for tax evasion, Grace stays with Karen—who hints strongly at wanting her to but denies doing so. Karen quickly tires of Grace's presence, though, and ultimately has her thrown out—literally—by her servants (Herschlag & Burrows, 2001). On another occasion, Grace endures countless insults to talk Karen into staying with her when she needs a place to stay—Karen is demeaning and cruel throughout Grace's endeavors (Lerner & Burrows, 2002). Grace embodies fairly conventional femininity insofar as her nurturing, caring, loving, and even childlike persona; Karen, conversely, is thoroughly and incorrigibly selfish, rude, and thoughtless.

Finally, a marked distinction between Karen and Grace as relevant to conventional femininity is their respective maternal inclinations. Grace harbors significant desires to have a child, a possibility she has explored with Will throughout the series, and by the final season she does so—given her nurturing and caring personality, this maternal yearning and its realization reads as consistent and natural. Karen, on the other hand, is notoriously nonmaternal; she has no biological children, although she has stepchildren through her marriage to Stan. She does not know exactly how many there are or what sex they are, however, and she does not know their names—her servants and her friends must remind her. Indeed, she employs a servant specifically because she resembles her, "in case the kids wake up crying in the middle of the night and want to be comforted." When she refers to her stepchildren, it is only in the most derogatory terms—they are fat or lazy or stupid, for instance. In one episode, Jack convinces her to attend her step-son's swim meet (Palmer & Burrows, 2001). Clearly taking her cue from the other parents around her, she cheers enthusiastically for her stepson, only to learn that the boy she is cheering for is not her stepson—she doesn't really know what he looks like. When he is finally pointed out to her, she boos him mercilessly for losing, assuming this is part and parcel of parental participation at a swim meet. Of course, she has been drinking heavily throughout the affair. The contrast between Karen and Grace seals the general differences between the two women on the count of femininity; although Karen is very feminine in appearance, in relation to Grace, it is a contrived, thoroughly artificial, even brittle femininity. Furthermore, with respect to their personalities and behavior, Karen conforms not at all to feminine conventions; it is Grace alone who manifests those qualities.

The other character against whom Karen is defined is Jack, but unlike Grace, Jack functions as the anchor for Karen's character, endowing it with substance via their congruence. Flamboyantly and unabashedly gay, Jack and Karen are kindred spirits; both are egocentric, materialistic, superficial, impulsive, and insensitive. They bond over others' misfortune and humiliation and are particularly amused when they are the cause of it. What is important about Jack in relation to Karen is that he is the only consistently featured character who provides her with some depth. Karen has a particular affection for Jack that she has for no one else. Although she is fond of her maid, Rosie, this character appears less regularly on the show, and Karen's affection for Rosie is presented more along the lines of dependency on the particular needs she fulfills. Karen's affection for Jack, however, is based on their simpatico. Often, Jack and Karen greet each other by Jack's saying, "Who's your daddy?" and Karen's responding, "You are," or by Karen's asking Jack, "Who's my poodle?" and Jack's responding, "I am."

Notably, whatever nurturing impulses Karen may experience—and they bear little resemblance to convention—are directed toward Jack. Because of her elitism and insensitivity, her care for Jack is typically condescending and patronizing, and it often takes the form of money; she will treat him to spending sprees or give him cash or credit cards, thus financing him in large part—he is notoriously unsuccessful, eternally unemployed. When Karen cuts him off periodically, he sulks until she comes around; and she always comes around because she feels sorry for him. Jack also is the conduit through which Karen is redeemed. When he is truly hurt or confused by something—much as a child might be—it is always Karen who steps in to comfort, protect, or reassure him. For instance, in one episode, Jack and Will—baffled by their obligation to throw a bachelor party for their heterosexual male friend—hire a female stripper (Kightlinger, Herschlag, & Burrows, 2000). Because the friend is unwilling to participate, the stripper performs for Will and Jack; while she is astride Jack, he becomes aroused. Struck by the prospect that he may be straight, Jack is inconsolable. Karen comforts him, reasoning with him in a very understanding way, and she also throws herself at him sexually, to prove that he is not straight—if he can resist her, he's got to be gay, she claims. All is resolved when Jack learns that the female stripper is a transsexual, but the fact remains that Karen is the person who cares for him most and can reach him the best. As such, Jack's character serves to round out Karen's character, rescuing it from becoming an acontextual caricature invoked merely for comic effect. Karen's performance is given substance, depth, and complexity, rescued from superficiality and endowed with the affection that Robertson (1996) claims is a crucial element of camp.

As foils and anchors, Grace and Jack, respectively, also serve to ground Karen Walker's camp performance firmly in the present. Flinn (1999) has argued about camp that turns on the female body, "When put in relation to the female body, camp's preoccupation with obsolescence and morbidity creates what might be called the 'aging diva' phenomenon. . . . The camped up forms of 'aging' femininity operate as the fleshy, excessive other to a more transcendent, cerebral masculinity" (pp. 443–444). Flinn (1999) notes that female celebrities like Gloria Swanson, Mae West, and Marlene Dietrich have become camp icons precisely by virtue of their excesses in terms of age or body or affiliation with death, in films and in life. Robertson (1996) concedes this point implicitly in her discussions of Mae West, Joan Crawford, and Madonna. The character of Karen Walker, however, is distinctive in this regard; although age is factored into her difference from Grace, it is not the defining feature. Drawn against contemporary figures of heterosexual femininity and gay masculinity, she is firmly anchored in the present, and her significance is relevant to those gendered and sexual discursive practices in particular. She is thus not isolated from a contemporary context, a tragic figure resurrected simply for a somewhat narcissistic nostalgia; rather, her camp performance, while playing to that nostalgia, assumes a distinctly political edge by virtue of its relationship to the characters that define it. As configured with the premises of the trope and spectacle that characterize her persona, the anchors and foils that lend definition to her character give rise to a fairly specific "take" on gender and sexuality; if that take is not guaranteed, it is nonetheless complex, layered, and logical.

Gay Man Trapped

As with the character of Xena, the culmination of this logic is sexuality. Karen Walker's camp performance functions as a discursive site of resistance with respect to sexual "alterity," as defined against heteronormative conventions, such that camp becomes the rhetorical means by which that alterity is articulated. Karen's camp performance initially may appear to advance an accessible—to consumers of mainstream popular culture—version of the "fag hag." *Fag hag* is a colloquialism often applied to heterosexual women who have one or more close relationships with gay men; however, as Robertson (1996) points out, the term is rife with derogatory meanings, as relevant to both the women and, of course, the men to whom it refers: "Rather than describe the love and friendship between women and gay men, the fag hag stereotype often seems to presume a failed object choice on the part of the woman, the 'hag'—that is, the fag hag chooses gay men because she 'can't get a man' (she is stereotypically unattractive) and/or because she desires a man who doesn't want her (she is stereotypically secretly, desperately attracted to gay men)" (p. 8). Furthermore, fag hags are popularly portrayed as wealthy, attractive, typically white women with some social cachet, thus making them desirable companions for gay men who aspire to move in sophisticated urban social circles—indeed, these women are often perceived as sponsoring, in a broad sense, their "fags" of choice.

As contextualized by gay masculinity on the show, then, the line between the rich-bitch socialite trope on which the character of Karen Walker is predicated and the fag hag is a fine one; thus it is a relatively easy conflation, suggesting a possible reading of the character that draws on aspects of the camp logic that we have identified. Karen's performance reflects especially the characterization of the fag hag; she is wealthy, she is Jack's primary source of funds, and she is his entrée into the world of the rich and famous, to which he so keenly aspires. In addition, she appears to spend much of her time with Jack—certainly more than she does with her family—and she engages in several activities with him, including going to gay clubs or to bathhouses. As noted, her most intimate relationship is with Jack.

But Karen deviates from the stereotype of the fag hag in several important ways; in the first place, she is quite attractive, and her sexual appeal to others is well established in the show. Second, although some scenes suggest that Jack's sexual technique—which he liberally employs with Karen in a playful fashion—is accomplished enough to make Karen weak with desire, her attitude toward him is quite condescending and pitying for the most part. Even when she is aroused by him—for example, during the making of a sexual harassment video, where he enacts inappropriate sexual behavior and she is beside herself with desire (Kohan, Mutchnick, & Burrows, 1999b)—her attitude is imperial, demanding that he repeat the behavior. In other words, her desire is for her own sexual gratification, not for him. Consequently, it is not the fag hag that Karen's camp performance insinuates and affirms in *Will and Grace;* rather, it is gay male sexuality that her camp performance offers, and it is, ironically, through her character—in tandem with but also more definitively than Jack's or Will's—that gay male sexuality is ultimately legitimized and made palatable for mainstream consumption.

This is primarily accomplished by the fact that Karen and Jack are very similar in their personalities, attitudes, and behaviors, which are, as we have discussed, "camped" to a great degree in the show via ironic, parodic, and excessive practices. As noted, each is superficial, highly egocentric, insensitive to others, materialistic, and possessed of a mean sense of humor that is most frequently manifest in the demeaning of others. For instance, they may compliment Grace effusively on an outfit or hairstyle that is rather ridiculous in order to convince her to go out in public wearing it; Karen and Jack follow her around, heckling her and inciting strangers to do the same (Kohan, Mutchnick, & Burrows, 1998). Similarly, they will "crank call" people who are ill—like Rosario, Karen's maid—and pretend to be physicians, advising her to engage in exercises that are excruciatingly painful while they giggle at her exclamations of pain (Herschlag & Burrows, 2005). Indeed, Karen and Jack are so similar that they are virtually indistinguishable; they engage in the very same activities and behaviors, and they usually anticipate what the other is planning.

The degree of similarity between Karen and Jack, not surprisingly, is the basis for their intimacy—they are the only ones who see each other vulnerable. Even if they exploit these occasions at the expense of the vulnerable one, they ultimately do comfort and even advise each other. Much of their intimacy is established by virtue of the high degree of sexual play in which they regularly engage. As such, their striking similarity to each other is also largely predicated on their sexualities. Essentially, Karen and Jack share the same sexual sensibility—a gay male sensibility, to be precise. Jack is notoriously promiscuous, in sharp contrast to Will, fulfilling a popular stereotype of gay men.[2] This is made evident by his references to numerous lovers, his casual attitude toward relationships, his fickleness when in relationships, and his high sex drive, as indicated by his frequently noted attraction to men. In addition, his behavior and actions are often crude and lascivious in recounting his sexual escapades, real or anticipated. Karen, significantly, mirrors Jack in this respect nearly exactly, save for the fact that she has been married twice. It is true that she was sexually repulsed by her grotesque first husband, Stan, and that her brief second marriage was unsatisfactory;[3] however, those marriages represent the epitome of conventional heterosexuality, and her rejection of both constitutes a rejection of that convention. This is made quite explicit in the case of her second marriage, where her rejection is attributed precisely to her balking at the idea of relinquishing herself and her desires for her new husband (Warfield et al., 2004). Karen, like Jack, muses frequently and lewdly on her sexual adventures and attractions. Her responses to sexual overtures mimic Jack's in terms of her inability to control her sexual impulses when aroused—again, her sexualization in this regard is established ironically and parodically in the context of her relation to the trope on which she is modeled and attendant anchors and foils, as well as the excess with which it is articulated. In other words, she is possessed of a stereotypically gay male sexuality, one that is marked by superficiality, promiscuity, and gratification. In one episode, in fact, Karen entertains having an affair with a man; as she prepares to meet him, stating to herself these intentions, Jack emerges from her bedcovers, saying, "I knew you were going to meet him; that's exactly what I would have done," confirming his and Karen's common sexuality (Barr & Burrows, 2002). In fact, Karen's close alliance with Jack is no doubt responsible, in part, for her cult status among gay men;[4] in one scene, this is explicitly addressed when Jack says to her, "You're like an icon to gay men. You've got the sass, the class, and the ass!" (Bardin, 1999, p. 30). Mullally also has said of her character that "[she] is the diva that [Jack's] always wanted to be" (Cagle, 1998, p. 48). We would suggest further that Karen's character is not simply aligned with and defined by gay men but is defined *as* gay male.

The most significant aspect of Karen's camp performance of sexuality, then, is that it is a performance of gay male sexuality and sensibilities, a feature that many theorists have identified as integral to camp historically (see, e.g., Babuscio, 1999; Cleto, 1999; Ross, 1999). What further endows Karen's performance with a camp sensibility is the fact that it is performed by a heterosexual woman who bears all of the hallmarks of conventional privilege and legitimacy: she is (and/or has been) married, wealthy, and powerful. Accordingly, Karen's camp performance justifies gay male sexuality in the conventionally mainstream context of popular culture. Furthermore—and most significant—that sensibility is conflated and thus endowed with upper-class status, the ultimate warrant of legitimacy. But more to the point, a reading of the character of Karen Walker as a performance of gay male sexuality—one that by definition challenges conventional discourses of gender and sexuality—is built on the collective foundation and peculiar configuration of the familiar rich-bitch trope; the over-the-top and paradoxical aesthetics that define the performance; and the other characters against whom the performance is drawn. Because each of these features in isolation is far from unique in a contemporary media environment, such a reading is not guaranteed—and as we have noted, elements of this logic may be selectively invoked to render any variety of readings with varying degrees of transgressive potential, such as the "fag hag." An apprehension of these features, however, specifically in relation to each other, yields a distinctive whole—a camp performance of a gay man by a historical paragon of conventional heterosexual femininity.

5

Macy Gray

Venus in Drag

Singer and songwriter Macy Gray arrived on the music scene to much critical acclaim in 1999 with her multiplatinum debut album, *On How Life Is*. Her voice alone is stylistically unique, described as a "strange squawk" (Chambers, Gordon, & Figueroa, 1999, p. 50), a "squeaky, hacked-silk rasp" (Gordinier, 1999, p. 46), and "Chaka Khan meets Betty Boop. Tina Turner on helium" (Brunner, 1999, p. 72). In fact, references to past icons of soul, rhythm and blues, and disco music are not accidental, for Gray's musical style is highly reminiscent of all of these genres and others. Her music has been compared to Billie Holliday, Eartha Kitt, Louis Armstrong, Al Green, Aretha Franklin, and Ella Fitzgerald (Chambers, Gordon, & Figueroa, 1999; Gordinier, 1999; Hudson, 1999). McKissack (2000) describes Gray's brand of fusion as "a vocal style that ranges from sixties soul and seventies funk to the bluesy women of the forties and the last time I heard a gospel choir get in good with the spirit" (p. 39).

Gray embodies the same unique aesthetic in dress and performances: "She's BECK's dust sister, a blur of glitter and fur, all four 'Lady Marmalade' girls tossed into a blender with the gitchy-gitchy knob turned all the way up" (Sheffield, 2001, p. 41). Her look is highly reminiscent of 1970s urban Black funk; Gray typically sports a wild head of "natural" hair—either dreads or an Afro—and she is given to wearing tight bell-bottom pantsuits, precarious platform shoes, long faux-fur coats, and gargantuan sunglasses. Her stage presence follows through on this promise; describing one of her concerts, Schaeble (2001) writes: "With her shimmery gold Pirates of Penzance outfit, wild Sideshow Bob hair and 15-piece backup band that looked like it's visiting from some '70s variety show, Gray stormed the stage of London's historic Old Vic Theatre in August to launch her eagerly anticipated second album, *The Id* (Epic), with a knockdown, drag-out funk fest that left the crowd screaming" (p. 54). Gray's "soul-funk . . . hippie chick" (Sheffield, 2001, p. 41) aesthetic distinguishes her from her musical contemporaries; it is an aesthetic inextricably laden with powerful allusions to African American culture in general and to a period of African American insurgence in particular.

She's a Soul Man

Gray leaves an indelible impression on her audiences, her eccentric individuality causing her to be "immediately identifiable in a sea of people who seem totally interchangeable" (Dougherty, 2001, p. 91). To witness her music is to embark on a trip through a psychedelic funk land of bluesy, jazz-inflected, and hip-hop rhythms, punctuated audibly by her "raspy, sleepy squeak of a voice" (Pantsios, 2000) and visually by her whacked-out stage presence—her "oversize head, shrub of hair, ghetto-not-so-fabulous wardrobe, and half-awake persona" (Browne, 2001). At 5'11" this African American woman cuts a commanding albeit gangly figure as she ambles across the stage in a dreamlike state. Her colorful cartoonish image summons a well-known trope, a Black funk sensibility made available to mainstream media audiences during the early 1970s in the popular television dance show *Soul Train* and in blaxploitation films such as *Sweet Sweetback's Baadasssss Song, Shaft,* and *Super Fly*. Gray is a visual parody of an amalgamated Black urban male stereotype, part harmless and inept spaced-out stoner and part precarious gun-toting, drug-pushing, "mack daddy," dressed to the nines and living by her own laws in a system ruled by "the [white] man."

The trope invoked in Gray's camp character is raced, classed, and gendered in particular ways, conflating African Americans with a seedy urban underworld characterized by drug addiction, prostitution, feral sex, and gun violence. A gritty city world of poverty governed by its own set of ethics, its inhabitants resort to the black market to find a way to beat the system. Those who do hold positions at the top of the social strata in this underworld are primarily African American men—pimps, drug lords, gang leaders. Gray's is a trope, then, that is gendered as masculine, epitomized in the characters of Shaft and Priest, the virile, hypermasculine stars of *Shaft* and *Super Fly,* respectively. These icons of Black popular culture present a striking model of

Black masculinity, men who are physically and economically powerful, heterosexually potent in their attraction to and domination of women, proud to be Black, and brazenly defiant of "the man." The trope summoned in Gray's camp character is saturated with the Black masculinity of a very specific moment in U.S. history.

In many ways, Gray unequivocally embodies this trope, as evidenced obviously, for example, in her visual signification of the Black urban stereotype as described above. Other less visual characteristics of Gray's performance, however, contribute to this Black-funk sensibility. Frequent allusions to her connection with illegal drugs, for example, made by herself and intimated in the press about her further align her with the trope. Her demeanor, both in interviews and onstage, supports an association with getting high. Critics describe Gray as a "nutcase," giving stage performances that are a "little spaced out" (Pantsios, 2000) and responding to interview questions with 1960s terms such as *cool* and *hip* (e.g., Dunn, 2002). Her lyrics, as well, frequently refer to drug use, such as in "Do Something":

> Lost in some ol' maze
> Some years have passed me by
> All I want to do is get high
> I'll get it together some other day.

And in "Still," Gray muses about her abusive relationship with a man who magnetically draws her in with the aid of mind-altering drugs:

> Wow! It gets better every time that we get high
> Then your crumbs of lovin'
> They somehow get me by.

Gray's musical scores invoke a psychedelic drug culture, as well. Her work has been described as having a "Janis Joplin–style sound" (Dougherty, 2001, p. 91), a reference not only to Gray's gravelly voice but also to the erratic rhythms of her tunes, similar to the 1960s maverick musician who also was aligned closely with drug culture. Gray's music is a mesmerizing "blend of old and new sounds—hip-hop, gospel, jazz, funk, blues and electronic dance music" (Pantsios, 2000), used to communicate fuzzy but fervent, overlapping emotions of vulnerability, yearning, desire, and satiation, all sentiments often linked with drug addiction.

Also like the Black urban male proto(stereo)type, Gray's camp character is steeped in violence. She is a "gun-packing sistah," a real force with which to be reckoned when things do not go her way. Her songs make the case for her willingness to take matters of injustice into her own hands, even brutally killing when necessary. In "I've Committed Murder," she shoots her boyfriend's female boss, when the "mean ol' bitch" fires him without pay:

> I said, "Give him the little bit of money you owe him"
> She said, "get back bitch I ain't giving you shit"
> I said, "you ol' bag, maybe you ain't heard but them are fighting words."

She commits the crime with no remorse, stating, "I don't feel bad about it" and "I have no intention of paying for my crime." In "Gimme All Your Lovin' or I Will Kill You," Gray again turns to guns as a solution, this time for unrequited love as she holds tight to her "AK" and threatens to "put one through" her lover's head, a man who turns out to prefer "girls with long and wavy hair" instead of her short and kinky Afro. Gray's sense of justice, understood by many scorned women in a world governed by men's rules, rationalizes the act:

> It's amazing what a gun to the head can do
> My baby loves me now as hard as he can
> My methods may be suspect
> But you gotta get love however you can.

In a world in which the vulnerable—those on the lower rungs of the class, race, or gender ladder—are frequently "done wrong," Gray's commanding presence of vigilante justice has considerable power. Her in-your-face noncompliant attitude infuses her presentation with an air of erratic and impulsive lunacy.

Gray's camp character also is saturated with sexuality and motivated by sexual pleasure in accordance with the trope that she invokes. In songs like "Freak like Me," she is a self-described "freak," someone who ignores the cultural admonition for self-restraint when it comes to sex. She loves sex, seeing it as a "beautiful thang." Her "Sexual Revolution" overtly calls for the celebration of the freak within, contrary to cultural mores:

Your mama told you to be discreet
And keep your freak to yourself
But your mama lied to you all this time

You've got to express what is taboo in you
And share your freak with the rest of us.

In "Sex-O-Matic Venus Freak," she unabashedly celebrates deviant sexual behavior and her feelings of being a "XX rated movie star" as she recalls a particularly carnal affair. The freak within her is a pulsating force not to be denied or confused with romantic love, as she explains in "Harry":

Don't want to be your girlfriend
But boy when you need the lovin'
Come and see me, Harry.

Here Gray again rejects the conventions of traditional feminine sexuality that prescribe women's vulnerability and subservience to men.

Gray's visual aesthetics, alliance with drug use, penchant for violence, erratic impulsive behavior, and attitude toward sexuality cohere to evoke a striking, potent trope of Black masculinity at the height of 1970s Black Power consciousness, in all its swaggering sexual prowess and renegade rejection of conventional, oppressive rules. Her performance deviates from the trope in important ways, however, constituting camp rather than a mere articulation or appropriation of it. The most obvious difference between Gray and the trope she invokes, of course, is that Gray is female while the trope is discoursed as decidedly male. This is a difference that causes Gray's enactment to bear resemblance to drag. In her performance, however, Gray does more than simply "act like a man." She blends aspects of femininity with her portrayal of Black urban masculinity in significant and often subtle ways. Her ardent but doleful expressions of her susceptibility, for example, distinguish her from her male counterparts. Her lyrics are marked by detailed descriptions of her yearnings for love that certainly include but go beyond the need or desire for sexual intercourse. In "Why Didn't You Call Me," for example, she plaintively asks the common question conventionally posed by many women of men who have dumped them; and in "Don't Come Around," she pleads with a former lover to leave her alone so that she might heal her "heart that's completely broke." Such expressions of vulnerability and subjection found more often in women's relational experiences distinguish and complicate Gray's performance of hypermasculinity.[1]

These expressions of vulnerability, however, are not accompanied by the typical prescription of subservience found in conventional representations of femininity. Instead, the manner in which Gray dovetails vulnerability with revelry of female sexuality marks her performance as conspicuously different. Her performance constitutes an amalgamation of a renowned Black male trope with powerfully resistive connotations with the female trope of the "sexual freak." A term introduced into mainstream parlance by funk artist Rick James in his 1980s hit "Super Freak," a freak is a woman out of control with sexual desire, urgently seeking men for her satiation, who of course, willingly oblige. *Freak,* then, most often connotes a subservient role for women in that it is presented from a masculine perspective as a fortuitous woman's problem that only men can fix. This is not the case in Gray's performance, however, as her aesthetic embodiment of a male sensibility, in tandem with her female "freakiness," results in a powerful presentation of female sexuality not predicated on vulnerability or subservience but that is edgy and certainly resistive to conventional norms and expectations. But Gray's performances, as politically edgy as they may be, are affectionate rather than contemptuous in homage to historical cultural stereotypes of race, class, and gender. In true camp form, she embraces lovingly, yet in exaggerated, parodic fashion, that which is critiqued.

Superfreak

To say that Macy Gray has style is to understate the obvious, and to describe that style as camp is highly fitting. Touted as a "one-of-a-kind star" (Sheffield 2001, p. 41), Gray embodies an aesthetic that is distinctive and noteworthy, to say the least. Critics have called Gray a "Saturday-morning-cartoon close up," in the spirit of *Fat Albert,* referring to the exaggerated manner in which she presents herself (Browne 2001, p. 80). Everything about Macy Gray is excessively outlandish, from her hair, makeup, and clothing to her helium-inflected "Betty-Boopish" voice to the ideas conveyed in her lyrics. Her appearance on the 2001 MTV Video Music Awards show was sartorially outrageous, as well, as she accepted her award in her sequined dress with "My Album Drops September 18th" embedded in the design, a satirical acknowledgment of her own commodification. In short, Gray is clownish, cartoonish, outrageous; she is excessive, liberally transgressing the boundaries of convention. It is in this vein that Gray's July 2004 Elton John Aids Foundation concert performance, where she performed nude but for a pair of Jimmy Choo shoes, is best understood. Even absent her trademark excessive couture, this performance was predicated on the same outrageousness and absurdity that characterizes Gray's public persona in all guises. More to the point, the excess that characterizes Gray is not that of mere unqualified indulgence; rather, so extreme is it in her case that it assumes caricaturish, ironic, and parodic—that is to say, camp—qualities.

Excess oozes from Gray's lyrics, as well, as she describes outlandish ideas and actions, most having to do with unrestrained sex. Her flagrant rejection of traditional societal mores, as exemplified in her call for "everybody in my underwear" as a sort of sexual revolution, is indeed excessive, as is her reference to and celebration of herself as a sexual freak. Her specific allusions to kinky sex acts—bondage, 69 positions, and "whip cream all over my skin"—pushes her beyond the limits of mainstream conventional sensibilities of sexual conduct. Perhaps the most unsettlingly excessive acts that Gray describes, however, have to do with gun violence. The act of pointing a gun at her lover's head in demand for sex, as she does in "Gimme All Your Lovin' or I Will Kill You," for instance, certainly surpasses conventional sexual relations; and her calculated decision in "I've Committed Murder" to kill her boyfriend's female boss—"the mean ole bitch who degrades him everyday"—as a means for avenging his loss of dignity is well beyond the realm of ordinary interpersonal relations. These lyrics are tinged with black humor, so that Gray comes across as amused and self-satisfied, indeed smug, rather than as an enraged vigilante. This tone, as well, adds a dimension of chilling excessiveness to Gray's persona.

As implied above, the spectacular dimension of Gray's performance is heightened as she is coded as not just flamboyantly sexual but as insane.

Gray continually teeters precariously on the edge of sanity, lapsing into bouts of lunacy brought on through mental depression and/or "addiction" to love, drugs, and sex. Her songs possess dimensions of dizzying flurries of madness, referring frequently to the "beast" or "war" within each of us that exists just below the surface of civility, waiting to be unleashed. Critics have even attributed her unique voice to her mental instability, equating her "high-on-helium rasp" to "the sound of gravel knocking around in her brain" (Browne, 2001, p. 80). Gray readily acknowledges her wackiness, stating blatantly—almost proudly—in "Relating to a Psychopath" that she's a demented psychopath with a twisted brain in need of medication so that her "feel better begins." The origins of her mental instability are unclear, but they are somehow related to sex and drugs. Indeed, she seems to be addicted to both, vacillating between tormented anguish and fantastic ecstasy. In "Caligula," she describes her lover as being a "favorite fix" that she's got to have again and again, noting that her particular addiction is to "fuckin', not lovin'." In "Oblivion," she celebrates a dreamlike state in which she can "create a world of her own" filled with love and magic, and invite "everybody in my underwear." To be in Gray's world is to be in constant tension between the worlds of restrained sanity and free madness in which her sexual "freak" is released.

Contributing to the camp sensibility that characterizes Gray's performance, juxtaposition is also present as apparently arbitrary and incongruous sensibilities. In large part, this is articulated lyrically and, accordingly, via alternate, disparate personas that Gray assumes. For instance, many of Gray's songs—such as "Gimme All Your Lovin' or I Will Kill You"—feature her as powerful and in control in her relationships, even aggressive to the point of violence. On the other hand, she also presents herself in other songs as vulnerable and passive in intimate relationships, as evidenced in "Why Didn't You Call Me," in which she waits forlornly for her lover, and in "Still," in which she portrays a willing victim of an abusive relationship.

Further examples of incongruity in Gray's performance turn on disjunctive representations of sexuality. Indeed, Gray's performance is infused with a representation of the sexual freak, in particular—she refers to herself as a "super Venus freak" in "Sex-O-Matic Venus Freak," for instance, and in various other songs expresses her voracious sexual appetites and availability. Historically, the sexual freak has been defined by decidedly masculine sensibilities and desires, such that the freak is a product of stereotypical male fantasy—the nymphomaniac who is always available for sex, rendering her passive, at best a projection of male pleasure. Yet in Gray's interpretation, her "freak within" regularly manifests in insanity—more to the point, a dangerous insanity, rife with violence and threat rather than mindless sensual passion.

Another apparently random, disjunctive feature of Gray's performance is her references to spirituality. Two songs, in particular, articulate strong messages of morality and accountability, a marked deviation from her other performances. In "I Can't Wait to Meetchu," Gray muses about meeting God, and in "Hey Young World, Part 2," she reminds youngsters that God is watching their actions. Although spirituality and morality are certainly not incommensurate with a powerful sexuality or even violence or insanity, they are not commonly linked in the popular consciousness. The spiritual dimensions of Gray's performance appear anomalous and dissonant, apparently haphazard aberrations from her freak and dangerous personas.

A key aesthetic of Macy Gray's performance is masculinity, achieved primarily through her dress and deportment and juxtaposed sharply with the very female sexual freak persona that she cultivates. Critics frequently note her masculine dress—big hats and loose-fitting pantsuits—in sharp contrast to the skimpy, seductive attire of many other female performers in the mainstream. This is not to say that Gray is asexual; on the contrary, she overtly performs sexuality, albeit a form of sexuality that is imbued with masculinity as conventionally discoursed. For instance, she has a ravenous sexual appetite that she seeks to satiate in a manner conventionally associated with men; she calls men up for "one-night stands," dismissing them once her sexual needs are satisfied. She communicates her unrelenting sexual needs in a forthright, unrepentant manner, refusing to apologize for or deny that she is motivated purely by sexual pleasure. Gray's sexuality, then, even in its "freakiness," is marked by assertiveness and power more likely to be associated with men rather than predicated on vulnerability and access, as typically found in mainstream representations of female sexuality. The kaleidoscopic gender and sexual play that mark her performance, in fact, squarely situate it as camp.

The masculine aesthetic in Gray's performance marks her as strikingly different from other Black women, in particular, available in popular media fare, historically and today, who are "mistresses of the come-on, all skin and slither" (Pantsios, 2000). While she might have selected from a virtual buffet of other women's styles from Black culture—sequin-gowned divas like Diana Ross, gold-chained female rappers such as Missy Elliott, midriff-baring "hoochie girls" like Li'l Kim—she chose instead a style most often associated with Black men and rife with controversial meaning in terms of race, class, gender, and sexuality. Furthermore, Gray's lyrics and perfor-mance establish the reference by turning on a powerful, assertive, even vio-lent sexuality—one that, more often than not, entails sexual domination. As noted, however, these references are balanced occasionally by lyrics and be-havior that endow Gray's performances with a more vulnerable, essentially more feminine, dimension; yet other instances reveal a potent and thor-oughly female sexuality available as a sexual freak. Each of these seemingly incommensurate representations—the mack daddy, the vulnerable woman, and the sexual freak—turn on gender, and they invite a resistive reading by virtue of their very juxtaposition.

The psychedelic excess, trumped up masculinity, and impenetrable in-sanity that constitute Gray's aesthetic create a kaleidoscopic spectacle. Look once and Gray is a benign carnie clown; turn slightly and she shifts into a parody of Black urban masculinity; turn once more and she morphs into an impulsive, precarious lunatic—all facets of the same captivating spectacle. All of these aesthetic avenues lead to a less conventional and more unsettling discursive construction, and none is wholly coherent or complete in itself. It is this very unsettling and reconfiguration of discursive meanings accom-plished through Gray's kaleidoscopic spectacle that renders her performance more than just "camp lite," creating camp with critical proclivity.

Diva Redefined

As we have argued in the foregoing chapters, the camp sensibility that char-acterizes Xena's and Karen Walker's respective performances inheres in large part in their definition as drawn against other characters, who serve as an-chors and foils for those performances. Anchors and foils similarly play an important role in defining Macy Gray's performance as camp and, further, endow it with a critical edge, although in the absence of a contained narra-tive, those characters emerge from the broader context of her peers: individuals with whom she is most likely to be compared and against whom she is most likely to be understood. That is, Gray is drawn against "characters" or performers in the broader context of the contemporary music industry—and, more specifically, within the contemporary musical genres that contextualize her: African American female performers who draw similar audiences and levels of visibility. Identifying Gray's peer group according to genre, however, is difficult, as Gray transcends musical genres. Her sound has been described as an unusual hybrid of rhythm and blues, hip-hop, soul, jazz, and funk, holding wide appeal for mainstream—and largely white—audiences, to the extent that she is notable for being more popular with white audiences than with Black (Pantsios, 2000; Samuels, 2001). Gray is not alone in this regard, however; in fact, a number of African American female singer/songwriters from the respective (and, in some cases, fused) genres that Gray encompasses with popular appeal to mainstream audiences may still be considered as Gray's contemporaries—for example, Mariah Carey, Mary J. Blige, Alicia Keys, and Whitney Houston. Three of her contemporaries, however—Beyoncé, Erykah Badu, and Lauryn Hill—emerge as particularly relevant to Gray's performance because of the highly distinctive, often "retro" aesthetic that characterizes each, showcasing via contrast the distinctive camp nature of Gray's performance and thus establishing a semiotic context for her critical potential.

At the time of this writing, Beyoncé is, arguably, the most popular African American female singer for mainstream audiences within the genre of hip-hop music. Like Gray, Beyoncé has crossover appeal in terms of genre and audience. Also like Gray, Beyoncé is associated with a particular style, albeit one that differs significantly from Gray's. Known as much for her sex appeal as for her music, Beyoncé permeates popular culture in various media venues. From the inception of her career as lead singer for the popular "girl group" Destiny's Child (often characterized in the press as hearkening back to the Supremes), Beyoncé has achieved even greater fame and notoriety as a solo artist and actress, via her roles in popular films such as *The Pink Panther* remake and *Austin Powers in Goldmember,* where she played Foxxy Cleopatra, a parody of a blaxploitation female action star.

Interestingly, both of these films, and her characters in them, are appropriately characterized as camp; this is especially true of Beyoncé's "soul sistah" role in *Austin Powers in Goldmember.* Given the lack of dimension and complexity to that character, as well as her passivity, however, it is better understood as an example of camp lite. This same quality is apparent in many of Beyoncé's stage and music video performances, where she might aesthetically reference cultural icons like Tina Turner or Diana Ross; the camp sensibility is certainly present in these cases, but it is firmly contained within a straightforward rendering of the sexual appeal of that character. Indeed, Beyoncé's sexuality as publicly discoursed, in general, is steeped in accessibility and passivity with a touch of exoticism, highly palatable to mainstream audiences and inoffensive to sensibilities highly informed by whiteness. Gray's aggressive, intimidating, and "take-charge" sexual persona, along with the unmistakable and unapologetic Black aesthetic in which it is steeped, stands in sharp relief to this seductive, conventionally feminine and "acceptably Black" sexuality, which functions as a foil for her camp performance. In fact, this distinction is focused and heightened when comparing Beyoncé's tongue-in-cheek performance of a 1970s Black aesthetic to Gray's: both constitute camp, but the depth and complexity—and thus the critical potential—of Gray's performance marks it as qualitatively distinct.

Erykah Badu is another of Gray's contemporaries who serves as a foil for her camp performance. In fact, parallels are often drawn between Badu and Gray primarily because of the strong Black aesthetic that characterizes them, although they each realize it differently. Both are African American singer/songwriters, and both have a unique musical style and visual aesthetic—the two have even collaborated musically (on the track "Sweet Baby" for Gray's *Id* album). Like Gray's, Badu's musical style is described as a unique mixture of rhythm and blues, hip-hop, soul, and jazz, and like Gray, Badu has crossover appeal, facilitating her success with mainstream audiences. Badu's Black aesthetic, however, which is powerfully Afrocentric, differs markedly from Gray's. Given to wearing African head wraps, long dreadlocks, beaded necklaces, and enormous bracelets, Badu's style is evocative of powerful, regal African women—feminine, strong, mystical, and infused with spirituality. Her aesthetic is not rendered at all parodically; on the contrary, her performance is rendered as "authentic" to the extent that it is presented in the public discourse as representative of her deeply personal, spiritual beliefs and identity. Gray's Black urban, Soul Train masculinity, with its highly parodic and cartoonish qualities, stands in sharp contrast to the reverence, gravity, and mystery that characterize Badu's style; indeed, that contrast contributes significantly to the camp sensibility of Gray's performance.

Yet a third contemporary of Gray's helps to establish the context for her camp performance via contrast. Described as one of the "leaders in the genre of hip-hop soul" (Toure, 1998), pushing the aesthetic envelope as well as the commercial, Lauryn Hill is an African American performer who, like Gray, has achieved popularity with mainstream audiences with her unique sound. In 1998, Hill burst onto the music scene with her hotly anticipated album, *The Miseducation of Lauryn Hill*. This debut album established Hill as a remarkably talented singer with an assertive, confrontational political consciousness, including a sophisticated awareness of race, and Hill became known more for her political messages than for her aesthetics. That aesthetic is drawn from the same 1970s era that informs Gray's performance, but it lacks the masculinity and is infused with more than a touch of rastafari: crocheted berets, cut-offs, dreadlocks, bell-bottoms, love beads, and lots of denim. But where Gray's performance is rife with incongruity and inconsistency, Hill's visual aesthetic is entirely consistent with her political consciousness, eschewing the campiness of her performance in favor of a reading of it as "authentic." Her lyrics address a myriad of sociopolitical issues, ranging from the struggles of single motherhood to the relationship of class to race. This, along with her work as the founder of a nonprofit organization dedicated to improving the quality of life for inner-city children, helps to confirm Hill's identity as activist in addition to performer. This imagery stands in sharp contrast to Gray, whose Black-funk sensibility clearly alludes to "Black Power" politics but is part of a kaleidoscopic pastiche that calls forth altogether different benchmarks for interpretation. Against Hill's grave and insightful body of work, Gray's comic performances of retro Black urban masculinity are endowed with a strong camp sensibility in part via their juxtaposition with Hill's more serious, politically inflected persona.

While foils such as Beyoncé, Badu, and Hill provide the context necessary for defining camp performances, other figures serve as semiotic anchors for them. In some instances, as we will argue in the case of Gwen Stefani, one individual can be identified as the anchor for the performance. In Gray's case, however, no single performer anchors her. Gray is evocative aesthetically of the 1970s P-Funk movement, but those musical artists (e.g., Parliament, Funkadelic, George Clinton, Bootsy Collins) do not represent the hybrid music associated with Gray, nor are they salient figures for contemporary audiences.[2] A more likely referent is Betty Davis, the late 1960s "funk femme fatale" perhaps best known for her wild sexuality, association with drugs and Jimi Hendrix, and brief marriage to jazz musician Miles Davis (Wang, 2001a). Indeed, critics have noted the similarities between Gray and Davis, commenting that Davis provides a foundation for Gray and that Gray embodies the quintessence of Davis's spirit, both musically and aesthetically. Davis's blending of blues, funk, and jazz in a unique voice that "beat you up, shook you down and left you begging for more" was eerily similar to Gray's idiosyncratic vocal style (Wang, 2001b). Her aesthetic of excess also rivaled Gray's spectacular presentation. Distinct in style from other soul singers of her time, Davis's costumes "went from rocking Daisy Duke shorts and cosmic go-go boots to an Afro-futurist Egyptian costume to jet black fishnet stockings with matching teddy" (Wang, 2001b). Equally excessive was her performance of female sexuality; her voracious sexual appetite, sated best via kinky sex, and her volatile sexual power created, as in Gray's case, a mesmerizing expression of female sexuality. The similarities between these two eccentric "funktresses" are many, but Davis's ability to function as an anchor for Gray's performance is limited in that Davis is not familiar to contemporary mainstream audiences; even at the height of her career, given the outré nature of her work, she remained on the periphery of popular culture, known primarily to Black audiences but never becoming a household name. In the late 1970s, she dropped out of sight from the musical scene, falsely rumored to have died from drug overdose. Her absence in popular cultural consciousness inhibits her ability to effectively anchor Gray's camp performance.

An artist much more available in contemporary popular cultural memory and similar—perhaps even inspirational—to Gray is the late Rick James, the early 1980s funk artist best known for his excessive aesthetic and highly sexualized persona, epitomized in his popular hits, "Super Freak" and "Give It to Me, Baby." Like Gray's, James's defining feature was excess, in both demeanor and visual aesthetic. His dress was notably outrageous; in platform shoes, sequined jackets, and wide-brimmed hats, he embodied the mack daddy stereotype. His deportment was excessive, as well; cashing in on the mainstream audience's appetite for pre-AIDS sex and unrestrained drug use, James promoted both in his lyrics, finding success until he was jailed for his drug addiction and physical abuse of women. The introduction of the term *freak* in popular parlance, in reference to irrepressible female sexuality, is attributed to him, made popular through his song of the same name:

> She's a very kinky girl
> The kind you don't take home to mother
> She will never let your spirits down
> Once you get her off the street.

It is this intimate association of James with the term *freak* that enables him to serve as an immediate and powerful semiotic frame for Gray's performance.

Indeed, Gray inhabits the freak persona in ways entirely consistent with James's depiction; however, ironically, and largely by dint of the reference, she also inhabits *James's* persona in terms of his aesthetic and performative excesses. As a contemporary icon, James contextualizes and grounds Gray's performance—not simply as a referent but as a foundation. Notable, of course, is the fact that he is a man, which may well speak to the fact that, save for the relatively forgotten Betty Davis, there are no women that serve this function in the popular consciousness, which speaks to the relative invisibility of Black women historically in popular culture and the rigid conventions that defined them when they were represented. But this also enhances the camp aesthetic, insofar as Gray both models James's sexist and misogynist concept of the freak *and* appropriates his very persona in doing so, turning conventionally gendered—and raced—conventions and expectations on their heads. In accordance with camp sensibility, Gray's comic performances of retro Black urban masculinity/female sexual freak are done with a "wink," revealing just a hint of critical distance between the performer and that which is performed.

MackFreak

In Gray's case, as in the cases of Xena and Karen Walker, the camp features of trope, spectacle, and anchors and foils culminate in an expression of sexual alterity. Interestingly, much of Gray's performance is masculine, from the masculine trope she borrows to her use of a Black male aesthetic to the masculine anchor that grounds her performance. But hers is not a "drag king" performance, a term used by Halberstam (1998)to describe the performance of women as men. Such femme pretenders, says Halberstam, create theater in a manner not unlike drag queens, performing in hyperbolic style elements of masculinity (e.g., pinstripe suit and goatee) and culminating in a dramatic revelation of their "true" gender: "Whereas a few male drag performers create drag drama by pulling off their wigs or dropping their voices a register or two, the femme pretender often blows her cover by exposing her breasts or ripping off her suit in a parody of classic striptease" (Halberstam, 1998, p. 249). Gray's performance of masculinity is different, however, in that there is no exposure of a "secret" gender. Rather, Gray's use of masculinity presents a particular articulation of sexuality: the embodiment of a hypermasculine Black-funk sensibility with an excessive freak aesthetic, resulting in a curious presentation of Black sexuality unhooked from gendered moorings. Such a performance of female masculinity that unhinges masculinity from maleness is consistent with Halberstam's discussion of the critical potential found in certain drag king performances, particularly those that denaturalize masculinity. Gray's coalescence of hypermasculinity and excessively sexualized femininity creates a discursive site of resistance for sexual alterity.

Although Black women historically have been invisible in popular culture, their contemporary representations—while perhaps more available—are problematic in terms of the sexuality expressed.[3] They are presented as blatantly sexual but vulnerable beings dominated in abusive relationships by their men, as in the case, for example, of Tina Turner and Whitney Houston, or they are depicted as divas whose sexuality is packaged, exoticized, and marketed to primarily white audiences, as in the case of Beyoncé (and Destiny's Child) and En Vogue. In either case, the Black women are not in control of their sexuality. In the case of hip-hop, Black female singers like Li'l Kim, Eve, and Missy Elliot present images of sexual agency. Their representations are troublesome, too, however, as they presuppose the commodification of sexuality, claiming "punanny as their most valuable asset" in obtaining wealth and power à la prostitution; thus, they fall short of critical effect (Morgan, 1997, p. 132). Finally, even those artists who exhibit a more complex Black female sexuality, such as Erykah Badu and Lauryn Hill, are coded in problematic ways—exotic and "other," as in the case of Badu's Afrocentric femininity, or politically and intellectually volatile, as in the example of Hill. Gray's hypermasculine, excessive performance, contextualized in its particular manner, however, signifies a challenge to these hegemonic representations of Black female sexuality.

Gray's camp performance of a masculine aesthetic serves a particular purpose in terms of articulating sexuality. Specifically, the primary means by which this critical potential is realized is through her ironic and parodic amalgamation of the mack daddy trope and the freak aesthetic. Gray appropriates the trope, in which she turns the commodification often assigned to Black female sexuality explicitly on its head. Whereas numerous Black artists, especially female rappers, have toyed with this notion of commodified sexuality, they have done so by positioning themselves in the "whore" position, albeit a whore with agency. The critical potential in this move is mitigated, however, in the reification of an age-old conception of female sexuality as that which is valuable only or primarily in its availability for others' consumption or as a means to an end. In co-opting the mack daddy trope, Gray fashions Black sexual power not predicated on access or vulnerability.

The appropriation of the trope in and of itself, however, does not present critical potential in that it employs a Black sexuality within the confines of commodification. Rather, it is the potent, highly ironic, and "spectacular" combination of the mack daddy persona with the freak aesthetic that facilitates sexual alterity. The freak aesthetic that Gray displays is coded as feminine, in accordance with the understanding of the term *freak* popularized by Rick James. As established earlier, a *freak* is a woman with an insatiable sexual appetite, a bad girl ("the kind you don't take home to mother") who rejects societal conventions for sex by giving into her sexual desires for kinky or alternative sexual practices and making herself readily available to men—anytime, anywhere. In this sense, she is coded as "abnormal" in her sexuality. Her insanity, however, is one that entices and enthralls men, who reap the benefits of its exploitation.

Rather than rejecting the "freakish" feminine aesthetic because of its problematical positioning of women's sexuality, Gray embraces the style in a larger-than-life fashion. In so doing, she retains a degree of female sexuality in her otherwise hypermasculine persona. Gray sidesteps the exploitation implied in the freak, however, by hyperbolizing the insanity associated with the freak aesthetic. Gray's insanity is not just wacky, mesmerizing in its nonsensical exhibition; it is perilous, even life-threatening. Whenever the freak appears, there is also the potential for extreme violence, not just "rough sex," as evidenced in "Gimme All Your Lovin' or I Will Kill You":

> Gimme all your lovin'
> Or I will kill you
> Put one through your head
> Gimme all your lovin'
> Or I will kill you
> And cry when you're dead.

In embellishing the insanity that comes with being a freak, Gray uses an aesthetic of excess to appropriate an otherwise problematic presentation of female sexuality, thwarting the easy objectification and fetishization that typically comes with the presentation of female sexuality. As such, the freak emerges as powerful and in control; her male partners are subject to *her* whims, pliant in the face of *her* desire. Insanity predicated on lack of sexual control is thus reconfigured in an apparently incommensurate way to endow Gray's freak with the utmost control. Thus, the erratic nature of the freak— the freedom that comes with the irrational logic of the aesthetic—provides a discursive instability that permits alterity. Further, the affiliation of insanity with female sexuality in particular adds an additional layer of meaning to Gray's performance. Female sexuality, typically defined in terms of its desirability for and accessibility to men, operates according to a different logic here. The combination of the masculine trope and feminine aesthetic results in more than just an embodiment of dichotomous masculinity/femininity found in gender performances à la drag. This is neither a "feminine man" nor a "masculine woman" nor even a performance of bizarre androgyny. Rather, Gray's performance showcases sexuality that is incongruously degendered in its excessive embrace of gendered tropes. The fusion created in the amalgamation effectively destabilizes both the trope and the aesthetic, unhinging their conventionally gendered meanings—particularly the agency associated with each—and thus enabling the expression of sexual alterity.

The critical potential of Gray's camp performance realized via the dissonant amalgamation of the mack daddy trope and the freak aesthetic depends on a certain primary response to the highly stylized trope. For the tension to work in the service of more than the reification of Black male sexuality as dangerous, exotic, and "other," the trope must be coded in a manner that is palatable to mainstream—primarily white—audiences. Gray enables the mainstream reception of Black male sexuality in her rendering of the trope as amusing. In her cartoonish embellishment of the pimp, she codes it as accessible, as "user friendly" for mainstream audiences who otherwise might find the trope disconcerting or even threatening. Whereas Black audiences may view Gray's performance on its own terms as an appropriation of Black culture or a dangerous reification of negative stereotypes of African Americans, white audiences are perhaps more inclined to find humor in Gray's parody of a Black male stereotype. Gray's exaggeration not only renders it laughable and thus palatable for broader mainstream, largely white audiences but, in so doing, strips the expression of Black male sexuality of its usual authority. The latter move is particularly significant for Black female sexuality, typically defined heteronormatively as subordinate to male sexuality.

The aesthetic dimensions of Gray's camp performances may be a primary reason for her popularity with white audiences. Further, the critical potential, expressed as sexual alterity, inherent in Gray's camp performance may be more likely realized with white audiences than Black ones. Critics (e.g., Browne, 2001) have noted that marketing Gray as an African American freak is a little "unsettling" for mainstream audiences, who find Gray mysteriously compelling in her spectacular exhibition of stereotypes. It is this very unsettling of discursive meanings accomplished through Gray's camp performance that renders Gray's performance camp with critical potential.

6

Gwen Stefani

Camp Vamp

Singer and songwriter Gwen Stefani made her pop-culture debut as lead singer of the band No Doubt, with the release of their first album, *Tragic Kingdom,* in 1995. The success of that album launched the group and Stefani, the only woman in the band, into the national and international spotlight, where they have remained as they continue to create highly successful music. Although the group has not permanently disbanded, in recent years Stefani has independently collaborated on songs with a number of popular artists, including Eve and Moby, to great critical and popular acclaim, and she has also embarked on a very successful solo career. In 2004, she released a highly successful solo album, *Love. Angel. Music. Baby. (LAMB),* which accelerated her already high profile, making her arguably one of the most popular contemporary musicians of the decade. In addition to her musical talent and success, Stefani has garnered considerable attention for her distinctive and trendsetting fashion sense. Described as "the poster girl for do-it-yourself chic" (Sherman, 2001, p. 271), Stefani—a conventionally attractive young woman—is wont to pair sequined bras with striped athletic pants and trainers or to wear nothing but frothy pink dresses for a period of time; she has dyed her hair various outrageous colors, from platinum to fuchsia to cobalt blue, and she wears it in distinctive ways—for instance, in pigtail braids or pulled back with a retro 1950s flowered headband; her makeup is vivid. Stefani has noted that her fashion incentive is to "look like a cartoon character" (Sherman, 2001, p. 271), a goal arguably realized with the 2005 launching of her own clothing line, LAMB (coinciding with the title of her solo album), to considerable fanfare and success. Marketed through Nordstrom department stores, its style reflected the dynamic and bizarre blending of fashion sensibilities that is Stefani's hallmark—a mix of Harajuku (referencing the highly "self-expressive," animé-inspired, and extreme Tokyo fashion scene, after the shopping district of the same name) and Alice in Wonderland, both of which, Stefani has noted, "I'm really into right now" (Huwig, 2005, p. 21).

Stefani's performances onstage and in music videos are similarly distinctive, often characterized alternately by intense and/or comic vamping, aggressive kick-boxing, diva "vogue"-ing, scrambling on top of sound systems, or glaring defiantly or staring vacuously into the camera. Although some dismiss her charm as "skank appeal" (Shoemer, 1997, p. 72), most have embraced Stefani as an innovative trendsetter. Selected as one of *People* magazine's 50 Most Beautiful People in 1997, she has been described as "bombshell meets goofball"; "a little bit Betty Boop, a little bit Buffy"; and "girly girl, meet riot grrrl" (Ali, 2001, p. 52; Gwen Stefani, 1997, p. 103; Toure, 2000, p. 69). Notable in nearly all characterizations of Stefani's style is its over-the-top, discordant, caricaturish, and totally unique quality; the fusing of seemingly not only incommensurate but entirely unrelated ideas, eras, icons, and sensibilities, with respect to music, fashion, and performance, is Stefani's stock in trade. While pastiche thoroughly characterizes Stefani's public persona, however, we suggest that a logical configuration of decidedly camp images and references can be identified in her performance—specifically, a constellation of the trope that frames it, the nature of the spectacle that characterizes it, and the anchors and foils that help to define it. In Stefani's case, that logic culminates in the articulation of a collective version of female sexuality that is certainly alternative and even resistive to convention—one distinguished by multiplicity, dynamism, agency, and power.

Sex and the Vintage Girl

The public persona that has become Gwen Stefani's trademark and that arguably alone secures her performance as camp is modeled on the vintage sex symbol, especially in the vein of Marilyn Monroe and Jayne Mansfield and also as modeled by, for instance, Jean Harlow and Betty Grable—her evocations of them, in fact, do much to qualify her performance as camp. Stefani assumes many aesthetic markers that align her with that trope; she is featured in a number of publicity shots that are clearly evocative of famous photographs of, for instance, Monroe and Grable, wearing the same clothing, hairstyle, and posing the same way; the cover of No Doubt's album *Tragic*

Kingdom featured her in just such a vintage style. Indeed, perhaps as a result of the powerful allusion to the vintage sex symbol in her public persona, Stefani was cast as Jean Harlow in the film version of Howard Hughes's life, *The Aviator*. But the reference to the vintage sex symbol is consistently apparent in Stefani's camp performance, especially on a visual level; although her hair color has ranged across the spectrum, she is most frequently available to media audiences as a platinum blonde, and her hair is almost always styled in the ultrafeminine, "soft curls" coif of the stereotypical—especially 1950s—blonde bombshell of a bygone era, regardless of its color. Her face, too, is highly reminiscent of these women in terms of how it is made up— featuring exaggerated, extremely vivid shades of lipstick, eye shadow, blush, and false eyelashes—as well as in terms of how it is typically lit: Stefani tends to be photographed and videotaped (for music videos) in an extreme white light, which renders her skin extremely white, her hair (typically) extremely platinum, and her makeup extremely garish, very much in keeping with the aesthetic of publicity and film shots of, for instance, Monroe, Mansfield, West, and Harlow.

Stefani also is characterized by many of the same ultrafeminine markers commonly associated with these women, especially her dress. Although her fashion sense is quite eclectic, staples of her wardrobe consistently feature stereotypically "sexy," feminine fabrics that were popular among celebrities like Monroe and Mansfield, like chiffon and sequins, worn in ways that accentuate her body—they are typically tight fitting and revealing— and, often, they are conspicuously vintage items: poodle-skirt dresses, brassieres, bustiers, and so forth. In addition, very much in the manner of Jayne Mansfield in particular, Stefani at one point was strongly associated with the color pink—it was featured prominently, even exclusively, in her clothing, in her music videos, and, as noted, in her hair, on occasion. In addition, Stefani often is featured with pink or red hearts onstage, in videos, and in her dress; the "valentine" heart is commonly associated with femininity, and in conjunction with the manifold other signifiers, it is especially reminiscent of the particularly sexy femininity of Mansfield and, to a lesser extent, Monroe, whose sexualities were commonly associated and even conflated with this icon of romantic love.

Also like these sex symbols of a bygone age, Stefani exhibits a blatant sexuality in terms of how she uses and positions her body; she poses and moves provocatively. In her music videos and stage performances, for instance, usually dressed in some variety of revealing clothing, Stefani typically gyrates sensuously and thrusts her hips. In music videos, she often rolls about, semiclothed, on a bed or on the ground; or she may simply stand provocatively on a street corner in a manner clearly designed to evoke prostitution. Although her physical performance is more blatantly sexual than those performances of the trope on which she is modeled, this dissonance arguably has more to do with the sensibilities of the respective eras in which those performances occurred. In any event, Stefani's sexuality and her apprehension as a sexual object are key to audiences' engagement with her and serve as further warrants for her relationship to the sex-symbol trope.

Finally, Stefani's references to the trope of bygone sex symbols are secured by virtue of the demeanor that she conveys, aside from the visual dimensions of her performance. Stefani consistently articulates a feminine naiveté that, even if it is not exclusive to the sex-symbol trope, is consistent with it. While Stefani's visual aesthetics, such as pink hearts and clothing, contribute to this persona, it is also apparent in her "girlish" demeanor: she often pouts, wears her hair in pigtails, and sucks on lollipops. In addition, her voice is quite girlish, not only in tone but—especially—in its expressiveness. For instance, in the song "I'm Just a Girl," she expresses vocally her inferior girlish status in a voice befitting that station; she also references children's scenarios in which girls are excluded from boys' activities, cultivating her innocent, naive persona. The song "Underneath It All" similarly articulates just such a persona, chronicling the determinedly romantic, highly unrealistic, and very naive love of a woman for a man who clearly doesn't reciprocate her affection. This particular representation of femininity, although not exclusive to the sex-symbol trope, was certainly modeled by women of that ilk, especially in the cases of Marilyn Monroe and Jayne Mansfield; their distinctly feminine guilelessness, naiveté, and subsequent vulnerability and accessibility were complemented highly and contributed greatly to their sex appeal. Indeed, their conflation of these dynamics was arguably the hallmark of their sex-symbol persona; Stefani's similar fusion of a girlish persona with her sexuality thus effectively establishes the sex symbol as the trope on which her performances are modeled.

Nonetheless, Stefani's performance constitutes camp as opposed to a simple appropriation or even homage to the sex-symbol trope, and that sensibility inheres as much in deviance from the trope as it does in straight-forward mimicry of it. Much of this deviance, not surprisingly, is a consequence of the spectacle that characterizes Stefani's performance; however, other features not readily understood as spectacle are responsible for that distinction as well. Chief among these is Stefani's propensity for transformation; although the qualities that characterize Stefani's performance as predicated on the sex-symbol trope are consistently available, they are featured in a variety of manifestations, many of them bizarre, both within and between specific performances. For instance, during Stefani's noted "pink" phase, that image was nonetheless quite consistent with and complementary to qualities and signifiers commonly associated with vintage sex symbols, especially given that Stefani, like those women, similarly conflated those markers with an overtly sexual persona. But Stefani is notorious for changing her image; during her career, she has also adopted a tough "street broad" persona, which typically has featured her wearing a beret with her hair in a long braid; low-slung, tight-fitting jeans; and a skimpy halter top. Conversely, she has also appeared, especially in stage performances, in trainers, athletic pants, athletic bra, and fingerless leather grip gloves; and as a "hippie chick" flower child, replete with bell-bottoms and psychedelic accessories. In a more recent incarnation, a distinct "Alice in Wonderland" aesthetic prevailed, replete with platinum pigtails, striped stockings, and pinafore dress. Across these various guises, however, she retains a sex-symbol sensibility stylistically, lyrically, performatively, and even aesthetically—that is, in terms of her hair, makeup, and naive feminine demeanor. That Stefani liberally manipulates the sex-symbol reference even as she maintains it as an important feature of her camp performance ensures an apprehension of that persona precisely as performed or constructed—that is, it asserts what Babuscio (1999) would identify as the theatricality of Stefani's performance.

Largely related to Stefani's metamorphoses, another point on which her performance diverges from simple appropriation or emulation of the vintage sex symbol is the fact that her dress—although frequently reminiscent in many respects of the dress, fabrics, and textures of the sex symbols on which her camp performance is predicated—often constitutes a distraction by virtue of its excessiveness. This excess is a primary feature of the spectacle that characterizes Stefani's performance, to be discussed momentarily; however, it is also relevant at this point because the sheer excessiveness of dress and fabrics almost exclusively associated with the sex symbol—in light of its contextualization within a sexualized performance—also serves to underscore the parodic nature of that performance. For instance, during her pink phase, Stefani wore extremely over-the-top tight pink chiffon dresses and pink satin pumps, her hair arranged in a classic 1950s wave; she typically completed the outfit with a matching chiffon scarf that trailed behind her for several yards. She has often appeared in clothing—for instance, pantsuits—in an intense heart print, and she often sports sequined heart bobby pins in her hair. She also often wears conventionally soft and lacy feminine fabrics in an extremely revealing manner, as well; for instance, in her music videos, she will appear dressed in gauzy, filmy material that is very form fitting, with her entire torso revealed. Similarly, she might assume the character of a streetwalker, wearing tight striped pants and a tight satin top, poised against a streetlight; but her face and hair are concealed by, respectively, large sunglasses and a demure scarf, classic 1950s feminine accoutrements, thus ensuring references to that era and to female sexuality, conflating the two in such a way that the allusion to the sex symbol, even in a novel context, is established. Stefani's simultaneous clear and consistent invocation and modification of the 1950s sex-symbol trope establishes her performance as camp; even as it confirms that trope as the premise on which that performance is based, it simultaneously distinguishes the performance from simple mimicry.

Stefani also is distinctive from the trope on which she models her performance with regard to a confrontational dimension to her demeanor. This may appear to contradict the feminine naiveté that is a consistent and significant feature of her performance, but, in fact, it does not; rather, Stefani manages to fuse the two in such a way that the allusion to the trope is secured even as it is modified. The confrontational aspect of Stefani's performance largely inheres in the fact that she consistently engages in sustained eye contact with the camera (and thus the viewer) whenever she performs, either onstage or in music videos. This may seem a rather minor detail, but it stands in sharp contrast to the demure, passive, notably averted gaze of many sex symbols—all the better to render them as sexual objects of desire. Even when those sex symbols established a gaze, it was almost never sustained; rather, the women would quickly, demurely look away, an action likely to preserve an apprehension of them as accessible and vulnerable. But

Stefani's gaze is constant, unflinching, and often on the level of a glare; she fixes the camera in her sights as she sings, never wavering, even when she is featured—as she is in some music videos—rolling about on the ground or in bed. Stefani is frequently depicted in a position higher than the viewer; although others have noted that this is a standard sexualizing photographic and filmic technique that mimics the sexual fetish of looking up a woman's dress, in Stefani's case, she is never wearing a dress or a skirt when this happens. Furthermore, she maintains eye contact with the camera throughout this, a fact that belies the intent of the shot as conventionally employed, which relies on an unsuspecting female rendered the object of an illicit gaze. In Stefani's performance, her visual height advantage, in conjunction with her unrelenting gaze and the fact that she is wearing pants, reads as a measure of control, even as she conveys a girlish pout or wounded innocence. Lyrically, as well, confrontation is paired with the vulnerability and accessibility of the trope, thus effectively tweaking it; for instance, during her stage performance of the song "I'm Just a Girl," the pouty chorus, which features the title of the song as the primary lyric, is alternated with Stefani's shrieking, "Fuck you, I'm a girl!" Her successful single "I Ain't no Hollaback Girl" is veritably dripping with assertiveness and confrontation, yet it is paired in the music video with trademark Stefani "come hither" platinum-blonde, sex-kitten naiveté. Again, these conflicting dynamics function simultaneously to secure Stefani's allusion to the sex-symbol trope even as they establish her deviance from it; together, they qualify the performance as camp. Moreover, the spectacle and contextual characters that further define that performance endow that camp sensibility with transgressive potential.

Hypergirl

As demonstrated in her invocation and "tweaking" of the trope of the vintage sex symbol, spectacle is Stefani's stock in trade, and it is this aspect that secures her performance as camp, as it is the nexus for the very irony, parody, and theatricality that have been identified as the hallmarks of camp (Babuscio, 1999). As with the other contemporary, potentially resistive camp icons we have assessed, spectacle is specifically and prominently characterized in Stefani's case by the twin axes of excess and juxtaposition. Certainly, a primary component of Stefani's spectacle is aesthetic excess, which is especially available in her physical presentation. Her dress, for instance, is consistently excessive; she often wears bizarre clothing, distinctive typically in terms of its extremely bright colors, shiny fabrics, and caricaturish qualities. She has similarly adopted extreme, cartoonish versions of, variously, a streetwise "tough broad" image, which featured her in lots of leather, fringes, chains, and a beret; and an exotic dancer, replete with a pantsuit made of netting with numerous strategic holes throughout, topped off with a red feather boa and performed within a giant red heart outline. Stefani typically presents thoroughly thematic performances onstage and in her music videos, yet another marker of the excess that characterizes her particular brand of camp. In her live performance for the 2003 Super Bowl halftime show, for instance, Stefani was accompanied by dozens of cheerleaders in keeping with the occasion and pushing it to a comic extreme. During her pink phase, which coincided with No Doubt's *Return of Saturn* album, the entire tour set was pink, and nearly all of the music videos during this period were shot with a pink cast: as chronicled by Toure (2000) during his interview of the band, "Gwen changes into a long, loose pink dress and slips on a pair of pink flip-flops. Neon pink has, by accident, become the official color of *Return,* a visual mantra for Gwen, who sports neon-pink hair and, onstage, pink jackets, wristbands and feather boas" (p. 69). In the music video "A Simple Kind of Life," Stefani was dressed in an over-the-top wedding dress and surrounded by heart shapes to convey romantic love; in the music video for "Luxurious," she is featured in an outfit highly reminiscent of Carmen Miranda, swathed in a tight-fitting sarong of a tropical print and sporting an elaborate headdress. As a final example, in the music video "Underneath It All," Stefani's character is tracked through a gradual shedding of various sexual personas that begin with a caricature of the femme fatale (lots of black, seamed stockings and garter, high heels, jewelry); progress through those of the exotic dancer (feather boas, heart props, strategically torn pantsuit) and hooker (provocatively posed on a street corner in tight Capri pants, high-heeled pumps, and a filmy lime-green top); and conclude in the vulnerable love-struck girl, wearing very little if any makeup, in her white bedroom, alternately bouncing and rolling about on her white bed, wearing white, and filmed in a soft blue-white light. All of these examples point to the extremes to which Stefani's performances are pushed in order to attain an excessive, caricaturish quality.

As noted, Stefani's hair and makeup also are consistently excessive, regardless of the guise du jour that she is adopting. In addition to the extreme colors that have variously characterized her hair, it is often styled in ways that render it conspicuous—for instance, in an extremely long braid; in a bouffant hairdo; or in a vintage spit-curl bob. Similarly, Stefani's lips are always an extremely bright shade of red—her favorite lipstick color is "Gash" (Sherman, 2001, p. 271), and her skin is made up to appear blindingly white, against which her heavily made-up, typically extremely colorful (sometimes sequined) eyes stand out in sharp relief. Regardless of how she presents herself, Stefani is never understated; to the contrary, she assumes an extreme persona that, essentially, constitutes a caricature and thus a parody of whatever image she has adopted. Accordingly, her performance is similarly redolent with theatricality and irony, staple features of camp.

Stefani's camp performance also is established by virtue of her use of juxtaposition, which does much to establish the irony on which that performance turns. Again, this irony is achieved primarily aesthetically, especially through her dress; Stefani is notorious for pairing highly incongruous articles of clothing or for wearing them in unconventional ways. Toure (2000) captures this aesthetic in his description of Stefani during the band's *Return of Saturn* tour: "The tall diva dynamo has her neon-pink hair pulled back and is rocking a black T-shirt with a pink cartoon cat, a white calf-length wool sweater-jacket held together by forty or fifty safety pins, and cranberry-colored toenails. She's the one who fills the room with her presence, playing coy, cartoonish sexy as well as badass hot mama" (p. 68). In other instances, she has frequently appeared onstage in loose athletic pants, trainers, and a conventionally "sexy" sequined bra, fostering a dissonance between conventional expectations of female sexuality and female assertiveness or even anti-sexuality: passive versus active, object versus subject. She has also appeared in bikini bottoms worn over baggy jeans, again recontextualizing an article of clothing typically associated with the sexualized female body by virtue of positioning it against its antithesis; she has appeared at award shows and the like dressed in, for instance, a conventional evening gown and combat boots. At other times, juxtaposition in Stefani's case does not simply turn on antithesis but on apparently random, unrelated pairings of articles of clothing or accessories. For instance, in her music video "Underneath It All," which chronicles Stefani's metamorphosis through several sexual but highly distinctive personas, she wears athletic gear while sporting a very large and ornate headdress reminiscent of warriors of the Roman Empire.

Juxtaposition is apparent in Stefani's performance in a variety of other ways, as well. She will pair colors, patterns, and textures that are highly incompatible, such as vividly striped red and white "candy cane" tights with sneakers, blue sequined short shorts, and a bikini top; or bell-bottom jeans, adorned with hand-painted words like *love* and *sex*, worn with an elegant silk bustier. Incongruence by way of juxtaposition also is apparent insofar as although Stefani is almost always featured in very revealing, very tight, barely-there bras, bikini tops, halter tops, and bustiers, she is extremely small breasted—she has absolutely no cleavage to speak of and almost no breasts. The fact that this physical feature, a staple of female sexuality in this culture, is blatantly flaunted despite its literal absence and in the context of Stefani's highly sexual, provocative dancing is more than a little ironic and arguably constitutive of parody. In some instances, the juxtaposition inherent in Stefani's performance is a consequence of eclecticism, as noted, but it still turns on a fundamental dissonance that functions ironically and points up the theatricality of that performance. For example, Stefani has been known to wear a *bindi* (a single jewel ornament) on her forehead and sometimes *barwatta* (jewels arranged over both eyebrows), traditional feminine religious symbols of the Hindu culture. Their appearance on her person in the context of her heavily made-up face, platinum blonde hair (sometimes arranged in a random series of tiny topknots all over her head), highly sexualized (in many respects, even if that sexualization is tweaked) demeanor, and quintessentially U.S. persona creates extreme dissonance. Another example of this sort of juxtaposition is apparent in the band's "A Simple Kind of Life" music video, in which Stefani, wearing a wedding dress, is featured running from the tuxedoed men of the wedding party, singing in front of a giant birth-control-pill dispenser, and standing in a roomful of tens of thousands of wedding cakes, which the male band members proceed to destroy violently. Again, as apparent in this example, juxtaposition predicated on irony and unexpected, sometimes bizarre, configurations are hallmarks of Stefani's performance.

Yet another way in which juxtaposition informs Stefani's performance is in her lyrics, especially as they emerge against her performances and music videos. For instance, and perhaps most obviously, in her song "I'm Just a

Girl" those lyrics are themselves rife with sarcasm, sung in the petulant tones of a young girl; Stefani chronicles her inferiority, albeit satirically, simultaneously implying her inability to be otherwise: "that's all that you'll let me be." Her music video, however, features a physically strong woman (Stefani) repeatedly frustrated in her various endeavors by boys and men. When Stefani performs this song onstage, she always includes a coda designed to energize the audience: "Fuck you, I'm a girl! Fuck you, I'm a girl!" (Heath, 1997, p. 38). The explicitly expressed femininity juxtaposed to conventionally unfeminine profanity contributes to a perception of the irony in the song and in Stefani's performance. Irrespective of the way in which it is manifest, the proliferation of juxtaposition as a key feature in Stefani's performance shifts and unsettles conventions and expectations, especially as relevant to female sexuality.

In many ways related to the juxtaposition that characterizes Stefani's camp performance, spectacle inheres in her frequent invocation of masculinity; although femininity—typically, excessive or hyperfemininity—is consistent throughout her public representation, masculinity is featured regularly, sufficient to constitute spectacle especially insofar as it stands in such sharp contrast to the aforementioned femininity. Some of this spectacle is articulated via her dress; as noted, she often appears in clothing more typically associated with men than with women, especially in the music industry, even if she usually pairs that clothing with ultrafeminine articles. For instance, she will wear sweatpants or other athletic gear that clearly has not been tailored to her body; she will wear low-slung, extremely baggy jeans; and she has appeared in the large, chunky jewelry, or "bling," often associated with male African American rappers.

But masculinity is primarily parlayed in terms of Stefani's physical performances. In the first place, her performances onstage and in music videos (e.g., "I'm Just a Girl," "Walking in a Spiderweb," Moby's "South Side," "Hey, Baby, Hey") often feature very physical, often aggressive movements; she will jump, kick, and throw punches as she sings, and she may yell or scream her lyrics during stage performances. She commonly races back and forth across the stage, clambering up giant speakers and jumping back onto the stage. That Stefani's body is relatively muscular and that she is very small breasted complements this physical performance. Her consistently bared torso captures the dissonance of femininity and masculinity very well, significantly more so than the average female musician featured in the mainstream, but it is always visible—very much in keeping with conventions of female sexuality in the contemporary music industry, and Stefani draws much attention to it as a feminine sexual feature in conventional ways, moving it provocatively as she dances. Furthermore, her torso often disappears on top into a revealing, very feminine bra and on bottom into quite masculine, extremely loose pants.

Masculinity is visible in Stefani's demeanor, which is often a product of her physical performance, but it is also apparent even when her physical performance is primarily or entirely feminine. That is, Stefani's camp performance is consistently characterized by confrontation, a characteristic typically associated with men rather than women. This confrontation is achieved largely by virtue of sheer consistency; that is, the confrontational attitude that Stefani projects is consistent across whatever guise she is assuming, be it masculine, ultrafeminine, sexual, vulnerable, or any combination thereof. In part, this is apparent in the lyrics of many of the songs that Stefani sings, like "I'm Just a Girl," "Walking in a Spiderweb," and "Underneath It All"; they are often accusatory, challenging, or satirical, chronicling a woman's dissatisfaction with or cynicism about men in her life. Stefani's vocalization of the lyrics contributes further to the confrontational sensibility; her voice will become louder and more "raw," deviating notably from the melody, as she articulates a particularly unflattering sentiment as her dissatisfaction crystallizes in the song.

As deceptively simple as it may appear, however, Stefani's unremitting eye contact in her music videos and stage performances is responsible for this confrontational demeanor in great measure, especially in the context of music industry conventions that almost exclusively cultivate women as objects to be gazed on, to have narratives projected onto, and to be rendered passively available to an implied male audience. Although Stefani's performance certainly implies a male audience simply by virtue of her consistent resistance to that convention, it concomitantly permits her to resist being positioned as an object, situating her instead as a subject. Accordingly, in contrast to the demure, vulnerable, and thus eminently (sexually) accessible woman fostered by music industry conventions, Stefani's performance endows her with considerable agency. Even when she is featured as unable to control a given scenario—as in, for instance, some of her songs or her music videos, like "A Simple Kind of Life" and "Underneath It All," both of which feature her as love struck but also as ironic and self-reflexive—she nonetheless exercises that agency via sarcastic, sometimes caustic, often unqualified, and always unrelenting commentary. Stefani's performance of masculinity—in conjunction with the excess and juxtaposition that similarly characterize her persona—functions to secure that persona as camp, insofar as irony, parody, and theatricality, under the guise of randomness and chaos, become the axes on which it turns.

No Hollaback Girl

Like Macy Gray, in Stefani's case, her contemporary peers—mainstream female musicians of a similar genre, level of success, and availability to mainstream public audiences—constitute important foils, functioning collectively as the contextual backdrop against which her performance emerges as camp and, more specifically, camp organized against a logic that invites reading of that performance as transgressive. Most prominent among these contemporaries are Britney Spears and Christina Aguilera, both popular female musicians who consistently have been featured with Stefani over the last few years in top-ten record lists, songs, and music videos. Thus, although a number of other women populate the contemporary popular music industry, Spears and Aguilera are the most comparable to Stefani in terms of genre and audience, as well as, to a considerable extent and specifically for our purposes, aesthetics. Drawn against these women, and in tandem with the particular manifestation of trope and spectacle as they occur in Stefani's performance, the camp sensibility that characterizes it—and more to the point, the resistive potential of that performance—is realized.

Like Stefani, Spears and Aguilera both are characterized by youth, beauty, flagrant sexuality, and other manifestations of excess. Spears, indeed, rode a wave of controversy into public consciousness, appearing as a highly sexualized schoolgirl in her music videos at the tender age of fifteen; she has continued to develop her sexual shtick, which often remains controversial in terms of its blatancy, given her extreme popularity with teen and pre-teen girls (who also constitute one of Stefani's major markets). Aguilera appeared on the contemporary popular music scene around the same time as Spears.[1] Although most critics find Aguilera, unlike Spears, to be extremely musically talented, her public persona has developed along the same lines: highly sexualized, as evident in overt and excessive stage and music video performances. Both of these women regularly engage in simulated "exotic" dancing in those performances, complete with extremely revealing dress and props (inspired by the theme of the particular role), for instance, and they often simulate sex with one or several other characters/dancers.

In fact, in addition to genre, audience, and level of success, Stefani's public persona has much in common with those of Spears and Aguilera; in the first place, like them, she uses sexuality and sexual performance as core themes. In addition, the three women share some physical resemblance: young, white,[2] attractive, typically sporting extremely, obviously dyed blonde hair, and they are all noted for the excessiveness of their dress—not only in terms of its sexual character but also in terms of its sheer flamboyance, as apparent in, for example, platform white go-go boots, a two-foot-high headdress studded with rhinestones (in Aguilera's case), and so forth. But Stefani is distinctive in a number of important ways; accordingly, given the superficial similarities that all of these women share, Spears and Aguilera become the landscape for the distinctiveness—and campiness—of Stefani's performance.

Although excess—especially excessive sexuality—is common across the performances of these three women, Stefani's articulation of it is distinctive; whereas Spears and Aguilera certainly push the envelope with respect to their performances on this count, Stefani's excess is manifest in character rather than behavior. Her dress, accessories, and details are precisely crafted in outrageous ways to achieve a particular theme or persona, and sexuality is a feature of that persona, rather than the other way around. Furthermore, Stefani is never depicted in sexual or romantic activity in her videos and performances—while other characters are often featured, they are either band members or characters who appear in ways that contribute to the theme, as when a bevy of cheerleaders appeared to accompany Stefani during her Super Bowl performance or when the Harajuku Girls serve as a bizarre, cartoonish, and thus ironic backdrop to a stage or music video performance. To the contrary, Stefani almost always appears solo, the camera breaking away to feature these other characters.

Excess also is featured in the dress of each of these women; in Stefani's case, it is a hallmark, and this is largely true of Spears and Aguilera as well. Stefani's use of excess in this regard, however, is distinctive on two counts: first, the premise for much of Stefani's excess is, as we have noted, the trope of the vintage sex symbol, which is a consistent thread throughout her various guises and performances. Conversely, although Spears and Aguilera both have donned "retro" looks on occasion, their visual aesthetic tends to be far more reflective of the ultrasexy contemporary heterosexual white girl/woman. Accordingly, by virtue of the reference to the sex-symbol trope, Stefani's performance achieves a measure of irony and parody, even as female sexuality is showcased and celebrated. Second, the outrageous quality of Stefani's dress inheres largely in the juxtaposition that characterizes it so thoroughly: pairing hyperfeminine and masculine articles of clothing; Hindu accoutrements with surfer-girl dress; pigtails, combat boots, and bright yellow secondhand faux-fur jacket with elegant evening wear. Spears and Aguilera, on the other hand, tend to be consistent in their self-presentations, again articulating a coherent version of contemporary overt female sexuality; although sexuality is a key element of Stefani's performance, it consistently occurs in dissonant contexts that ultimately serve to disrupt convention. Put another way, there is a degree of ironic humor, parlayed as playful outrageousness, that pervades Stefani's performance; conversely, while outrageousness and even humor do mark Aguilera's and Spears's performances, their personas over the arc of their careers tend to suggest an investment in being taken "seriously," especially as women—an interest signaled, arguably, by Aguilera's more recent incarnation as a classic (and relatively "classy") 1930s torch singer.

Finally, as noted, a level of confrontation and aggression characterizes Stefani's performance, qualities that are absent in their truest sense from Aguilera's and Spears's performances. Although confrontation is arguably conveyed in their performances as they develop a story of sexual or romantic conquest, it is employed as a means of sexual invitation; for instance, when Aguilera confronts a man in her music video, they immediately engage in very erotic dancing. In addition, both Aguilera and Spears perform very much within the constraints of conventional female sexuality, insofar as they position themselves as passive, sexual objects for an implied male viewer. Their physical performances contribute largely to this, for their performances often mimic precisely conventions of the female exotic dancer. But both women are also characterized by vulnerability and accessibility, parlayed, for instance, by video representations that feature them, forlorn and downcast yet downright sexy, waiting for their implied lovers to appear and restore them to happiness. Spears especially is notable in this regard; her provocative "Lolita" persona continues to be cultivated even as she has entered motherhood and approaches her late twenties—recast perhaps in disturbingly classed ways but retained nonetheless. Conversely, Stefani's performances are rife with confrontation that does not conclude in her sexual availability; her sexuality defies easy access. Furthermore, the sheer outrageousness of her dress as well as her relative lack of endowment deflects the conventional male gaze and thus resists or at least qualifies Stefani's being positioned as a passive object of sexual desire.

Although Spears and Aguilera, as comparable peers in the contemporary music industry, bolster an apprehension of Stefani's performance as camp, other, more physically proximate foils are or have been available and notable in Stefani's case. As lead singer and the only female member of the band No Doubt, Stefani occupied center stage in ways that endowed her with a presumption of agency. How she was constituted in relation to the other band members is significant, however, especially as viewed through the lens of camp. That is, in music videos, album covers, photographs, and interviews, the other members play impassive "straight men" to Stefani's frenetic energy and her eclectic and sometimes bizarre aesthetic. First, in visual representations, rather than being depicted individually, the band members typically are presented as a collectivity hovering in the background. In sharp contrast to Stefani's bright and even jarring plumage, they are attired in nondescript jeans, slacks, and T-shirts or sometimes in suits and ties. Even when they are presented individually, however, as in the music video for "It's My Life," they remain generic and essentially interchangeable—in that video, they each enter Stefani's life only to be systematically killed off by her, and none is really distinguishable from the others.[3] Their passivity relative to Stefani in the public discourse and entertainment fare is a key characteristic as well; they are invariably reactive to her, cultivating a perception that she is a dynamic and powerful agent. This is the case even when evidence to the contrary is available; although Stefani's romantic relationship with guitarist Tony Kanal for several years early in the band's career was fodder for popular coverage, that relationship was very much framed in such a way that she was constructed as the agent, up to and including the dissolution of the relationship—despite her openness about the fact that he terminated the relationship, much to her dismay and devastation (Ali, 2001, 2004; Eliscu, 2005; Toure, 2000). This was perhaps most obvious in her characterization as canny and strategic on the heels of that breakup, as she was credited as using that experience to her benefit, to write and sing several hit songs that set her on the path to a highly successful solo career (Ali, 2004; Eliscu, 2005).

During that solo venture, in fact, Stefani has included as part of her performance shtick—in concert, in music videos, in photographs, and on album covers—an entourage of four apparently Japanese women, or "Harajuku Girls," who also are Stefani's backup dancers. Named after a schoolgirl subculture and Tokyo's famed fashion and shopping district, these women are dressed garishly and made up excessively, "like futuristic comic-book heroines in high-fashion-meets-punk getups—knee-high boots, cutesy mini-dresses, [and] extreme makeup" (Fiore, 2004), a visual manifestation of the contemporary and over-the-top world of consumerism and style (see, e.g., Walker, 2005). Aesthetically, they mirror Stefani, and there is certainly a camp sensibility about them by dint of excess, dissonant ensembles, or actions discordant with visual cues—for instance, the geisha might be strongly evoked in their makeup and behavior, but they may be wearing candy-striped tights with stiletto ankle boots and leather bustiers. This dissonance could suggest some manner of subversive play or parody, in the way that we have suggested that Stefani's performance could be apprehended, with regard to gender and perhaps even as relevant to consumerism. On the other hand, quite unlike Stefani, they are quite passive and reactive, not to mention exoticized and fetishized in arguably problematic ways, invoked as decorative and objects of a voyeuristic gaze. In reality, the four women are "plain Jane American girls," but they only converse in Japanese in public (rumored to be a contractual obligation), and they alter their facial expressions and move their bodies as a unit, "seemingly on cue" (Kubo, 2005, pp. 36–37). Organized precisely in relation to Stefani in terms of their performances (indeed, they appear whether or not the songs, music videos, or public appearances have any relevance to them), their presence clearly hampers a reading of their collective performance as transgressive. But for that very reason, while the exoticization of the Harajuku Girls remains highly problematic on the basis of race, possibly "the worst kind of cultural hijacking" (Kubo, 2005, p. 36), especially as it intersects with gender, the resistive potential of Stefani's camp sensibility as relevant to gender and sexuality is drawn out and more sharply defined—thus realizing their function as foils for such a reading. In this vein, albeit problematically, the Harajuku Girls could well be understood as an embodiment of camp lite, against which resistive camp is drawn and, in this case, literally emerges. At the same time, their presence provides considerable camouflage for that same transgressive potential.

While foils function as the backdrop for Stefani's camp performance, that performance also is defined by an anchor that grounds the performance and endows it with particularly critical significance. For Stefani, that anchor is Madonna. Although Madonna remains active in the mainstream, she is not Stefani's contemporary. Madonna's legacy contributes greatly, nonetheless, to the semiotic context for Stefani's performance. Madonna did and continues to do much to "push the envelope" of female sexuality in mainstream popular culture, especially by venturing performances and images never before available in that context; indeed, so risqué were some of these performances that censorship and withdrawal of sponsorship have been common events throughout Madonna's career. Madonna's performances also have been characterized by some of the same features that qualify Stefani's performances as camp: irony, excess, and satire. For instance, in stage and music video performance, Madonna has parodied Marilyn Monroe; she has appeared dressed in a man's suit under which she sported highly sexualized feminine lingerie; and she has appeared as a female "mack daddy," thus employing, on various occasions, all of Stefani's repertoire staples of excess, juxtaposition, and dissonance. Indeed, these and other features have led Robertson (1996) to identify Madonna as "feminist camp," if problematically so.

It is our contention that although Madonna has had and continues to have camp moments, her performance is not consistently camp, unlike Stefani's case. Arguably, that Madonna is not consistently camp may well be a function of the fact that she was and continues to be an innovator with regard to disrupting the confines of female sexuality in popular culture; because the camp sensibility is often subtle and duplicitous, relying largely on established, shared references and assumptions, it likely would have been less effective than other, more overt means to that end. Indeed, when Madonna does invoke camp, we would submit that it also serves as a means to the end of this very innovation rather than an end unto itself. Nonetheless, both Madonna's innovation on the count of female sexuality and the similarity of her strategies in that regard to Stefani function to contextualize—anchor—Stefani's performance insofar as female sexuality, in particular, emerges as both the nexus and the contested terrain of that performance. That sexuality is a prominent feature of Stefani's performance is clear, even absent its apprehension in the context of Madonna's body of work; however, that context ensures that all other references—to gender, to culture, to style, to era—are understood in terms of their relevance to female sexuality.

As foils and anchors, Britney Spears, Christina Aguilera, the No Doubt band members, the Harajuku Girls, and Madonna all function to endow Stefani's performance with semiotic significance. As foils, Spears and Aguilera ensure an apprehension of Stefani's camp sensibility insofar as the dissonance, satire, and irony that characterize her performance—unlike theirs—become starkly apparent. Albeit in different ways, the No Doubt male band members and the Harajuku Girls serve as benchmarks for Stefani's agency. As an anchor, Madonna ensures that Stefani's performance is apprehended first and foremost as turning on female sexuality as a site of contention. Importantly, without these referents in the broader context of contemporary popular culture, Stefani's performance would likely be lost in the vortex of pastiche, randomness, and self-reflexivity that characterizes that culture; indeed, they are vital, if implicit, components of her camp performance.

Collage Girl

Stefani's camp performance turns on sexuality at every stage, as determined by the trope on which that performance is predicated, the spectacle that characterizes the performance, and the foils and anchor that contextualize it. These elements configure a logic that culminates in a decidedly transgressive representation of female sexuality. Specifically, Stefani's performance constitutes a site of struggle insofar as it negotiates sexuality within conventions of mainstream contemporary popular culture—accordingly, her performance reflects that context to the extent that white, heterosexual, middle-class female sexuality is its locus. Although excessive female sexuality is increasingly familiar and available in that context, such representations do not challenge said conventions so much as they intensify them. The excess that characterizes Stefani's performance, however, in tandem with its other notable qualities, conversely manipulates and challenges those conventions.

Perhaps the most subversive feature of Stefani's performance of female sexuality is that it is infused with agency. As we have argued, this is a marked departure from mainstream conventions that endorse passivity and availability as a cornerstone of acceptable female sexuality, generally articulated in terms of positioning women as objects of sexual desire for an implied male viewer and by virtue of projecting a vulnerable demeanor that establishes their accessibility and tandem inability to resist. Exceptions to this, in fact, generally are evinced as playful or strategic ploys of sexual invitation such that those conventions are ultimately reified and reinforced. In the contemporary music industry of which Stefani is a part, these conventions are readily apparent, both historically, in terms of the tropes on which Stefani draws, and currently, in terms of the anchors and foils that benchmark her persona. As we have established, however, Stefani's performance clearly defies these standards, even as its invokes them; although feminine naiveté is a hallmark feature of that performance, it is coupled with confrontational and even aggressive actions and behaviors that complicate if not belie her accessibility. Similarly, although Stefani's performance is certainly sexualized, categorical objectification of her is complicated by virtue of a variety of disruptive tactics, including her confrontational attitude; her outrageous, excessive dress, which often borders on the bizarre; the incongruity of her dress, actions, behaviors, and various combinations thereof; and the powerful allusions consistently present in her performance to explicit or implied referents that themselves constitute familiar icons of popular culture. All of these strategies resist easy objectification and uncomplicated sexualization of Stefani by at least complicating if not deflecting attention away from the sexual components of her performance. The fact, too, that she is not featured onstage or in music videos as the literal object of another person(s) desire ensures that her agency is not mitigated; rather, she is consistently featured "solo," accompanied only occasionally in the background by her band members. In addition, although many of her song lyrics chronicle her passion for and vulnerability to a lover, those lyrics are frequently ironic, as is her vocal interpretation of them. Accordingly, her agency is never compromised, even when her control may falter.

A second way in which Stefani's performance challenges conventions of mainstream female sexuality is by pointing up its artifice. This is accomplished primarily aesthetically, via her appearance, as well as in the way she uses her body. Stefani, in fact, employs many of the trappings of conventional female sexuality—her hair and makeup are highly consistent with it, and much of the clothing she wears is familiar to audiences of mainstream popular culture as standard "sexy" female attire: lacy bras; high heels; tight, revealing clothing; garter belts; and so forth. Furthermore, her offstage persona, which inevitably informs her public persona for audiences, is highly conventional: she is married and has a child. But Stefani's performance disrupts these conventions even as it invokes them, implicitly and explicitly. The excessiveness of her performance is responsible for this in part. As noted, her hair and makeup are a study in extremes, and her dress, too, is typically excessive; she has worn, for instance, a gauzy pantsuit with the back and torso completely absent (save for barely covering her breasts), its sleeves trailing several yards behind her. But excess alone is not sufficient in this regard, for as noted, excessive female sexuality that is nonetheless predicated on established norms is not particularly subversive. In Stefani's case, excess assumes a subversive sensibility in conjunction with other features of her performance, most notably the juxtaposition that results in significant dissonance relative to those very norms. Her pairing of extremely feminine, typically sexualized articles of clothing with other, totally incongruous items functions to decontextualize them such that their potency as signifiers of female sexuality is qualified and even rendered arbitrary. Her flaunting of her extremely small breasts in highly sexualized feminine wear similarly disrupts accepted norms of female sexuality; female breasts, of course, are firmly ensconced in the cultural psyche as objects of sexual fetishization, and this is typically manifest in the mainstream as at least very visible—in terms of cleavage and burgeoning flesh—if not very large breasts. Stefani, on the contrary, has none of the above; indeed, she often appears to be literally flat-chested in her sequined, revealing halter tops and her sinuous bustiers. The dissonance that inheres by virtue of the juxtaposition and incongruity that so thoroughly infuse Stefani's performance functions to complicate an apprehension of the conventional trappings and connotations of female sexuality. That is, by virtue of their decontextualization and, as important, their *re*contextualization as props, they are submitted instead as contrived and arbitrary signifiers of female sexuality, to be assumed, manipulated, or rejected at will, rather than inherent features of it.

The very features that function to establish the artifice of conventional female sexuality in Stefani's performance similarly serve to suggest an alternative (to mainstream discursive conventions) concept: that female sexuality is dynamic, complex, layered, and multidimensional. The dissonance that characterizes Stefani's public persona does much to establish especially the latter two sensibilities. Her eclectic clothing styles, coupled with her sexual performance, resist an easy read of her as sexually passive and, thus, available; they also suggest, however, that any and all of the personas that she is performing at a given time constitute viable sexual ways of being. For instance, when she dances seductively while wearing a lacy brassiere and combat pants in a music video, all the while staring defiantly into the camera, she is performing sexual control, conventional sexualized femininity, alternative femininity (again, especially as suggested by her flaunting of very small breasts), and masculinity. Indeed, Stefani often literally layers her clothing, such that she may wear thong underwear over jeans or a bra over a T-shirt; frequently, this layering involves the pairing of conventionally feminine and masculine articles of clothing, simultaneously sexualizing and decontextualizing them in a way that cultivates a more complicated apprehension of them as sexualized items and, by extension, of the woman wearing them.

Stefani's eclecticism is not limited to the masculine-feminine dichotomy, although this is a frequent manifestation. She has also enlisted a number of hyperfeminine features that are dissonant with respect to era, culture, or age: for instance, she has appeared wearing her hair in a conventional 1940s hairstyle with go-go boots and cropped Girl Scout T-shirt; she has appeared wearing the traditional forehead decorations of Hindu women and otherwise decked out in "surfer chic" attire; and she has appeared with her hair in pigtails, wearing a childlike pinafore, fishnet stockings, and impossibly high platform shoes. Thus, her performance does not simply suggest an assumption of or even merging with conventional masculine sexuality; to the contrary, it suggests that femininity and female sexuality—for Stefani's performance is always characterized by the sexual—are infinite in terms of their manifestations and expressions.

That Stefani is notorious for her chameleon-like penchant for change—she almost never is available to the public in the same guise more than once—contributes significantly to this interpretation. Per Stefani's performance, female sexuality—like her various guises—is a vast repertoire of limitless potential for innovation and exploration from which one may choose. It is not static, limited to a handful of hackneyed clichés defined and sanctioned by discursive convention—for example, virgin, whore, good-girl-turned-bad, femme fatale, dominatrix, nymphomaniac. Although Stefani does not necessarily reject any of these tropes categorically, she never assumes any of them in their entirety, and when she does invoke them in her performance, they are consistently complicated by virtue of their recontextualization with highly dissonant elements. Stefani's performance of female sexuality is predicated on depth and complexity and transformation; it is advanced as constantly shifting and evolving and reconfiguring itself, at—importantly—the will of the person whom it characterizes. This is perhaps the most subversive feature of Stefani's performance—that, indeed, it is a performance and, furthermore, that it can be created, modified, expressed, and interpreted ad infinitum.

Conclusion

Camp Sites

The resistive potential of camp is not guaranteed, nor, perhaps, is it even characteristic, an observation demonstrated, ironically, by the fact that a camp sensibility pervades contemporary media fare. The general congruence between camp and contemporary sensibilities that we have identified arguably renders it a natural fit for the contemporary mediascape, and many camp theorists have noted the proliferation of "camp lite" or "pop camp" in that context (M. Booth, 1983; Robertson, 1996; Ross, 1999; Sontag, 1964). Camp of this variety, these critics argue, is more accurately understood as an appropriation of camp, wherein whatever resistive potential that it may offer has been evacuated, and camp is instead utilized as a mechanism of nostalgia—for instance, as apparent in the release of films that hearken back to the rather kitschy cultural (media) staples of yore. *The Brady Bunch, Charlie's Angels, The Stepford Wives, Bewitched, The Dukes of Hazzard,* and *Dynasty* are but a few examples of this. This appropriation of camp is entirely consistent with media critics' caution that such rearticulations camouflage highly conventional discourses of privilege. For instance, the discourses of gender, class, race, and sexuality available in all of these films are blatantly stereotypical, even offensive; however, they are made available and rendered above reproach precisely because of their ironic, nostalgic camp frame. That is, under the rubric of affectionate nostalgia for the cultural trappings of the past, and assuming (if not articulating) a supposedly enlightened vantage point, these texts are rendered irreproachable, even as they resurrect and reproduce dominant discourses. As such, camp has undeniably been manipulated and reconfigured to become yet another hegemonic tactic in the increasingly vast repertoire of contemporary media practices. Indeed, precisely because of its congruence with contemporary sensibilities and its moorings in established cultural icons, most of which have secured icon status through mediated venues, camp is arguably an ideal vehicle for conventional discourses seeking to disclaim themselves.

But given the relatively risqué and arguably resistive origins of camp, we have tried to show that a closer inspection of camp in contemporary popular culture is warranted. Our interest has not been to redeem "pop camp"—for indeed, it is widespread in popular culture, and the vast majority is remarkably free of reflection, let alone critical potential. This is so despite, or perhaps partly because of, the occasional overt (arguably pseudo-self-reflexive) disclaimer, such as the inclusion of a token, highly stereotypical, and ultimately self-negating gay man as one of the "wives" in the 2004 remake of *The Stepford Wives*. Nor are we interested in reifying a rigid distinction—and attendant elitism—between "authentic" and "pop" camp per se. Rather, we have attempted to demonstrate that certain of the myriad "camp lite" texts and performances that litter the contemporary media landscape feature some of the critical, resistive potential that camp theorists have identified as a key element of authentic camp; we have also tried to illustrate where and how, precisely, a camp sensibility intersects with particular, contemporary cultural aesthetics. Because of camp's critical "home" in gender and sexuality, we were drawn to what appeared to be camp performances of femininity by women—namely, the characters of Xena and Karen Walker, as well as the singers Macy Gray and Gwen Stefani. In part, our interest in examining female camp performances of femininity was informed by our suspicion that a critical sensibility might be more available in those instances than in conventional "drag" performances. The subversive potential of drag is fairly blatant, so that when it does appear in contexts of constraint, it is often managed in such a way as to defuse and neutralize any critical potential—for example, by trivializing or demeaning the performers. Furthermore, given the high congruence between conventionally defined femininity, in particular, and contemporary media hallmarks of artifice, excess, and performance, we speculated that female performances of femininity in the context of contemporary popular media might be likelier to afford camouflage for a critical camp sensibility, if indeed it is available in a given performance; masculinity conventionally has not been construed as performative or contrived in the same way or to the same extent as femininity. In an effort to discover what made these camp performances distinctive, we identified a specific configuration of certain rhetorical premises that constituted a particular discursive logic, culminating in a critical articulation of gender and sexuality—specifically, of female sexuality.

These premises, as we have established, include trope, or the connection of the camp performance to a genre of past cultural icons; spectacle, or excessive, parodic, and dissonant aesthetic performance; and anchors and foils, contemporary cultural benchmarks that are invoked in such a way as to position the camp performance for a critical reading. In isolation of each other, none of these premises is inherently critical—indeed, they are staple features of camp lite, as well as authentic camp. That is, tropes are common to most camp performances; spectacle of some sort or another is a key characteristic of camp; and the relation of the camp artifact or performer to other characters or contextual considerations also serves to point up a camp sensibility. Unlike most of the camp available in the contemporary landscape of the popular media, however, the way in which each of these aspects is configured in these particular performances assumes a highly distinctive pattern—a logic—that "maps" the performances in such a way as to culminate in a critical conclusion regarding gender and sexuality. In the following section, we note that, unlike camp-lite fare, each one of these features is present in the camp performances that we have identified, albeit manifest in unique ways in each performance, and furthermore, they are configured against each other to render a distinctive logic.

Trope: Base Camp

The trope on which each of these performances draws is a necessary component of—indeed, a first premise for—the resistive camp sensibility that they embody in the context of the aesthetics that characterize contemporary media practices. As many theorists have noted, parody is a staple feature of camp historically, and gender—more precisely, femininity—is typically the axis on which such parody turns. Parodic femininity is certainly apparent in the performances of Macy Gray, Gwen Stefani, Karen Walker, and Xena; however, it is manifest in distinct and significant ways, in large part attributable to the contemporary media context in which these performances occur.

Like parody, trope as utilized in these performances is recognizable by virtue of the similarities that inhere between the object of the performance and the performance itself. Historically, however, camp—especially but not exclusively as available in drag—either turns on the parody of a specific individual (e.g., Cher, Barbra Streisand, Judy Garland, Gloria Swanson) or an abstract concept (e.g., femininity, elitism). Conversely, these performances elect neither of these routes, instead venturing a third option: invoking familiar *genres* of gender organized around a particular sensibility that alludes to a set of individuals who, importantly, are familiar to audiences precisely via the very mainstream popular mediated contexts in which the camp performances themselves occur. Stefani, for instance, by parodying and celebrating the vintage sex symbol, invokes the specters of Marilyn Monroe, Jean Harlow, Jayne Mansfield, Betty Boop, and others; Gray's performance alludes to icons of 1970s Black male funk sensibility, most readily accessible in the television variety show *Soul Train* and the films *Shaft* and *Superfly,* featuring the characters of John Shaft and Priest, respectively; Karen Walker's character hearkens back to classic "rich bitches" like Alexis Carrington in *Dynasty* and Bette Davis in *Whatever Happened to Baby Jane* and *All About Eve;* and Xena evokes the Amazon warrior most familiar to audiences from films, television shows, and even comic books such as Wonder Woman and Sheena, Queen of the Jungle. In each case, the women allude to "all of the above" yet none in particular. In so doing, these camp performances may resist apprehension as "merely" parodying specific individuals and thus as being confined to them—even if some of them may be called forth for particular audiences—as opposed to ironizing an established cultural form, thereby illuminating that very form as such.

The parodies that constitute, in part, these camp performances are in fact composites—each represents an amalgam of generic gendered sexuality embedded in the popular (mediated) consciousness and clearly associated with the trope in question. Camp is achieved via the eclecticism that characterizes the performances within their respective genres. Karen Walker's extreme wealth, elitism, callousness, and sense of entitlement are correlated qualities that are uniquely associated, in women, with the wealthy, bitchy socialite; Gwen Stefani often features a "mix" of fashions and hairstyles that reference any number of sex symbols simultaneously and thus secure the reference; Macy Gray's dress and behavior are a composite homage and "play" on 1970s Black funk masculinity; and Xena's historical location in a bygone era, her superpowers, her fighting skills, and her costuming all warrant the allusion to the Amazon warrior trope.

Specific features of each performance ensure an apprehension of those performances in terms of their respective tropes, largely by invoking the hallmarks of a number of historically popular media figures that fit under that rubric; concomitantly, however, no singular character or individual is clearly, specifically referenced. Configuring the parodic dimension of camp in this way ensures that it is the *essence* of each trope that serves as the cornerstone in each case; that essence is specific constructs of gender and sexuality, and specifically femininity and female sexuality, manifest in different ways in each performance. Parodying the tropes in this way thus affords a critical edge to these camp performances; it is less likely that they might be dismissed as "sending up" specific characters or individuals. Thus, the denigration that many critics cite as inherent in parodic stagings of femininity is, if not obviated, at least significantly problematized. Indeed, denigration is further offset by the fact that each of these women—Gray, Stefani, Karen Walker, and Xena—inhabits these highly recognizable tropes thoroughly and consistently in her performance; the nonetheless obvious invocation of the tropes is not variously assumed and discarded. In this respect, each performance fulfills Robertson's (1996) assessment that "camp depends on our simultaneously recognizing stereotypes as stereotypes to distance ourselves from them and at the same time recognizing, and loving, the hold and power those stereotypes have over us" (p. 142). In this sense, the employment of particular media tropes, or generic figures, in camp performance seems particularly well suited to securing a critical camp sensibility.

Furthermore, and as relevant to the "recombination" motif of myriad contemporary mediated texts, each camp performance invokes a secondary, complementary, arguably less established or "mainstream," yet highly significant "companion" trope that turns very explicitly on sexuality. In Xena's case, the Amazon warrior is rendered alongside the dominatrix; Karen Walker's "rich bitch" is conflated with the "fag hag"; the "mack daddy" that Macy Gray embodies is synthesized with the sex "freak"; and the ultrafeminine, innocent 1950s girl-next-door that Gwen Stefani portrays is presented in tandem with the more aggressive and risqué sex symbol of the same era. In each case, this particular reconfiguration of cultural tropes prompts a more nuanced apprehension of them in terms of discerning points of dissonance and congruence between them and the performances themselves. Moreover, the irony that characterizes their eclectic recombination cultivates a relatively critical awareness of gender and sexuality as performances per se: each of these women is very clearly performing several versions of gender and sexuality, a fact that contains far greater critical significance and thus potential than simply "performing"—or parodying—a particular woman.

Although similarities to the tropes invoked secure the appropriate references, rather than reproduce the discursive conventions on which those tropes rely, deviations from them provide these performances with their critical edge—they serve as springboards for the deconstruction and reframing of gender and sexuality. Indeed, those points of deviation are significant; for instance, unlike the Amazon warrior trope on whom Xena is modeled, Xena is masculine in ways other than physical—she is emotionally stoic and rugged, aggressive in her violence, and regularly battling darker impulses. Also, significantly, not only is she not defined by a relationship with a man or men, her primary—and intimate—relationship is with a woman. Likewise, Karen Walker's rich-bitch socialite is not clearly defined by a man, and references to an invisible husband simply point up his inability to control her. Further, unlike her prototype, Karen is crass and crude, sexually explicit and lascivious. Macy Gray incorporates the female sexual freak in her invocation of the urban black male "mack daddy" sensibility, and Gwen Stefani layers her performances with various historical and cultural tropes of femininity.

The tropes on which each of these camp performances turns function, in part, as entrees into the forum of contemporary mediated popular culture, thus establishing trope as very likely the inevitable, necessary first premise of camp in that context. After all, those tropes are products of that culture and are thus familiar to media audiences, at least by virtue of the sheer self-reflexivity that is characteristic of contemporary mediated texts or their constant recirculation and recombination of historical and current media fare. Self-reflexivity is highly complementary and conducive to camp sensibilities, so perhaps it is not surprising that the contemporary popular mediascape is rife with camp lite, characterized by the purely nostalgic, acontextual, and entirely unreflective resurrection of historical trends and icons, especially as fodder for media fare. The deviations from form apparent in the camp performances of Xena, Karen Walker, Gray, and Stefani are significant, however, as are the specific points at which they diverge, such that they appear to contain a potentially critical dimension. Such deviance does not compromise their cultural currency; rather, contemporary mediated texts are at least as profoundly characterized by pastiche and irony as they are by self-reflexivity, such that quirky or bizarre riffs on established media tropes could be attributed to sophisticated, camp lite media shtick—hip, trendy "pomo" images predicated on the very pomo terms that constitute their context.

In fact, the inconsistent, relative, insubstantial, and incoherent qualities of the contemporary media environment provide not only an ideal back-drop but ideal camouflage for texts that manipulate those very qualities in particular ways, serving to invest seemingly inchoate texts and images with meaning rather than divesting them of it, as contemporary sensibilities are typically understood. Many scholars have described the ways in which dominant discourses can be identified in ostensibly liberatory contempo-rary media fare by virtue of strategic appropriations and configurations of the aesthetic features of that fare (Condit, 1989, 1992; Harms & Dickens, 1996; Shugart, Waggoner, & Hallstein, 2001). We suggest that camp is ideally poised to engage in precisely such strategic (re)configurations in the context of contemporary popular media fare but to the ends of resistance and sub-version rather than hegemonic control.

This potential is illustrated in the camp performances of Xena, Walker, Gray, and Stefani as relevant to gender and sexuality; the respective—culturally sanctioned and media legitimate—tropes on which each perfor-mance turns are not dismantled but are reconfigured, reconstituted as sig-nifiers of and ciphers for sexual alterity that ultimately redefine femininity and female sexuality. Xena's warrior-princess-with-a-dash-of-dominatrix is redefined as an icon of lesbian sexuality; Karen Walker repositions the rich bitch/fag hag as not only social sanction for but actual incarnation of gay male sexuality; Macy Gray's indelibly feminine fusion of the mack daddy and the sexual freak creates an innovative, powerful, and heretofore un-available space for Black female sexuality; and Gwen Stefani's multiple, dy-namic, ever-shifting female sexual personae—from naive girl-next-door to sexual vixen—suggest the infinite and unlimited nature, scope, and freedom of female sexuality. These camp performances accomplish a potentially pro-foundly subversive feat: they each employ tropes that historically have functioned as models of constraint and reconstitute them as avenues of possibility. Although the reconfigurations of cultural tropes in these cases alone do not guarantee a resistive camp sensibility, they do constitute its vital—and powerful—first premise.

Spectacle: Camp Fireworks

Whereas the trope aspect of these women's performances functions as the grounds for contemporary camp, spectacle functions as its warrant, securing a camp sensibility that ultimately creates a discursive space for alterity within a context of constraint. Consistent with the existing literature on camp as historically available, spectacle as apparent in these women reflects all of the characteristics typically associated with camp—irony, parody, aestheticism, theatricality, and resistance. These characteristics assume a particular shape, however, in the context of contemporary, mainstream, and mediated popular culture. As noted relative to how trope functions to advance a camp sensibility in that context, much of this is attributable to the self-reflexivity and pastiche that characterize contemporary mediated texts, such that irony and parody, for instance, inhere precisely to the extent that the audience is familiar with implicit popular culture references on which those sensibilities turn.

At first blush, the spectacular dimensions of the performances of Xena, Karen Walker, Macy Gray, and Gwen Stefani seem entirely consistent with other media spectacles readily available in contemporary popular culture, the vast majority of which are hardly suggestive of resistive potential. Female spectacle, in particular, is widely available in contemporary popular culture, evidenced, as we have noted, in the bodies of Beyoncé, Paris Hilton, Britney Spears, Christina Aguilera, Jennifer Lopez, and Carmen Electra, and it is typically rendered in such a way as to reify and reinforce dominant discourses of femininity and female sexuality as alternative chic rather than political resistance. But the spectacular performances of the women we are examining are best understood as camp, and resistive camp more specifically, and the distinctiveness of those performances can be apprehended rhetorically. That is, particular rhetorical strategies characterize spectacle in these cases, constituting highly refined versions of established camp devices.

The key rhetorical features of spectacle in all of these camp performances are excess and juxtaposition, which are configured in specific ways and function to abrade conventions of femininity in a mainstream context. Caricaturing established popular cultural references serves as a vehicle for critical potential: Xena's parodic dominatrix, Karen Walker's over-the-top rich bitch fag hag, Macy Gray's outrageous sexual freak, and Gwen Stefani's trumped up sex kitten provide the viewing space that fosters a critical camp sensibility, particularly potent for gender. This, as Russo warns, is a "specifically feminine danger" (Russo, 1986, p. 213), as women play with the boundaries of their constraints, embracing rather than retreating. Making a spectacle of oneself is "stepping into the limelight" in ways that are out of turn—too young, too old, too early, too late. Simply put, it is *too much*. But it is precisely that dicey flirting with feminine danger that is necessary for critical potential. Playing with fetish must always raise the stakes of the game; otherwise it's just reification of stereotypes (Silverman, 1993, p.87).

As we have noted, many feminist theorists and critics have identified the particular shape assumed by female or feminine spectacle: functionally, it becomes fetishized, the object of an implied male gaze, such that the feminine is reduced to excessive, visual display for consumption as a sexual commodity. Some theorists have complicated this logic, for instance by introducing drag as a site of rupture of these conventions of particularly feminine spectacle (see, e.g., Butler, 1990, 1993; Newton, 1999). We contend that the spectacles that Stefani, Gray, Karen Walker, and Xena embody and represent similarly function, like drag, to schism these conventions by invoking them in especially discordant ways. Indeed, the strategies that characterize their performances are highly evocative of drag and especially of those features that qualify it as resistive—blurring and problematizing gendered social assumptions via incongruity, for instance, and ironizing aesthetic excess via parodic representations. Butler (1990) argues that such strategies render visible the performative nature of gender: via drag, "we see sex and gender denaturalized by means of a performance which avows their distinctness and dramatizes the cultural mechanism of their fabricated unity" (p. 364). Indeed, the peculiar configuration of qualities that characterize these performances arguably constitutes them as drag.

As many theorists have noted, the relationship between drag and camp is close-knit, and dissonance that turns on excess also is a staple feature of camp performances historically. Such incongruent dissonance is apparent in these camp performances, particularly manifest in juxtapositions of femininity with masculinity. Newton (1999) argues that "camp usually depends on the perception or creations of *incongruous juxtapositions*" of extreme characterizations (p. 103) to interrupt and problematize conventional expectations. In a more abstract sense, Britton (1999) identifies this same quality in his argument that camp's aesthetics are only recognizable as a deviation from a norm (p. 138). Camp requires a "sense of perversity in relation to bourgeois norms" (p. 138), which can be secured via excess or incongruity or both. Such incongruent dissonance is apparent in the camp performances of Xena, Walker, Gray, and Stefani, particularly manifest in juxtapositions of femininity with masculinity. As noted by Newton and Britton, however, the dissonance and excess that characterize these contemporary camp performances are not in themselves unique; indeed, so integral are these features to camp as historically understood that their absence in these cases would be conspicuous and grounds to challenge our argument that these performances are, in fact, camp.

But these performances also are constituted against the backdrop of contemporary popular culture, and as such, they are configured in distinctive ways. Specifically, the spectacular dimensions that secure the camp sensibility of these performances turn on particular renditions of excess and juxtaposition that ultimately constitute an appropriation of the conventions of spectacle as widely available in mainstream media fare—excessive, dissonant, random, eclectic, and highly sensational images and texts. Erickson (1998) has noted that the hegemonic function of spectacle inheres, at least in part, in the fact that spectacles "rhetorically or randomly appropriate images of iconic, historic, or significant sites, events, and audiences" (p. 150); our contention is that particular, strategic, and ultimately camp configurations of spectacle, such as those enacted by Stefani, Xena, Gray, and Karen Walker, constitute an appropriation—perhaps more accurately a reappropriation—of spectacle to the end of disrupting conventional discourses of gender and sexuality.

The aestheticism that appears to define contemporary female camp performances in the current mediated environment thus appears to be manifest as spectacle. The points of convergence and divergence of these contemporary performances of camp with historical performances are notable and significant. Again, sufficient overlap exists to warrant these contemporary instances as camp, especially with respect to the excess and irony that have always characterized camp. But contemporary camp, at least as evident in the performances of Gray, Stefani, Xena, and Karen Walker, appears to be rhetorically distinctive, especially insofar as irony is secured in these performances. We have argued that this distinctiveness is largely due to the aesthetics and sensibilities that define contemporary popular culture, the context in which these performances occur. That is, the landscape of mainstream popular culture today is rampant with dissonance and excess, such that simple invocation of these sensibilities is not sufficient to constitute spectacle, let alone evoke the specter of alterity—historically, the hallmark of camp irony. By manipulating these very aesthetics in particular ways, however—specifically, by employing the contemporary sensibilities of popular culture in novel and strategic ways—these performances are able to secure a camp sensibility even as they maintain congruence with the very conventions that would constrain them.

Anchors and Foils: Camp Benchmarks

The pastiche-laden, fragmented, and chaotic landscape of contemporary media fare poses particular challenges for interpretation and assessment. Audiences are left to make sense of infinitely various and seemingly incoherent ideas and images, often to hegemonic ends, such that said incoherence and variety either paralyze audiences or are strategically rendered in order to secure acquiescence with conventional discourses. Contemporary incarnations of camp also are predicated on apparent randomness and incoherence, however, as demonstrated in the performances of Macy Gray, Gwen Stefani, Xena, and Karen Walker, and they reflect well the landscape of contemporary popular culture. But our contention is that even while this reading (and arguably others) is readily available, a critical one *also* is available. Key to this critical potential in contemporary camp, as we have argued throughout this study, is a discursive logic characterized not only by well-known icons and spectacular aesthetics but by benchmarks—foils and anchors—within the text or the contemporary semiotic landscape, providing vantage points for viewers, promoting narrative coherence, and facilitating a critical reading of the camp performances.

Parody is a hallmark of camp—conventional icons and ideas are "sent up" in playful, often affectionate, and sometimes critical ways. But the icons and ideas that serve as fodder for the parody do not occur in a vacuum; rather, the context in which they occur provides necessary and meaningful traction. By virtue of contrast, foils—or characters juxtaposed with the camp performers—furnish that traction in important ways. These foils are contemporary repositories of the irony that characterizes camp, predicated on distance achieved via incongruous contrasts between the thing and its context or association (Babuscio, 1977, p. 41). Given that the performers we have examined appear in different mediated milieus, foils may be fixed and physically present, as with Xena and Karen Walker; or they may be constituted intertextually, via comparable peers in a given medium, as with Gray and Stefani. In *Xena: Warrior Princess,* the boy-child Joxer and eunuchlike Salmoneus perform humorous displays of emasculated gender, modeling sexual impotency and thus pointing up the sexual potency of Xena's character. Karen Walker's sexual potency is thrown into sharp relief via her juxtaposition with Grace's comical, bumbling female sexuality. In the broader context of the contemporary music industry, and with particular genres, Macy Gray's and Gwen Stefani's camp performances are rendered critical, as well, when considered against their peer group of more conventionally feminine female musical artists such as Beyoncé and Christina Aguilera.

While foils offer viewers perspectival vantage points via contrast, anchors do so via a principle of congruence. In his work explaining the intimate relationship between form and content in persuasion, Burke (1954) explains the human desire for congruence, especially prevalent in times of great conceptual change. He notes that piousness, for instance, is not "confined to the sphere of churchliness" but rather is the general sense of appropriateness that something goes properly with something else, a "response that extends throughout the texture of our lives" (p. 75). The principle of congruence operates in these contemporary female camp performances via anchors— contemporary icons and characters that give new readings for the camp performers. Ironically, the critical reading is achieved in large part because of the sense of piety that is enabled via the anchors. That is, even as these camp performers are enacting a type of resistance to dominant discourse, they do so in a way that promotes congruence, and this facilitates a sense of appropriateness. Given that the cases that we have studied occur in different mediated contexts—precisely contained television shows, in two cases, and the far more diffuse music industry in the other two—anchors play out in different ways and, respectively, to somewhat different effect. In all cases, however, they provide considerable semiotic traction to the camp performances, especially insofar as their critical potential is concerned.

Whereas foils operate disjunctively, anchors function somewhat analogically, operating on a principle that an object is like another one in important ways. Gwen Stefani, for instance, is anchored by Madonna in the popular consciousness, whose legacy, we have argued, contributes to the semiotic impact of Stefani's performance. Having blazed a trail of excessive female sexuality and given the notable aesthetic parallels between the two women, Madonna grounds Stefani's performance in ways that enable a critical reading, especially in terms of female sexuality. Likewise, Rick James serves as an anchor for Macy Gray, providing a heavily ironic semiotic frame for Gray's camp performances. Without James's "Superfreak" construct and aesthetic in the late 1980s, Gray's performance loses critical significance. In both cases, the logic of camp works only if the viewers are familiar with the anchors, as it is not always the case that anchors are conjured overtly within performances. Instead, anchors serve to semiotically ground the contemporary camp performances for critical effect. In this sense, too, anchors are distinct from the tropes that serve as the historical, iconic referents for these camp performances; while tropes are stereotypes or clichés whose meaning transcends the character in archetypal fashion, anchors are not so endowed with archetypal significance. Yet anchors perform an important function in the logic of camp, demonstrating once again the prevalence of intertextuality, especially in a contemporary mediated context.

Anchors, however, are not limited to their analogical function. The cases of Xena and Karen Walker suggest that anchors may serve a redemptive function, as well. Gabrielle's character, as we have seen, serves as a moral guide for Xena, "correcting" her rigidly masculine persona via her presentation of pure, unspoiled femininity. In her interactions with Xena, Gabrielle brings out Xena's vulnerabilities and nurturing capacities, redeeming her otherwise inappropriate character. Likewise, in *Will and Grace,* Jack redeems Karen Walker's character, serving as a conduit for her vulnerabilities and compassion for others. Here, both Gabrielle and Jack function discursively to provide a sense of satisfaction for viewers that is akin to Burke's notion of piety or appropriateness. Just as foils promote a contrast necessary for the emergence of irony and parody, anchors foster a sense of congruence that is related to appropriateness and ultimately to affection that marks the performances as camp and speaks to the homage and affection that, as many scholars have argued, are staple features of camp.

Our analysis of anchors and foils in the performances of Xena, Karen Walker, Macy Gray, and Gwen Stefani suggests the important role that contextual cues play in these performances as camp, even when those cues simultaneously function as camouflage or are dismissed as random "noise." Camp sensibilities emerge via the principles of congruence and contrast, camouflaged as incoherence, recirculation, and self-referentiality. But anchors and foils do more than help to secure the camp status of these performers; they also help to secure their critical potential with viewers. That critical potential depends on a delicate balance of both congruence and contrast, as conventional order is being disrupted in the promotion of alternative perspectives. Anchors and foils, in the cases of contemporary female camp performers, operate in the service of this dual function—defining the performers as camp, while simultaneously securing their resistive potential.

Camp Sex

The features to which we have attended in the preceding chapters—trope, spectacle, and anchors and foils—constitute the premises of a unique discursive logic of "resistive" camp available in the contemporary mediated environment. In each of the cases that we have assessed, those premises culminate, or logically conclude, in an articulation of sexual alterity—that is, as defined against normative heterosexuality. Given camp's long and close affiliation with gender and sexuality, especially in the context of gay male culture in general and drag culture in particular, this is hardly surprising (Babuscio, 1999; Britton, 1999; Cleto, 1999; Dyer, 1999; Ross, 1999; Sontag, 1999); gender and sexuality are arguably the default fodder for camp, and it may well be the case that "critical" camp—at least as historically available—always turns on those axes.

Many scholars have attested to the performative nature of gender in general and, with its more obvious and highly visible aesthetic trappings, of femininity in particular. Noting this distinction, Halberstam (1998) has argued that, at the very least, masculinity is discursively naturalized in a manner altogether different from femininity; masculinity tends to be constructed as "authentic," in sharp contrast to the myriad and overtly strategic practices and performances that characterize femininity. Thus, femininity is an obvious, perhaps even inevitable, camp *ground,* an ideal and endless field from which to mine the aesthetic and ironic sensibilities on which camp turns.

For this reason, contemporary aesthetic practices and sensibilities are especially intriguing and significant on a number of levels, insofar as they intersect with camp and, in particular, its peculiarly gendered legacy. Contemporary cultural sensibilities are characterized powerfully, if not primarily, by an emphasis on artifice, on image, and on the superficial, qualities that align it seamlessly with the performative. As we have suggested throughout our analysis of contemporary camp, contemporary popular culture and, more specifically, the contemporary media environment constitute an ideal camp *site.* Of course, the chasm that separates the two, as many have argued, is the critical sensibility that at least accompanies if not infuses camp; thus, the distinction between "authentic" camp and "pop camp," or "camp lite."

But we suggest that this is where gender—particularly femininity—enters into the frame, with particular historical and political significance. Extreme and excessive performances of femininity continue to abound in contemporary media fare as they have historically, if not necessarily more than masculine performances then certainly more visibly. Because femininity offers a ready-made and seemingly inexhaustible supply of the highly visible artifice that fuels contemporary aesthetic practices, it is not surprising that feminine performances are so regularly "camped" in popular culture. Accordingly, the alignment of femininity, camp, and contemporary aesthetics is highly congruent and remarkably fluent, their convergence perhaps even inevitable. Given the historical significance of femininity for camp, however, it is also highly volatile; that is, femininity has long served as the critical flashpoint of camp to the end of critique, however pointed or diffuse, of conventional discourses of gender and sexuality. In this one arena, camp arguably has the critical advantage over other mediated aesthetic sensibilities with respect to resisting its own co-optation by contemporary sensibilities: as femininity is the "home turf" of camp, it is likely far more available to be constituted and configured in such a way as to make available—if not foreground—an "old-school" critical camp sensibility. Our attempt here has been to identify precisely the ways in which camp might be configured rhetorically for transgressive ends.

Of course, as historically practiced, critical camp performances have entailed cross-gender enactments, as epitomized by the drag queen in gay male culture, the popularly designated origin of camp. As several critics have contended, however, this is an unnecessary and unwarranted limiting of the possibilities and permutations of camp, in part informed by gendered biases on a number of levels. Scholars have noted not only that women can and do camp but that the shape that camp assumes on their bodies opens up additional and different critical possibilities. Robertson, for instance, has argued that camp in such contexts features a distinctly feminist edge. We concur, and we would venture that within the critical potential of the camp performances we have identified, that feminist edge might well be apparent. In addition to our interest in identifying the rhetorical logic of contemporary critical camp performances, however, we depart from Robertson insofar as we would submit that, in these cases, the emphasis is less on a particular political objective or set of objectives than on conventional camp sensibilities: that is, directed to the disruption and complication of conventional discourses of gender and sexuality in general *for its own sake*. This certainly does not depoliticize camp; on the contrary, it may render it more diffuse and thus more pervasive, defined by a critical sensibility rather than agenda. In the broadest sense, this is arguably feminist; however, our contention is that these camp performances are characterized far less by the articulation of a particular position or perspective than in the *reconfiguration* of gender and sexuality to that same end: the *unlimited* reconfiguration of gender and sexuality. While we assert that a coherent pattern can be identified in these performances to the end of qualifying them as critical, we acknowledge that they are critical insofar as they disrupt convention, in decidedly inconsistent and unpredictable ways.

The fact that gender and sexuality are reconfigured in tandem with each other is notable, as well. Their tight conflation has been chronicled extensively by scholars across disciplines, including those attending to camp. But what is intriguing in this case is their relationship or, perhaps more accurately, proportions to each other: that is, each camp performance of femininity renders a distinctive rendition of sexual alterity, as drawn against convention, or normative heterosexuality. Sexual alterity, of course, is readily available in contemporary mainstream media fare, and we do not suggest that these performances are distinctive merely insofar as they articulate it. So prevalent are representations of sexual alterity—especially homosexuality and most especially gay male sexuality—that they arguably have carved out their own fairly de rigueur niche in popular cultural fare, assuming a chic and trendy status. But as many critics have pointed out, visibility is no guarantor of legitimacy; as Walters (2001) notes, "We may be *seen,* now, but I'm not sure we are *known*" (p. 10). In most cases in mainstream mediated texts, gay characters are desexualized and depoliticized, depicted only in contexts and communities that reflect and reproduce heteronormative conventions and privilege. Another prevalent mode of representation of sexual alterity in mainstream media programming features gay characters for their heuristic value for heterosexuality—that is, they are rendered as conduits or catalysts for the development of "straight" characters. The increased availability of representations of sexual alterity in contemporary mainstream media fare is effectively illusory insofar as only a particular kind of sexual alterity is made available, primarily in the form of gay men, and even those representations are both constrained by and redolent of heteronormative sensibilities and conventional heterosexual sensibilities.

In each of these camp performances, however, sexual alterity is not explicit or always even visible, for that matter, nor is it articulated consistently across the performances. Rather, respective incarnations of sexual alterity emerge in each instance as a logical conclusion of the peculiar, kaleidoscopic configuration of trope, spectacle, and anchors and foils. Despite significant variance in premises and their configurations, it is sexual alterity that consistently emerges, and this is significant insofar as the playing field of femininity appears to be the one common denominator. This confirms the tight conflation of gender and sexuality, but it might also indicate that femininity is "ground zero" for the critique, negotiation, and even resistance of gendered and sexual conventions. Moreover, it may be the case that, given the emphasis on artifice and image that is the cornerstone of contemporary aesthetic practices and, accordingly, the contemporary mediascape, femininity—rather than those aesthetic practices per se—constitutes the actual camouflage necessary for de- and reconstruction: these practices simply intersect with femininity in highly congruent and fortuitous ways, despite the fact that they might be wielded more broadly as strategies of domination. This suggests further that, in the context of popular culture, the critical potential of camp is more likely to be realized in or on the bodies of women, insofar as female performances of femininity may be more difficult to identify as such and thus more unstable and difficult to govern—that is, to appropriate—than male performances of femininity. Of course, the instability and even volatility of femininity has long been recognized and embraced as a (arguably *the*) cornerstone of camp; as such, the convergence of the trilogy of camp, femininity, and contemporary aesthetic practices and sensibilities at this historical moment is simultaneously "natural," seamless, and thus one of very few sites in contemporary, mainstream, mediated popular culture that might retain possibilities and margins of resistance. Furthermore, the new modalities and venues afforded by popular, mainstream media fare suggest innovative ways in which critical potential in a contemporary context of constraint might be realized via camp, in particular as relevant to the contemporary mediascape. What distinguishes that site rhetorically and critically warrants attention, scholarly and otherwise.

Mapping Camp: Logics and Logistics

The camp performances that we have assessed are configured in such a way as to constitute a discursive logic, such that sexual alterity is not presented as the premise or overt focus of those performances; that is, they are not articulated *as* representations of sexual alterity on their face. Rather, a critique of sexual alterity emerges only subsequent to attendance to the particular configuration—or logic—that is constituted by the premises we have identified and how they engage each other: trope, spectacle, and anchors and foils. Absent those cues, these camp performances easily dissolve into the pastiche-laden landscape of popular culture that serves as their context; however, on recognizing said cues and their relationship to each other, the logic of this "critical camp" emerges. The audience must complete that logic, which culminates in an argument regarding sexual—and gender—alterity.

The dimensions that this logic assumes have significant implications for the role of rhetorical analysis and rhetoric more broadly in a contemporary context, for that logic is very much located at the intersection of a conventional form and a contemporary aesthetic. While the strategic form and function of logic emerge somewhat intact despite an ostensible rejection of order and coherence, what has altered is its object: the definitive and inevitable conclusion. As we have noted, despite the logic that undergirds these performances to the end of rendering a critical reading, that reading is by no means guaranteed—and in fact, some or all of the premises may be foregrounded at the expense of others to render any variety of alternative viable readings. As suggested by these cases, the rhetorical force of logic in a contemporary venue that appears to be "illogical" seems to lie in the configuration of premises—or the situation of signs and symbols in relation to each other—rather than in the conclusion itself. In this way, the fluidity and amorphousness that are hallmarks of contemporary sensibilities assert themselves indelibly on the rhetorical conventions of logic, altering the "movement" of the argument from its usually inevitable linear march to its conclusion.

This rhetorical derailing can be seen, for instance, in an examination of how the logical form of the enthymeme plays out in the camp performances that we have examined. Each of these camp performances constitutes a particular discursive logic, and the conclusion of that logic—predicated on the configuration of trope, spectacle, anchors and foils peculiar to each case— is a rhetorical case for sexual alterity, distinctive to each performance. As we have noted, this "camp logic" is contingent on the audience, who must attend to the cues, as well as their relationship to and configuration with each other, available in each performance, which is itself heavily steeped in the conventional codes and sensibilities of contemporary mainstream media fare. As such, the logical conclusion must be realized by the audience. In this regard, the logic of resistive camp is highly reflective of enthymematic reasoning, wherein the audience must cooperate with the rhetor in constructing a given rhetorical argument to the end of (self)persuasion (Bitzer, 1959; Cronkhite, 1966). The camp performances that we have examined are consistent with this historical conception of the enthymeme insofar as they rely on audience inferences in terms of securing the premises of camp as embodied in the characteristics that we have identified.

Further, the enthymematic character of contemporary, resistive camp, as we have described it, is arguably not unique to the contemporary mediascape. Aden (1994) has argued that the enthymeme may well constitute the reasoning modus operandi in a "postmodern" world. One of the defining features of this world is "the proliferation of signs and their endless circulation.... [Thus] the 'already said' is being constantly recirculated" (J. Col-

lins, 1992, pp. 331–333). In its capacity to produce, circulate (and recircu-
late), and combine (and recombine) signs ad infinitum, the contemporary
mediascape is an ideal vehicle for, as well as an active producer of, the sensibilities that Aden describes. Speaking to political arguments presented in
a contemporary mediated forum in particular, he notes that "the content
of [mediated] arguments presented to the public consists of the 'already
said' fragments, from which individuals construct their own interpretations"
(Aden, 1994, p. 55). For Aden, the distinctive feature of enthymematic reasoning in a "postmodern [mediated] age" is the sheer volume of signs ("fragments") available to contemporary audiences, which increases exponentially
the possible number of interpretations of "public arguments" by individuals
(p. 63). Accordingly, suggests Aden, the contemporary media might best be
apprehended as the purveyor of a "public sphere of discourse rather than a
public sphere of argument" (p. 62).

We submit, however, that, especially in contemporary venues and for the
very same reasons, signs or fragments may well be combined—configured—
in particular ways to, if not guarantee an interpretation, construct a relatively systematic and complex discursive logic that affords some definition
to its premises in such a way as to invite and cultivate a particular interpretation. The camp performances that we have assessed, thoroughly steeped in
contemporary sensibilities and characterized by media conventions and aesthetic practices that reflect those sensibilities, constitute just such examples
of configured and "layered" enthymematic logic. Furthermore, although we
concur with Aden that the contemporary media in general and mediated
texts in particular are better understood as agents of discourse than of argument, we do not find them any less powerful or influential because of it—
arguably, they are potentially more so.

Another important point of departure between enthymematic logic as
historically understood and the logic that, we argue, these camp performances embody is, again, that rather than simply contributing premises
(albeit within parameters established by the text), the audience also must
draw the logical conclusion of those premises—in these cases, an articulated challenge to conventions of gender and sexuality. This distinction
does not negate the logic of these performances; however, it does illustrate
the foregrounding of premises and their relationship to each other without
privileging the conclusion and accordingly points to a profound relationship

between irony and the enthymeme—more specifically, between contemporary incarnations of each.

Irony operates in the negotiation of meaning—specifically, in the incongruity between literal and intended meanings (see, e.g., W. Booth, 1974; Foss & Littlejohn, 1986; Olson & Olson, 2004; Swearingen, 1991; Terrill, 2003). Audiences that encounter the incongruity are compelled to resolve the dissonance and proceed to identify the underlying, less obvious, elements that afford congruence to the ironic statement or event. Many theorists assert that, as with the enthymeme, the collusion that inheres between the audience and the ironist necessitated by successful detection likely results in increased compliance, making irony a highly effective rhetorical device (W. Booth, 1983; Wilde, 1982). Perhaps not surprisingly, irony has been identified as something of a leitmotif of postmodernity, characterized as it is by a seemingly infinite number of random, incoherent, and often inconsistent ideas and images (J. Collins, 1989; Harms & Dickens, 1996; Jameson, 1991). Some critics have argued that the overwhelming degree of dissonance, ironic or otherwise, characteristic of postmodernism may well render all meaning suspect, with the net result being cynicism at best and paralysis at worst (Harms & Dickens, 1996; Jameson, 1991; Moore, 1996). Others are more optimistic, however, citing the distinctively subversive potential of "postmodern irony," contingent as it is on variety, dissonance, incoherence, and contradiction as measured against dominant discourses and sensibilities (Bernard, 1992; Blair, 1992; Hutcheon, 1991, 1992; Nadaner, 1984; Waring, 1992). Hutcheon (1991), for instance, argues that postmodern irony can assume either of two forms, deconstructive or constructive, both of which contain endemic resistive potential: "The first is a kind of critical ironic stance that serves to distance, undermine, unmask, relativize, destabilize. . . . Here *marginality* becomes the model for internal subversion of that which presumes to be central. The other, constructive kind of irony . . . , works to assert difference as a positive. . . . This irony's focus is on *liminality,* where . . . [i]rony opens up new spaces, literally between opposing meanings, where new things can happen" (pp. 30–31). The risk of postmodern irony, however, is that given that it is defined by and predicated on the conventional premises, it risks reifying and reproducing the very meanings it seeks to subvert—that is, postmodern irony simultaneously reiterates and contradicts dominant representations (e.g., Bernard, 1992).

As many camp scholars have noted, and as we have reiterated in this study, irony is a critical, defining feature of camp (Babuscio, 1999; Case, 1999; Flinn, 1999; Newton, 1972; Sontag, 1964). That is, camp turns on "incongruous juxtapositions" (Newton, 1972, p. 103) and the "recontextualization of signs" (Flinn, 1999, p. 440), inviting and arguably prompting the audience to engage the incongruity in a way that demands participation to secure the camp sensibility. What distinguishes camp from conventional irony—indeed, what may establish the irony in this case as truly camp—is that, rather than being confronted with apparent dissonance (the literal meaning) and then seeking resolution in the way of identifying congruence (the intended meaning), audiences are confronted with apparent *congruence* initially but are prompted to attend to the incongruities that belie it. For instance, in the case of drag, which epitomizes camp, audiences apprehend a man who remarkably resembles a woman—sometimes, a particular woman, like a cultural icon. The similarity constitutes the literal, or superficial, meaning; however, on engaging the incongruities in that performance, the audience may identify the intended meaning, which turns on a playful—and subversive—take on the constructed, artificial nature of gender and sexuality. This distinction is not at all inconsistent with postmodern irony, however, which engages dissonance in a variety of ways. Hutcheon (1992) has argued that the very strength—and subversive potential—of postmodern irony lies in its ability to cultivate paradox rather than transcend it.

The camp performances that we have identified, occurring as they do in a contemporary context and abounding with those sensibilities—for instance, as defined by their multiple points of reference with respect to tropes, anchors, and foils; the highly excessive and often dissonant configurations and characteristics that spectacle assumes in each case; and attendant multiple possible interpretations—may be understood as prime examples of contemporary irony or irony apprehended in the context of contemporary cultural aesthetic practices and sensibilities. We concur that they are. They are more than just that, however: specifically, the multiple iron*ies* of which these performances consist constitute the premises for the enthymematic discursive logic that culminates in a particular rhetorical—and resistive—case regarding gender and sexuality. That is, rather than the fairly straightforward and transient incongruity contained in a given instance of irony, the multiple ironies that make up the premises of this camp logic are configured together in such a way as to cultivate a particular interpretation. So, the audience not only participates in securing the ironic readings *within* each premise; importantly, those premises engage and build on each other to encourage the logical conclusion—a subversive representation of female sexuality. As such, the ironies are employed to the end of making an argument, but one in which the audience must participate at every step—and rhetorical logics are reoriented accordingly to foreground premises rather than conclusions.

We do not suggest that this logic and its conclusion are self-evident or guaranteed. On the contrary, by virtue of these performances' contextualization in a broader mediascape characterized by contemporary sensibilities and their formal congruence (and confluence) with those very sensibilities, at least as likely an interpretation of these camp performances is that they are wholly consistent with discursive conventions. Audiences may not participate at all in the construction of this discursive logic, content with the "literal" meanings presented to them, or their participation may be incomplete at any point: in either of these cases, the irony is lost, as is the resistive potential of the performances. But this does not detract from our point that contemporary aesthetic practices and sensibilities serve, collectively, as both ideal vehicle and camouflage for these camp performances. Indeed, as theorists of both the enthymeme and irony have noted, the risks associated with each—that is, of the audience not "getting it"—is great (Aden, 1994; Bitzer, 1959; W. C. Booth, 1974; Foss & Littlejohn, 1986). Nonetheless, when they do "work"—that is, when the audience successfully contributes to or participates in them—their rhetorical effectiveness is significant, even profound. For those audiences who not only engage the ironies apparent at the level of trope, of spectacle, and of anchors and foils but apprehend them *in relation to* each other, the camp performances of Xena, Karen Walker, Macy Gray, and Gwen Stefani culminate in the logical conclusion of sexual alterity—that is, in the subversion of conventional discourses of gender and sexuality. In this regard, as with any text, the audience is a key determinant in how a text will be read.

But what our analysis of resistive camp logic suggests is that we must also engage particular mediated *texts*—not simply their interpretations—as sites of contestation. That is, rather than assume that contemporary mediated texts are inherently and authentically random and incoherent, thereby granting unlimited interpretive agency to the audience, and rather than assume that all such texts have been manipulated and reconfigured by the political economy that drives mediated texts to embody hegemonic messages, rendering at least an impoverished if not essentially passive audience, we began our project with the assumption that, just as the aesthetic practices and sensibilities that characterize contemporary media fare can serve as ideal camouflage for dominant ideologies, perhaps resistive moments can exist in media fare under the same guise, occupying an ambiguous, liminal space that invites a resistive reading even as it conforms to hegemonic conventions and constraints. We are intrigued by what Fiske (1986) refers to as "the collision between discourses" in any given text:

> Neither the text, nor the dominant ideology, can ever control all the potential meanings that this collision produces. The fissures in the text which allow for meanings that escape the control of the dominant are at their most apparent and most exploitable when the text is composed of discourses or other elements which are related by association rather than by the laws of [formal] logic or cause and effect. The laws of association are looser, more resistant to closure and admit of greater reader participation in the negotiation of meaning. (pp. 401–402)

The camp performances that we have identified result in a particular rhetorical phenomenon—and logical form—that is better understood as a "double text," wherein a distinct and coherent message seemingly at odds with a superficial reading can be identified in and emerge from the text contingent on the cues foregrounded and attended to by the audience. In this sense, they function as something of a figure-ground or "magic eye" perceptual illusion, where a distinctive and wholly coherent image emerges out of a large, seemingly random and abstract pattern on attending to particular visual cues. In these cases, resistive readings coexist with their own appropriations. In these texts, both dominant and resistive messages can be identified, contingent on the cues to which the audience attends; accordingly, these texts may be better considered conjoined than conflated.

Conjoined texts challenge prevailing, if contradictory, assumptions regarding both the manufacture of the text and its ideological moorings, as well as the agency or passivity of the audience, as we have suggested. Furthermore, conjoined texts suggest alternative ways of considering "intertextuality"—as understood both in terms of the intersection between a given text and its audiences (and their experiences), as well as the intersection and layering of multiple, especially mediated, texts and discourses. As Fiske (1986) has argued, "we may not be able to predict the actual reading that any one empirical viewer may make, but we can identify the textual characteristics that make polysemic readings possible, and we can theorize the relation between textual structure and social structure that make such polysemic readings necessary" (p. 394). These camp performances suggest that texts that occur within a mainstream context of constraint demand closer scrutiny as specifically rhetorical artifacts, as they may well be more nuanced than cultural critics might presume, on all sides of the debate. In the case of these camp performances, the very rhetorical devices that define the context of constraint in which these performances occur constitute the premises for the resistance available in those texts: they are merely configured in distinctive ways so as to articulate a contrary discursive logic. This suggests that, at least in conjoined texts but perhaps in a contemporary mediated context more broadly, a critical sensibility—afforded via the complication of signs, discourses, and practices—is of far more significance than a particular critical agenda or stance.

That the performances that we have assessed occur in a mediated context largely characterized by fluidity, dynamism, instability, and therefore accessibility—whether those features are apprehended as fabricated or "authentic"—is highly significant as well. Arguably, these sensibilities are a required backdrop for the conjoined texts that these performances embody. That is, the pastiche-laden and chaotic context of the contemporary mediascape provides the ideal camouflage, by virtue of its "random pattern," for particular configurations—discursive logics—to be organized and made available to audiences. Although we remain quite skeptical of contemporary media fare in terms of the political economy that governs it, we submit that there exist opportunities within various texts for, at least, negotiation of conventional discourses, if not resistance. The manifestation of these dynamics in camp performances, in particular, is notable, for camp arguably serves as an ideal vehicle for critical schism and negotiation, functioning metaphorically as a Trojan horse that, albeit absent a revolutionary coup, smoothly infiltrates the mainstream arena and imports critical sensibilities, sidestepping the essentially modernist and thus nonviable (in that context) trappings of a critical agenda. Certainly, problematic representations accompany their presence—after all, they serve as camouflage, and one's "reading" of the text may well be limited to those superficial interpretations. But these camp texts—and perhaps others—also are characterized by rather cheeky manifestos that, significantly, are not buried under or constrained by the dominant discourses that contextualize them but are, instead, always available and in plain view.

We hope that our analysis of camp in contemporary, mediated contexts also illuminates the utility and value of a specifically rhetorical sensibility in identifying and assessing sites of political struggle. As this project suggests, a critical rhetorical attitude both enables and animates the apprehension of the political dimensions of public discourses and texts thereof. That is, discernment of exactly how power is negotiated and managed in cultural texts requires an apprehension of the rhetorical dimensions of that negotiation—and, more specifically, how resistive discourses are configured in a context of notorious restraint. We would suggest further that a rhetorical sensibility is especially vital in contemporary cultural contexts, including mediated ones, insofar as what constitutes sites of contestations—as well as where and how they are available—is increasingly difficult to discern. A rhetorical sensibility is thus not simply useful but increasingly necessary for the negotiation of this novel and complicated terrain; we have employed it to the end of examining how gender and sexuality, including as they engage race and class, are destabilized and resisted even as they are framed by normativizing conventions—conventions that present themselves to be anything but normativizing. As our cultural forms and practices continue to shift, expand, and develop, and given that those forms and practices are always already political, our abilities to engage and critique them must evolve accordingly. As this project suggests, a particularly rhetorical sensibility is especially—even ideally—suited to precisely that endeavor.

Notes

Introduction

1. Although Xena and Karen Walker are fabricated characters rather than "real" individuals, given our founding assumption that gender and sexuality are performed, our interest is in examining the performances that constitute the fictional character in each case—as represented and available in electronic and print media—rather than in "actual" identities. As such, our focus in each case is on the textualization of those characters.

2. In addition to close textual readings, we use a case-study approach in our assessment of camp performances, believing that the records of cultural practice, or texts, are best studied within "the wider range of social, economic, political, institutional, economic, and belief systems" (Rosteck, 1999, p. 232). Camp texts must be contextualized by historical and concurrent discourses, as well as within their broader material conditions—including the political economy that guides and arguably drives their production.

Chapter 2

1. Quoted in "User Comments" by moonspinner55 (26 June 2005). Internet Movie Database. Retrieved June 26, 2006, from http://www.imdb.com/title/tt0160127/usercomments.

Chapter 4

1. Although Will, the other (and lead) gay man featured on the show, would seem to be configured in a significant capacity in relation to Karen, he is not. Their characters have far fewer interactions with each other than either of them do with Grace and Jack, and when they do engage, Will is construed primarily as a target for her homophobic one-liners. On this count, Will is more on a par with Rosario in terms of how Karen is drawn against him. In Will's case, this may have something to do with the fact that his is a very paternalistic character (see, e.g., Shugart, 2003), and as such has far less relevance to Karen's character than to Grace's and Jack's.

2. For a discussion of the "heterosexualization" of the character of Will Truman on the show, see Battles & Hilton-Morrow, 2002; and Shugart, 2003.

3. In the penultimate season, motivated initially by a desire to exact revenge on her (presumed deceased, at the time) husband's mistress, Karen commences an affair with and eventually marries that woman's father. The marriage ends on their wedding day, however, immediately on her new husband's chronicling (in appreciation) Karen's sacrifices to be with him.

4. Although the popularity of "gay-themed" television shows and films with heterosexual women—and, in fact, the specific targeting of that audience for such fare—has been addressed in the popular and trade literature (e.g., Fitzgerald, 2003; Smith, 2005; Vasquez, 2005), their popularity with gay audiences remains undaunted and, as some critics have argued, distinctive, insofar as the "inside" humor and references and the "pleasure" that gay audiences derive from those texts (e.g., Keller, 2002; Walters, 2001). If, however, the phenomenon of gay-themed programming's resonating with heterosexual women is beyond the scope of this analysis, it demands greater attention, for instance in terms of complicating the constitution of "mainstream" audiences and how heteronormativity and gay sensibilities may be implicated and/or intersect in ways relevant to gender as well as sexuality.

Chapter 5

1. Our point here is not that women and men have inherently different relational experiences as a result of biological considerations but that their relationships often feature conventional gender constructions (e.g., feminine as vulnerable, masculine as dominant).

2. "P-funk" is a subgenre of funk music that was popular in the 1970s and is commonly associated with George Clinton and the bands Parliament and Funkadelic.

3. Undoubtedly, the historical practice of representing Black women as "mammy," "Sapphire," or "Jezebel" complicates a Black woman's performance of masculinity in different ways from a white woman's portrayal of masculinity. For more on the intersections of race and class in representations of women, see P. H. Collins, 1990; hooks, 1990; and Perry, 2003.

Chapter 6

1. Although Stefani predates both of these women in terms of her career, her proliferation into the mainstream popular music industry occurred at about the same time.

2. Although Aguilera has some Latin heritage, she is overwhelmingly presented as white in the dominant public discourse.

3. In fact, this issue was discussed in the popular press as the band's playful response to the press's representation of Stefani as moving on to a solo career and "getting rid" of her band mates to that end (see, e.g., Ali, 2004).

References

Aden, R. C. (1994). The enthymeme as postmodern argument form: Condensed, mediated argument then and now. *Argumentation and Advocacy, 31*(2), 54–63.

Ali, L. (2001, Dec. 24). Far beyond a shadow of No Doubt. *Newsweek, 138*(26), 52.

Ali, L. (2004, Sep. 6). It's my life. *Newsweek, 144*(10/11), 90.

Babuscio, J. (1977). Camp and the gay sensibility. In R. Dyer (Ed.), *Gays and film* (pp. 40–57). London: BFI.

Babuscio, J. (1999). The cinema of camp (*aka* Camp and the gay sensibility). In F. Cleto (Ed.), *Camp: Queer aesthetics and the performing subject* (pp. 117–135). Ann Arbor: University of Michigan Press.

Bader, H. (Writer), & Merrifield, A. (Director). (1997). Been there, done that [Television series episode]. In S. Sears (Producer), *Xena: Warrior Princess.* New Zealand: Pacific Renaissance Pictures.

Bakhtin, M. (1968). *Rabelais and his world* (H. Iswolsky, Trans.). Cambridge: Massachusetts Institute of Technology Press.

Bardin, B. (1999, Nov. 23). Cover girl. *Advocate, 798,* 30–34.

Barr, A. (Writer), & Burrows, J. (Director). (1999). Object of my rejection [Television series episode]. In D. Kohan & M. Mutchnick (Producers), *Will and Grace.* Studio City, CA: National Broadcasting Company.

Barr, A. (Writer), & Burrows, J. (Director). (2000). He's come undone [Television series episode]. In D. Kohan & M. Mutchnick (Producers), *Will and Grace.* Studio City, CA: National Broadcasting Company.

Barr, A. (Writer), & Burrows, J. (Director). (2001a). Crouching father, hidden husband [Television series episode]. In D. Kohan & M. Mutchnick (Producers), *Will and Grace.* Studio City, CA: National Broadcasting Company.

Barr, A. (Writer), & Burrows, J. (Director). (2001b). Mad dogs and average men [Television series episode]. In D. Kohan & M. Mutchnick (Producers), *Will and Grace.* Studio City, CA: National Broadcasting Company.

Barr, A. (Writer), & Burrows, J. (Director). (2002). And the horse he rode in on [Television series episode]. In D. Kohan & M. Mutchnick (Producers), *Will and Grace.* Studio City, CA: National Broadcasting Company.

Bartlett, N. (1988). *Who was that man? A present for Mr. Oscar Wilde.* London: Serpent's Tail.

Battles, K., & Hilton-Morrow, W. (2002). Gay characters in conventional spaces: *Will and Grace* and the situation comedy genre. *Critical Studies in Media Communication, 19*(1), 87–105.

Baudrillard, J. (1983a). *Simulations.* New York: Semiotext(e).

Baudrillard, J. (1983b). *In the shadow of the silent majorities.* New York: Semiotext(e).

Beaver, H. (1999). Homosexual signs (in memory of Roland Barthes). In F. Cleto (Ed.), *Camp: Queer aesthetics and the performing subject* (pp. 160–178). Ann Arbor: University of Michigan Press.

Bell, E. (1993). Performance studies as women's work: Historical sights/sites/citations from the margin. *Text and Performance Quarterly, 13*(4), 350–374.

Bennett, T. (1986). Introduction: Popular culture and "the turn to Gramsci." In T. Bennett, C. Mercer, & J. Woollacott (Eds.), *Popular culture and social relations* (pp. xi–xix). Milton Keynes, UK: Open University Press.

Bergman, D. (1993). *Camp grounds: Style and homosexuality.* Amherst: University of Massachusetts Press.

Bernard, K. (1992). Ironing out the differences: Female iconography in the paintings of Joanne Tod. In L. Hutcheon (Ed.), *Double talking: Essays on verbal and visual ironies in Canadian contemporary art and literature* (pp. 134–144). Toronto: ECW.

Best, S., & Kellner, D. (1991). *Postmodern theory.* New York: Guilford Press.

Best, S., & Kellner, D. (1997). *The postmodern turn.* New York: Guilford Press.

Best, S., & Kellner, D. (1999). Debord, cybersituations, and the interactive spectacle. *Substance: A Review of Theory and Literary Criticism, 28*(3), 129–156.

Birdsell, D. S. (1993). Kenneth Burke as the nexus of argument and trope. *Argumentation and Advocacy, 29,* 178–185.

Bitzer, L. (1959). Aristotle's enthymeme revisited. *Quarterly Journal of Speech, 45*(4), 399–408.

Blair, S. B. (1992). Good housekeeping: Virginia Woolf and the politics of irony. In D. W. Conway & J. E. Seery (Eds.), *The politics of irony: Essays in self-betrayal* (pp. 151–169). New York: St. Martin's.

Booth, M. (1983). *Camp.* London: Quartet.

Booth, M. (1999). *Campe-toi!* On the origins and definitions of camp. In F. Cleto (Ed.), *Camp: Queer aesthetics and the performing subject* (pp.66–79). Ann Arbor: University of Michigan Press.

Booth, W. C. (1974). *The rhetoric of irony.* Chicago: University of Chicago Press.

Booth, W. C. (1983). *The rhetoric of fiction.* Chicago: University of Chicago Press.

Bradford, S. (Writer), & Burrows, J. (Director). (2000). Alice doesn't lisp here any-more [Television series episode]. In D. Kohan & M. Mutchnick (Producers), *Will and Grace*. Studio City, CA: National Broadcasting Company.

Bradford, S. (Writer), & Burrows, J. (Director). (2002a). Hocus focus [Television series episode]. In D. Kohan & M. Mutchnick (Producers), *Will and Grace*. Studio City, CA: National Broadcasting Company.

Bradford, S. (Writer), & Burrows, J. (Director). (2002b). The honeymoon's over [Television series episode]. In D. Kohan & M. Mutchnick (Producers), *Will and Grace*. Studio City, CA: National Broadcasting Company.

Britton, A. (1999). For interpretation: Notes against camp. In F. Cleto (Ed.), *Camp: Queer aesthetics and the performing subject* (pp. 136–142). Ann Arbor: University of Michigan Press.

Bronski, M. (1984). *Culture clash: The making of gay sensibility*. Boston: South End Press.

Brookey, R. A. (1996). A community like *Philadelphia*. *Western Journal of Communication, 60*(1), 40–56.

Brookey, R. A., & Westerfelhaus, R. W. (2001). Pistols and petticoats, piety and purity: *To Wong Foo*, the queering of the American monomyth, and the marginalizing discourse of deification. *Critical Studies in Media Communication, 18*(2), 141–156.

Browne, David. (2001, Sep. 21). Freudian slip. *Entertainment Weekly, 616*, p. 80.

Brunner , R. (1999, July 30). There's something about Macy. *Entertainment Weekly, 496*, p. 72.

Burke, K. (1954). *Permanence and change: An anatomy of purpose*. New York: Bobbs-Merrill.

Burke, K. (1962). *A rhetoric of motives*. Cleveland: World Publishing.

Burke, K. (1969). *A grammar of motives*. Berkeley, CA: University of California Press.

Butler, J. (1990). *Gender trouble: Feminism and the subversion of identity*. New York: Routledge.

Butler, J. (1993). *Bodies that matter: On the discursive limits of "sex."* New York: Routledge.

Butler, J. (1999). From interiority to gender performatives. In F. Cleto (Ed.), *Camp: Queer aesthetics and the performing subject* (pp. 361–368). Ann Arbor: University of Michigan Press.

Butler, J. (2004). *Undoing gender*. New York: Routledge.

Cagle, J. (1998, Dec. 25). Breakouts. *Entertainment Weekly, 464/465*, 46–51.

Campbell, K. K., & Jamieson, K. H. (1978). *Form and genre: Shaping rhetorical action*. Falls Church, VA: Speech Communication Association.

Capsuto, S. (2000). Alternate channels: The uncensored story of gay and lesbian images on radio and television. New York: Ballantine.

Case, S.-E. (1999). Toward a butch-femme aesthetic. In F. Cleto (Ed.), *Camp: Queer aesthetics and the performing subject* (pp. 185–199). Ann Arbor: University of Michigan Press.

Chambers, V., Gordon, D., & Figueroa, A. (1999, Aug. 16). Macy Gray makes a scene. *Newsweek, 134*(7), 50.

Chen, K.-H. (1986). MTV: The (dis)appearance of postmodern semiosis, or the cultural politics of resistance. *Journal of Communication Inquiry, 10*(1), 66–69.

Cleto, F. (1999). Introduction: Queering the camp. In F. Cleto (Ed.), *Camp: Queer aesthetics and the performing subject* (pp. 1–42). Ann Arbor: University of Michigan Press.

Cloud, D. L. (1992). The limits of interpretation: Ambivalence and stereotype in *Spenser: For Hire. Critical Studies in Mass Communication, 9,* 311–324.

Cloud, D. L. (1996). Hegemony or concordance? The rhetoric of tokenism in "Oprah" Winfrey's rags-to-riches biography. *Critical Studies in Mass Communication, 13,* 115–137.

Collins, J. (1989). *Uncommon cultures: Popular culture and postmodernism.* New York: Routledge.

Collins, J. (1992). Postmodernism and television. In R. C. Allen (Ed.), *Channels of discourse, reassembled* (pp. 327–353). Chapel Hill: University of North Carolina Press.

Collins, P. H. (1990). *Black feminist thought.* New York: Routledge.

Condit, C. M. (1989). The rhetorical limits of polysemy. *Critical Studies in Mass Communication, 6,* 103–122.

Condit, C. M. (1992). Hegemony in a mass-mediated society: Concordance about reproductive technologies. *Critical Studies in Mass Communication, 9,* 311–324.

Cooper, B. (1999). The relevancy and gender identity in spectators' interpretations of *Thelma and Louise. Critical Studies in Mass Communication, 16,* 20–42.

Cooper, B. (2000). "Chick flicks" as feminist texts: The appropriation of the male gaze in *Thelma and Louise. Women's Studies in Communication, 23*(30), 277–306.

Cooper, B. (2001). Unapologetic women, "comic men," and female spectatorship in David E. Kelley's *Ally McBeal. Critical Studies in Media Communication, 18*(4), 416–436.

Cooper, B. (2002). *Boys Don't Cry* and female masculinity: Reclaiming a life and dismantling the politics of normative heterosexuality. *Critical Studies in Media Communication, 19*(1), 44–63.

Cooper, B., & Pease, E. C. (2002). "Don't want no short people 'round here": Confronting heterosexism's intolerance through comic and disruptive narratives in *Ally McBeal. Journal of Communication, 66,* 300–318.

Core, P. (1984). *Camp: The lie that tells the truth.* London: Plexus.

Cronkhite, G. (1966). The enthymeme as deductive rhetorical argument. *Western Speech, 30*(2), 129–134.

Danesi, M. (1994). Introduction: Thomas A. Sebeok and the science of signs. In T. A. Sebeok, *Signs: An introduction to semiotics* (pp. xi–xvii). Toronto: University of Toronto Press.

Daniels, L. (2000). *Wonder Woman: The complete history.* San Francisco: Chronicle Books.

De Lauretis, T. (1984). *Alice doesn't: Feminism, semiotics, cinema.* Bloomington: Indiana University Press.

Debord, G. (1976). *The society of the spectacle.* Detroit: Black and Red.

Diamond, E. (1996). Introduction. In E. Diamond (Ed.), *Performance and cultural politics* (pp. 1–12). New York: Routledge.

Doane, M. A. (1982). Film and masquerade: Theorizing the female spectator. *Screen, 23,* 74–87.

Doane, M. A. (1987). *The desire to desire: The woman's film of the 1940s.* Bloomington: Indiana University Press.

Doane, M.A. (1991). *Femmes fatales: Feminism, film theory, psychoanalysis.* New York: Routledge.

Dollimore, J. (1999). Post/modern: On the gay sensibility, or the pervert's revenge on authenticity. In F. Cleto (Ed.), *Camp: Queer aesthetics and the performing subject* (pp. 221–236). Ann Arbor: University of Michigan Press.

Dougherty, S. (2001, March 12). Shades of Gray. *People, 55*(10), 91.

Dow, B. J. (2001). *Ellen,* television, and the politics of gay and lesbian visibility. *Critical Studies in Media Communication, 18*(2), 123–140.

Dunn, J. (2002, Oct. 31). Macy Gray. *Rolling Stone, 908,* 69.

Dyer, R. (1999). It's being so camp as keeps us going. In F. Cleto (Ed.), *Camp: Queer aesthetics and the performing subject* (pp. 110–116). Ann Arbor: University of Michigan Press.

Eliscu, J. (2005, Jan. 27). Gwen cuts loose. *Rolling Stone, 966,* 36–40.

Erickson, K. V. (1998). Presidential spectacles: Political illusionism and the rhetoric of travel. *Communication Monographs, 65,* 141–153.

Evans, N. (1998). Games of hide and seek: Race, gender, and drag in *The Crying Game* and *The Birdcage. Text and Performance Quarterly, 18*(3), 199–216.

Farrell, T. B. (1989). Media rhetoric as social drama: The Winter Olympics of 1984. *Critical Studies in Mass Communication, 6,* 158–182.

Finch, M. (1999). Sex and address in *Dynasty*. In F. Cleto (Ed.), *Camp: Queer aesthetics and the performing subject* (pp. 143–159). Ann Arbor: University of Michigan Press.

Fiore, R. (2004, Dec. 17). Girls club. *Entertainment Weekly, 797*, 21.

Fiske, J. (1986). Television: Polysemy and popularity. *Critical Studies in Mass Communication, 3*, 391–408.

Fiske, J. (1987). *Television culture*. New York: Methuen.

Fiske, J. (1989). *Understanding popular culture*. New York: Routledge.

Fitzgerald, T. (2003, July 24). Whole world of buzz over "Boy meets boy." *Media Life*. Retrieved March 14, 2006, from http://www.medialifemagazine.com/news2003/jul03/jul21/4_thurs/news4thursday.html

Flinn, C. (1999). The deaths of camp. In F. Cleto (Ed.), *Camp: Queer aesthetics and the performing subject* (pp. 433–457). Ann Arbor: University of Michigan Press.

Flores, L. A. (1996). Creating discursive space through a rhetoric of difference: Chicana feminists craft a homeland. *Quarterly Journal of Speech, 82*(2), 142–157.

Foss, K. A., & Littlejohn, S. W. (1986). *The Day After:* Rhetorical vision in an ironic frame. *Critical Studies in Mass Communication, 3*, 316–336.

Frankel, D. (2000, Feb. 28). Action fights back. *Mediaweek, 10*(9), 18.

Fraser, A. (1988). *The warrior queens*. New York: Knopf.

Frentz, T. S., & Rushing, J. H. (2002). "Mother isn't quite herself today": Myth and spectacle in *The Matrix. Critical Studies in Media Communication, 19*(1), 64–87.

Frye, N. (1957). *Anatomy of criticism: Four essays*. Princeton, NJ: Princeton University Press.

Gabriel, S. (Writer), & Burrows, J. (Director). (2005). The birds and the bees [Television series episode]. In D. Kohan & M. Mutchnick (Producers), *Will and Grace*. Studio City, CA: National Broadcasting Company.

Gifford, D. (1984). *The international book of comics*. Toronto: Royce.

Giroux, H. A. (2000). *Impure acts: The practical politics of cultural studies*. New York: Routledge.

Gitlin, T. (1986). Looking through the screen. In T. Gitlin (Ed.), *Watching television* (pp. 3–8). New York: Pantheon.

Goldman, R., & Papson, S. (1994). The postmodernism that failed. In D. R. Dickens & A. Fontana (Eds.), *Postmodernism and social inquiry* (pp. 224–253). New York: Guilford.

Gordinier, J. (1999, Aug. 16). Give in to a neo-soul pleasure machine. *Fortune, 140*(4), 46.

Grabe, M. E. (2002). Maintaining the moral order: A functional analysis of *The Jerry Springer Show. Critical Studies in Media Communication, 19*(3), 311–328.

Gregg, R. B. (1978). Kenneth Burke's prolegomena to the study of the rhetoric of form. *Communication Quarterly, 26*(4), 3–13.

Gronbeck, B. (1978). Celluloid rhetoric: On genres of documentary. In K. K. Campbell and K. H. Jamieson (Eds.), *Form and genre: Shaping rhetorical action* (pp. 139–161). Falls Church, VA: Speech Communication Association.

Gross, L. (2001). *Up from invisibility: Lesbians, gay men, and the media in America.* New York: Columbia University Press.

Grossberg, L. (1983). The politics of youth culture: Some observations on rock and roll in American culture. *Social Text, 8,* 104–126.

Grossberg, L. (1989). MTV: Swinging on the (postmodern) star. In I. Angus & S. Jhally (Eds.), *Cultural politics in contemporary America* (pp. 254–268). London: Routledge.

Grossberg, L. (1996). Toward a genealogy of the state of cultural studies: The discipline of communication and the reception of cultural studies in the United States. In C. Nelson & D. P. Gaonkar(Eds.), *Disciplinarity and dissent in cultural studies* (pp. 131–148). New York: Routledge.

Gwen Stefani. (1997, May 12). *People, 47*(18), 103.

Halberstam, J. (1998). *Female masculinity.* Durham, NC: Duke University Press.

Halberstam, J. (2005). In a queer time and place: Transgender bodies, subcultural lives. New York: New York University Press.

Hall, S. (1980). Encoding/decoding. In S. Hall (Ed.), *Culture, media, language: Working papers in cultural studies, 1972–79* (128–138). London: Hutchinson.

Hall, S. (1997). The centrality of culture: Notes on the cultural revolutions of our time. In K. Thompson (Ed.), *Media and cultural regulation* (pp. 203–219). Thousand Oaks, CA: Sage.

Hall, S. (2000). Racist ideologies and the media. In P. Marris & S. Thornham (Eds.), *Media studies: A reader* (pp. 271–282). New York: New York University Press.

Hanke, R. (1998). The "mock-macho" situation comedy: Hegemonic masculinity and its reiteration. *Western Journal of Communication, 62*(1), 74–94.

Harms, J. B., & Dickens, D. R. (1996). Postmodern media studies: Analysis or symptom? *Critical Studies in Mass Communication, 13,* 210–227.

Hasian, M. (2002). Nostalgic longings and imaginary Indias: Postcolonial analysis, collective memories, and the impeachment trial of Warren Hastings. *Western Journal of Communication, 66*(2), 229–256.

Hauser, G. A. (2002). *Introduction to rhetorical theory* (2nd ed.). Prospect Heights, IL: Waveland.

Heath, C. (1997, Jan. 5). Snap! Crackle! Pop! *Rolling Stone, 759,* 36–44.

Hebdige, D. (1991). *Subculture: The meaning of style.* London: Routledge.

Henry, W. A., III, & Browning, S. (1990, Nov. 8). The lesbians next door. *Time, 136*(19), 78–80.

Herschlag, A. (Writer), & Burrows, J. (Director). (2001). Prison blues [Television series episode]. In D. Kohan & M. Mutchnick (Producers), *Will and Grace.* Studio City, CA: National Broadcasting Company.

Herschlag, A. (Writer), & Burrows, J. (Director). (2005). Partners [Television series episode]. In D. Kohan & M. Mutchnick (Producers), *Will and Grace.* Studio City, CA: National Broadcasting Company.

Holman, C. H., & Harmon, W. (1992). *A handbook to literature* (6th ed.). New York: Macmillan.

Hontz, J. (1997, March 17). *Xena, Rosie, ET* top syndie sweeps. *Variety, 366*(7), 27.

hooks, b. (1990). *Yearning: Race, gender, and cultural politics.* Boston: South End.

Hudson, H. (1999, Dec.). Listen to the music. *Lesbian News, 25*(5), 40.

Hutcheon, L. (1991). *Splitting images: Contemporary Canadian ironies.* Toronto: Oxford University Press.

Hutcheon, L. (1992). Double talking: Essays on verbal and visual ironies in Canadian contemporary art and literature. Toronto: ECW.

Huwig, P. (2005, May). Gwen Stefani. *Lesbian News, 30*(10), 20–21.

Inch, E. S., & Warnick, B. (2002). *Critical thinking and communication: The use of reason in argument* (4th ed.). Boston: Allyn and Bacon.

Isherwood, C. (1954). *The world in the evening.* London: Methuen.

Isherwood, C. (1999). From *The world in the evening.* In F. Cleto (Ed.), *Camp: Queer aesthetics and the performing subject* (pp. 49–52). Ann Arbor: University of Michigan Press.

Jameson, F. (1983). Postmodernism and consumer society. In H. Foster (Ed.), *The anti-aesthetic: Essays on postmodern culture* (pp. 111–125). Seattle: Bay.

Jameson, F. (1991). *Postmodernism, or, The cultural logic of late capitalism.* Durham, NC: Duke University Press.

Janetti, G. (Writer), & Burrows, J. (Director). (2003). Fagmalion Part Two: Attack of the Clones [Television series episode]. In D. Kohan & M. Mutchnick (Producers), *Will and Grace.* Studio City, CA: National Broadcasting Company.

Jhally, S. (1995). *Dreamworlds II* [video recording]. Northampton, MA: Media Education Foundation.

Jhally, S., & Lewis, J. (1992). Enlightened racism: *The Cosby Show,* audiences, and the myth of the American Dream. Boulder, CO: Westview Press.

Kaplan, E. A. (1987). *Rocking around the clock: Music television, postmodernism, and consumer culture.* New York: Methuen.

Keller, J. R. (2002). *Queer (un)friendly film and television.* Jefferson, NC: Mcfarland.

Kellner, D. (2003). Cultural studies, multiculturalism, and media culture. In G. Dines

& J. M. Humez (Eds.), *Gender, race, and class in media* (2nd ed., pp. 9–20). Thousand Oaks, CA: Sage.

Kightlinger, L. (Writer), & Burrows, J. (Director). (2004). Ice cream balls [Television series episode]. In D. Kohan & M. Mutchnick (Producers), *Will and Grace*. Studio City, CA: National Broadcasting Company.

Kightlinger, L. (Writer), & Burrows, J. (Director). (2005). Sour balls [Television series episode]. In D. Kohan & M. Mutchnick (Producers), *Will and Grace*. Studio City, CA: National Broadcasting Company.

Kightlinger, L., Herschlag, A. (Writers), & Burrows, J. (Director). (2000). An affair to forget [Television series episode]. In D. Kohan & M. Mutchnick (Producers), *Will and Grace*. Studio City, CA: National Broadcasting Company.

Kohan, D., & Mutchnick, M. (Producers). (1998–2006). *Will and Grace* [Television series]. Studio City, CA: National Broadcasting Company.

Kohan, D., Mutchnick, M. (Writers), & Burrows, J. (Director). (1998). New lease on life [Television series episode]. In D. Kohan & M. Mutchnick (Producers), *Will and Grace*. Studio City, CA: National Broadcasting Company.

Kohan, D., Mutchnick, M. (Writers), & Burrows, J. (Director). (1999a). Big brother is coming [Television series episode]. In D. Kohan & M. Mutchnick (Producers), *Will and Grace*. Studio City, CA: National Broadcasting Company.

Kohan, D., Mutchnick, M. (Writers), & Burrows, J. (Director). (1999b). Terms of employment [Television series episode]. In D. Kohan & M. Mutchnick (Producers), *Will and Grace*. Studio City, CA: National Broadcasting Company.

Kubo, E. (2005). Harajuku girls coopted. *Japan Inc., 64,* 36–41.

Lerner, G. (Writer), & Burrows, J. (Director). (2000). Sweet and sour charity [Television series episode]. In D. Kohan & M. Mutchnick (Producers), *Will and Grace*. Studio City, CA: National Broadcasting Company.

Lerner, G. (Writer), & Burrows, J. (Director). (2002). Boardroom and a parked place [Television series episode]. In D. Kohan & M. Mutchnick (Producers), *Will and Grace*. Studio City, CA: National Broadcasting Company.

Lizer, K. (Writer), & Burrows, J. (Director). (2001). My uncle the car [Television series episode]. In D. Kohan & M. Mutchnick (Producers), *Will and Grace*. Studio City, CA: National Broadcasting Company.

Lizer, K. (Writer), & Burrows, J. (Director). (2003). Dolls and dolls [Television series episode]. In D. Kohan & M. Mutchnick (Producers), *Will and Grace*. Studio City, CA: National Broadcasting Company.

Lockford, L. (1996). Social drama in the spectacle of femininity: The performance of weight loss in the Weight Watcher's program. *Women's Studies in Communication, 19*(3), 291–312.

Lotterstein, R. (Writer), & Burrows, J. (Director). (1999). Yours, mine, and ours [Television series episode]. In D. Kohan & M. Mutchnick (Producers), *Will and Grace.* Studio City, CA: National Broadcasting Company.

Lotterstein, R. (Writer), & Burrows, J. (Director). (2000). My best friend's tush [Television series episode]. In D. Kohan & M. Mutchnick (Producers), *Will and Grace.* Studio City, CA: National Broadcasting Company.

Lyotard, J.-F. (1984). *The postmodern condition.* Minneapolis: University of Minnesota Press.

Martindale, D. (1999). Batgirl, Bionic Woman, Wonder Woman, and now Xena, TV's warrior princess. *Biography, 3*(4), 90–95.

McGee, M. C. (1980). The "ideograph": A link between rhetoric and ideology. *Quarterly Journal of Speech, 66,* 1–16.

McKerrow, R. E. (1989). Critical rhetoric: Theory and praxis. *Communication Monographs, 56,* 91–111.

McKissack, F. (2000, March). The question of the cradle. *Progressive, 68*(3), 38–39.

McRobbie, A. (1994). *Postmodernism and popular culture.* London: Routledge.

McRobbie, A. (2000). *Feminism and youth culture.* New York: Routledge.

Messaris, P. (1997). *Visual persuasion: The role of images in advertising.* Thousand Oaks, CA: Sage.

Miller, T. (1998). *Technologies of truth: Cultural citizenship and the popular media.* Minneapolis: University of Minnesota Press.

Moore, M. P. (1996). From a government of the people to a people of the government: Irony as rhetorical strategy in political campaigns. *Quarterly Journal of Speech, 82,* 22–37.

Morgan, J. (1997). The bad girls of hip-hop. *Essence, 27*(11), 76.

Morner, K., & Rausch, R. (1991). *NTC's dictionary of literary terms.* Lincolnwood, IL: National Textbook.

Morreale, J. (1998). *Xena: Warrior Princess* as feminist camp. *Journal of Popular Culture, 32*(2), 79–87.

Morris, C. E., III (1998). The responsibilities of the critic: F. O. Mathiesson's homosexual palimpsest. *Quarterly Journal of Speech, 84*(3), 261–283.

Morris, C. E., III (2002). Pink herring and the fourth persona: J. Edgar Hoover's sex crime panic. *Quarterly Journal of Speech, 88*(2), 228–244.

Moruzi, N. C. (1993). Veiled agents: Feminine agency and masquerade in "The Battle of Algiers." In S. Fisher and K. Davis (Eds.), *Negotiating at the margins: The gendered discourses of power and resistance* (pp. 255–277). New Brunswick, NJ: Rutgers University Press.

Mulvey, L. (1975). Visual pleasure and narrative cinema. *Screen, 16,* 6–18.

Mutchnick, M., Kohan, D. (Writers), & Burrows, J. (Director). (2006). The finale [Television series episode]. In D. Kohan & M. Mutchnick (Producers), *Will and Grace.* Studio City, CA: National Broadcasting Company.

Nadaner, D. (1984). Intervention and irony. *Vanguard, 13,* 13–14.

Nelson, C. (1999). The linguisticality of cultural studies. In T. Rosteck (Ed.), *At the intersection: Cultural studies and rhetorical studies* (pp. 211–225). New York: Guilford Press.

Nelson, C., & Gaonkar, D. P. (Eds.). (1996). *Disciplinarity and dissent in cultural studies.* New York: Routledge.

Newton, E. (1972). *Mother camp: Female impersonators in America.* Englewood Cliffs, NJ: Prentice-Hall.

Newton, E. (1999). Role models. In F. Cleto (Ed.), *Camp: Queer aesthetics and the performing subject* (pp. 96–109). Ann Arbor: University of Michigan Press.

OKT profile: Megan Mullally. (2001, Sep./Oct.). *Oklahoma Today, 51*(6), 19.

Olson, K. M., & Olson, C. D. (2004). Beyond strategy: A reader-centered analysis of irony's dual persuasive uses. *Quarterly Journal of Speech, 90*(1), 24–52.

O'Neill, M. (1997, Dec. 29). Lucy Lawless. *People, 48*(26), 78–80.

Ono, K. A., & Sloop, J. M. (1995). The critique of vernacular discourse. *Communication Monographs, 62,* 19–46.

Osborn, M. (1967). Archetypal metaphor in rhetoric: The light-dark family. *Quarterly Journal of Speech, 53,* 115–126.

Osborn, M. (1977). The evolution of the archetypal sea in rhetoric and poetic. *Quarterly Journal of Speech, 63*(4), 347–363.

Palmer, K. (Writer), & Burrows, J. (Director). (1999). To serve and disinfect [Television series episode]. In D. Kohan & M. Mutchnick (Producers), *Will and Grace.* Studio City, CA: National Broadcasting Company.

Palmer, K. (Writer), & Burrows, J. (Director). (2001). Swimming pools . . . movie stars [Television series episode]. In D. Kohan & M. Mutchnick (Producers), *Will and Grace.* Studio City, CA: National Broadcasting Company.

Pantsios, A. (2000, March 4). Profile: Macy Gray. *Hear/Say: America's College Music Magazine.* Retrieved July 18, 2007, from http://web.archive.org/web/20040316224817/ http://www.hearsay.cc/features/articles/03-07-04-00/MacyGray.html

Perry, I. (2003). Who(se) am I? The identity and image of women in hip-hop. In G. Dines & J. M. Humez (Eds.), *Gender, race and class in media* (2nd ed., pp.136–148). Thousand Oaks, CA: Sage.

Phelan, P. (1993). *Unmarked: The politics of performance.* New York: Routledge.

Piggford, G. (1997). Who's that girl? Annie Lennox, Woolf's *Orlando,* and female camp androgyny. *Mosaic, 30*(3), 39–58.

Poster, M. (1990). *The mode of information: Poststructuralism and social context.* Chicago: University of Chicago Press.

Procter, D. E. (1990). The dynamic spectacle: Transforming experience into social forms of community. *Quarterly Journal of Speech, 76,* 117–133.

Rea, S. (2003, June 27). Angels fulfill a host of jiggly new fantasies. *The Philadelphia Inquirer,* p. W04.

Reich, J. L. (1999). Genderfuck: The law of the dildo. In F. Cleto (Ed.), *Camp: Queer aesthetics and the performing subject* (pp. 254–265). Ann Arbor: University of Michigan Press.

Riviere, J. (1929). Womanliness as masquerade. *International Journal of Psychoanalysis 10,* 303–313.

Robbins, B., & Myrick, R. (2000). The function of the fetish in *The Rocky Horror Picture Show* and *Priscilla, Queen of the Desert. Journal of Gender Studies, 19*(3), 269–281.

Robertson, P. (1996). *Guilty pleasures: Feminist camp from Mae West to Madonna.* Durham, NC: Duke University Press.

Rosenstock, R. (Writer), & Burrows, J. (Director). (2000). Love plus one [Television series episode]. In D. Kohan & M. Mutchnick (Producers), *Will and Grace.* Studio City, CA: National Broadcasting Company.

Ross, A. (1999). Uses of camp. In F. Cleto (Ed.), *Camp: Queer aesthetics and the performing subject* (pp. 308–329). Ann Arbor: University of Michigan Press.

Rosteck, T. (1999). A cultural tradition in rhetorical studies. In T. Rosteck (Ed.), *At the intersection: Cultural studies and rhetorical studies* (pp. 226–247). New York: Guilford Press.

Russo, M. (1986). Female grotesques: Carnival and theory. In T. de Lauretis (Ed.), *Feminist studies/critical studies* (pp. 213–229). Bloomington: Indiana University Press.

Russo, M. (1995). *The female grotesque: Risk, excess, and modernity.* New York: Routledge.

Salholz, E., & Glick, D. (1993, June 21). The power and the pride. *Newsweek, 121*(25), 54–61.

Samuels, A. (2001, April 9). Wall of soul. *Newsweek, 137*(15), 56.

Schaeble, M. (2001, Nov.). Hail Britannia! *Flare, 23*(11), 54.

Schulian, J. (Writer), Green, B. S., & Perez, J. (Directors). (1995). Pilot: The warrior princess/the gauntlet/unchained heart [Television series episode]. In S. Sears (Producer), *Xena: Warrior Princess.* New Zealand: Pacific Renaissance Pictures.

Schwichtenberg, C. (1993). Madonna's postmodern feminism: Bringing the margins to the center. In C. Schwichtenberg (Ed.), *The Madonna connection* (pp. 129–145). Boulder, CO: Westview Press.

Sears, S. (Producer). (1995–2001). *Xena: Warrior Princess* [Television series]. New Zealand: Pacific Renaissance Pictures.

Sears, S. (Writer), & Alexander, J. (Director). (1995). Hooves and harlots [Television series episode]. In S. Sears (Producer), *Xena: Warrior Princess.* New Zealand: Pacific Renaissance Pictures.

Sears, S. (Writer), & Jacobson, R. (Director). (1997). The dirty half dozen [Television series episode]. In S. Sears (Producer), *Xena: Warrior Princess.* New Zealand: Pacific Renaissance Pictures.

Sedgwick, E. K. (1999). From Wilde, Nietzsche, and the sentimental relations of the male body. In F. Cleto (Ed.), *Camp: Queer aesthetics and the performing subject* (pp. 207–220). Ann Arbor: University of Michigan Press.

Sender, K. (2004). *Business, not politics: The making of the gay market.* New York: Columbia University Press.

Sheffield, R. (2001, Aug. 11). PopEye. *Rolling Stone, 881,* 41.

Sherman, H. (2001, Oct.). Gwen Stefani. *InStyle, 8*(12), 271.

Shields, V. R., & C. Coughlin. (2000). Performing rodeo queen culture: Competition, athleticism, and excessive feminine masquerade. *Text and Performance Quarterly, 20*(2), 182–202.

Shoemer, K. (1997, Jan. 13). Skanks, but no skanks. *Newsweek, 129*(2), 72.

Shugart, H. A. (2001). Parody as subversive performance: Denaturalizing gender and reconstituting desire in *Ellen. Text and Performance Quarterly, 21*(2), 95–113.

Shugart, H. A. (2003). Reinventing privilege: The new (gay) man in contemporary popular media. *Critical Studies in Media Communication, 20*(1), 67–91.

Shugart, H. A., Waggoner, C. E., & Hallstein, L. O. (2001). Mediating third-wave feminism: Appropriation as postmodern media practice. *Critical Studies in Media Communication, 18*(2), 194–210.

Silverman, D. (1993). Making a spectacle, or is there female drag? *Critical Matrix, 7*(2), 69–89.

Singer, B. (1988). Film, photography, and fetish: The analyses of Christian Metz. *Cinema Journal, 27*(4), 4–22.

Sloop, J. M. (2000). Disciplining the transgendered: Brandon Teena, public representation, and normativity. *Western Journal of Communication, 64* (2), 165–189.

Sloop, J. M., and Olson, M. (1999). Cultural struggle: A politics of meaning in rhetorical studies. In T. Rosteck (Ed.), *At the intersection: Cultural studies and rhetorical studies* (pp. 248–265). New York: Guilford Press.

Smith, S. (2005, Nov. 21). Forbidden territory. *Newsweek, 146*(21), 60–62.

Sontag, S. (1964). Notes on camp. *Partisan Review, 31*(4), 515–530.

Spitz, M. B. (Writer), & Burrows, J. (Director). (2000). There but for the grace of Grace [Television series episode]. In D. Kohan & M. Mutchnick (Producers), *Will and Grace.* Studio City, CA: National Broadcasting Company.

Spivak, G. (1983). *Displacement: Derrida and after.* Bloomington: Indiana University Press.

Stockwell, A. (1996, Aug. 20). Flirting with Xena. *Advocate, 713/714,* 81–84.

Swearingen, C. J. (1991). *Rhetoric and irony: Western literacy and western lies.* New York: Oxford University Press.

Tavener, J. (2000). Media, morality, and madness: The case against sleaze TV. *Critical Studies in Media Communication, 17*(1) 63–85.

Terrill, R. E. (2003). Irony, silence, and time: Frederick Douglass on the fifth of July. *Quarterly Journal of Speech, 89*(3), 216–234.

Tetzlaff, D. (1991). Divide and conquer: Popular culture and social control in late capitalism. *Media, Culture, and Society, 13,* 9–33.

Toulmin, S. (1958). *The uses of argument.* Cambridge, UK: Cambridge University Press.

Toure. (1998, Aug. 12). The Miseducation of Lauryn Hill: Review. *Rolling Stone.* Retrieved March 8, 2007, from http://www.rollingstone.com/reviews/album/93007/the_miseducation_of_lauryn_hill

Toure. (2000, July 6). No Doubt. *Rolling Stone, 844/845,* 68–72.

Tseelon, E. (2001). Introduction: Masquerade and identities. In E. Tseelon (Ed.), *Masquerade and identities: Essays on gender, sexuality, and marginality.* New York: Routledge.

Tyler, C. (1999). Boys will be girls: Drag and transvestic fetishism. In F. Cleto (Ed.), *Camp: Queer aesthetics and the performing subject* (pp. 369–392). Ann Arbor: University of Michigan Press.

Vasquez, D. (2005, June 27). Pondering the promise of MTV's logo. *Media Life.* Retrieved June 17, 2006, from http://www.medialifemagazine.com/News2005/jun05/june27/2_tues/news3tuesday.html

Waggoner, C. E. (1997). The emancipatory potential of feminine masquerade in Mary Kay Cosmetics. *Text and Performance Quarterly, 17*(3), 256–272.

Waggoner, C. E., & Hallstein, L. O.(2001). Feminist ideologies meet fashionable bodies: Managing the agency/constraint conundrum. *Text and Performance Quarterly, 21*(1), 26–46.

Walker, R. (2005, June 19). Love. Angel. Product. Baby. *New York Times Magazine, 154,* 27.

Walters, S. D. (2001). *All the rage: The story of gay visibility in America.* Chicago: University of Chicago Press.

Wander, P. (1983). The ideological turn in rhetorical criticism. *Communication Studies, 34,* 1–18.

Wang, O. (2001a). Funk's femme fatale. *San Francisco's Bay Guardian.* Retrieved July 18, 2007, from http://www.sfbg.com/noise/23/bdavis.html

Wang, O. (2001b). Betty Davis: Game is her name. Retrieved Feb. 1, 2003, from http://www.O-dub.com/articles/betty.html

Warfield, S., Lizer, K., Greenstein, J., Marchinko, J. (Writers), & Burrows, J. (Director). (2004). I do, oh, no, you di-in't [Television series episode]. In D. Kohan & M. Mutchnick (Producers), *Will and Grace.* Studio City, CA: National Broadcasting Company.

Waring, W. (1992). Mother(s) of confusion: End bracket. In L. Hutcheon (Ed.), *Double-talking: Essays on verbal and visual ironies in Canadian contemporary art and literature* (pp. 145–157). Toronto: ECW.

Wilde, A. (1982). Horizons of assent: Modernism, postmodernism, and the ironic imagination. Baltimore: Johns Hopkins University Press.

Winter, T. (Writer), & Jones, G. (Director). (1996). The giant killer [Television series episode]. In S. Sears (Producer), *Xena: Warrior Princess*. New Zealand: Pacific Renaissance Pictures.

Winter, T. (Writer), & Levine, M. (Director). (1995). The cradle of hope [Television series episode]. In S. Sears (Producer), *Xena: Warrior Princess*. New Zealand: Pacific Renaissance Pictures.

Wolf, N. (1991). *The beauty myth: How images of beauty are used against women*. New York: Anchor.

Wrubel, B., Barr, A. (Writers), & Burrows, J. (Director). (2001). Something borrowed, someone's due [Television series episode]. In D. Kohan & M. Mutchnick (Producers), *Will and Grace*. Studio City, CA: National Broadcasting Company.

Index